Reaching Out

David W. Johnson
University of Minnesota

Reaching Out

Interpersonal effectiveness and self-actualization

Fifth Edition

ALLYN AND BACON
Boston London Toronto Sydney Tokyo Singapore

Editor-in-Chief, Education: Nancy Forsyth
Editorial Assistant: Christine Nelson
Cover Administrator: Linda Dickinson
Manufacturing buyer: Louise Richardson
Editorial-Production Service: P. M. Gordon Associates

Library of Congress Cataloging-in-Publication Data

Johnson, David W.
    Reaching out : interpersonal effectiveness and self-actualization /
David W. Johnson. —5th ed.
        p. cm.
    Includes bibliographical references and index.
    ISBN 0-205-14770-4
    1. Interpersonal relations. 2. Interpersonal communication.
3. Interpersonal conflict. 4. Self-actualization (Psychology)
I. Title.
HM132.J64 1993
302.3'4—dc20   92-30074
                                                                    CIP

Printed in the United States of America
10 9 8 7 6 5 4 3 2 1   97 96 95 94 93 92

Photo Credits

page 28 (bottom): ©Sepp Seitz/Woodfin Camp, Inc.
page 302: ©Sepp Seitz/Woodfin Camp, Inc.
page 312: ©Michael Heron/Woodfin Camp, Inc.

Contents

Preface

Reaching Out seeks to provide the theory and experience necessary to develop effective interpersonal skills. It is more than a book that reviews current psychological knowledge on how to build and maintain friendships. It is more than a book of skill-building exercises. The theory and exercises are *integrated* into an *experiential approach* to learning about interpersonal skills.

I wish to thank many people for their help in writing this book. My younger sister, Edythe Holubec, contributed the questions the reader will find in the text and helped revise and improve many parts of the book. My secretary, Judy Bartlett, stepped in to handle many of the bothersome details and greatly facilitated the publication. I owe much to those psychologists who have influenced my theorizing and to my colleagues with whom I have conducted various types of experiential learning sessions. Whenever possible, I have tried to acknowledge the source of any exercises that are not original in this book, but a few of the exercises are so commonly used that the originators are not traceable. If I have inadvertently missed giving recognition to anyone, I apologize.

Special thanks go to the many friends who have helped me improve my interpersonal skills and to my wife, Linda Mulholland Johnson, who contributed her tireless support to the rewriting of this book. All photographs not otherwise credited were taken by the author. Finally, I wish to thank Nancy Valin Waller, who drew the cartoon figures appearing in the book.

D.W.J.

1 *The Importance of Interpersonal Skills*

THE RELATIONSHIP IMPERATIVE

A friend is one
to whom one may pour
out all the contents
of one's heart,
chaff and grain together
knowing that the
gentlest of hands
will take and sift it,
keep what is worth keeping
and with a breath of kindness
blow the rest away.

> *Arabian proverb*

A new student enters the school lunchroom. He looks around trying to decide where to sit. He knows no one, but has high hopes. In that lunchroom may sit individuals who will later become close friends, companions, girl friends, and even a future wife. Or, if things go wrong, individuals sitting in that lunchroom may reject, dislike, belittle, and ridicule him. As the new student stands in the doorway it seems as if his whole life hangs in the balance. Will he make friends? Will people like him? Will he fall in love? All else pales in comparison.

We are created, not for isolation, but for relationships. At heart, we are not a thousand points of separated light but, rather, part of a larger brightness. *To live is to reach out to others.* "People who need people are the luckiest people in the world," a popular song tells us. That includes all of us. Initiating, developing, and maintaining caring and committed relationships is the most important (and often the most underestimated) activity in our lives. From the moment we are born to the moment we die, relationships are the core of our existence. We are conceived within relationships, are born into relationships, and live our lives within relationships. We are dependent on other people for the realization of life itself, for survival during one of the longest gestation periods in the animal kingdom, for food and shelter and aid and comfort throughout our lives, for the love and education necessary for social and cognitive development, for guidance in learning the essential competencies required to survive in our world, and for fun, excitement, comfort, love, personal confirmation, and fulfillment. Our relationships with others form the context for all other aspects of our lives.

Interpersonal relationships take many forms. Some people are only casual acquaintances; others become spouses or lovers. Some relationships last. Others end in boredom or distress. And sometimes you may be lonely, wanting relationships you do not have. Whether relationships begin, deepen, or end largely depends on your interpersonal skills.

We are not born instinctively knowing how to interact effectively with others. Interpersonal and group skills do not magically appear when they are needed. Many individuals lack basic interpersonal skills, such as correctly identifying the emotions of others and appropriately resolving a conflict, and often their social ineptitude seems to persist as they get older. Their lives typically do not go well. Individuals who lack social skills find themselves isolated, alienated, and at a disadvantage in vocational and career settings. The relationships so essential for living productive and happy lives are lost when basic interpersonal skills are not learned.

In this chapter the importance of interpersonal relationships for personal well-being, for the well-being of society, and for self-actualization will be examined. In addition, the specific interpersonal skills needed to build and maintain relationships will be discussed, along with the procedures for learning interpersonal skills from the experiential exercises included in this book. In subsequent chapters, each major interpersonal skill will be discussed at length.

INTERPERSONAL RELATIONSHIPS

People reach out to others because they have goals they wish to pursue that require the participation of other people as well as themselves. Social encounters are profoundly cooperative in the sense that they are improvised jointly by all present. When you participate in a genuine social encounter you and the other person are creating a "story" as you go along. You create action and dialogue that fit the situation. You and the other person coordinate your actions to maximize your mutual satisfaction.

Relationships are built on *interdependence.* You are interdependent if you share mutual goals with another person (such as repairing a car, playing chess, or enjoying each other's company). You are interdependent if what you want to do requires the other person to coordinate his or her actions with yours (such as playing tennis). When you are interdependent with another person, a change in the state of the other person causes a change in your state and vice versa. If you are sad, the other person feels concern, and if the other person is happy, you feel pleased. When the actions of other people are required for you to achieve your goals (and vice versa), and when what happens to them affects you (and vice versa), you and they are interdependent and in a relationship.

In order to form a relationship you have to interact. All interaction is based on a cycle of perceiving what the other person is doing, deciding how to respond, taking action, and then perceiving the other person's response. When a boy and a girl, for example, see each other, the boy suddenly has a goal—to meet her. He interprets her glance as an indication that she shares that goal. He decides to make a humorous comment to initiate a conversation. He acts on the decision by walking over to her and saying, "Beautiful day!" She interprets his action as meaning he would like to get to know her, decides she would like that also, and takes action. She looks at the rain outside, laughs, and says, "If you're a duck." As the interaction continues, the cycles become faster and faster and more automatic. Neither the boy nor the girl think the other is thinking consciously of what to say or do, yet both are engaged in a *cycle of social interaction* that includes perceiving (sensing, organizing, interpreting) the other person's actions, deciding how to respond, act, and perceive the other person's response. This cycle occurs throughout any kind of social interaction, from routine everyday conversations to special exchanges such as being interviewed for a job or giving a speech. It is fundamental to all interpersonal interaction and provides the context in which individuals build and sustain relationships.

The social interaction cycle begins with perception. *Perception* is the process of gathering sensory information and assigning meaning to it. Perception occurs in three stages. Your eyes, ears, nose, skin, and taste buds gather information. Your brain selects from among the items of information gathered and organizes them. Finally, your brain interprets and evaluates the information. What you perceive, furthermore, is unique to you. No two people will sense, organize, and interpret the same events in quite the same way. Perception provides a unique, but not necessarily an accurate, view of events. Sometimes the level of inaccuracy is insignificant; sometimes you completely misperceive what is taking place.

What we perceive is affected by many factors, including our expectations. In Figure 1.1, read the phrases in the triangles. If you are not familiar with this test you probably read the three triangles as "Paris in the springtime," "Once in a lifetime," and "Bird in the hand." But if you look closely you will see something different. Many people tend not to see the repeated words because they do not expect them to be there. We are so familiar with the phrases that our active perception stops once we recognize the phrase.

After perceiving what the other person has done, you decide how to respond and then take action, while at the same time continuing to perceive how the other person is reacting to what you are doing. As two people engage in this repeating cycle, they coordinate their behavior. The repeating cycle of perceiving, deciding, acting, and perceiving is fundamental to all social interaction (Figure 1.2).

As you enter the repeating cycle of social interaction, you have (1) a set of *goals* based on your needs, interests, personality, and relevant roles; (2) a set of *roles* (male or female, adult or child, teacher or student, host or guest) that affect how you interact with the other person; and (3) a *mood* based on personality, past events, other's behavior, physical setting, and significance of the interaction. The interaction takes place within a *physical setting* in which the purpose of the setting (church or playground), color, noise, and lighting affect mood and the rules that prescribe appropriate behavior. The *nature of the occasion* (party, wed-

FIGURE 1.1

FIGURE 1.2:   Cycle of Social Interaction

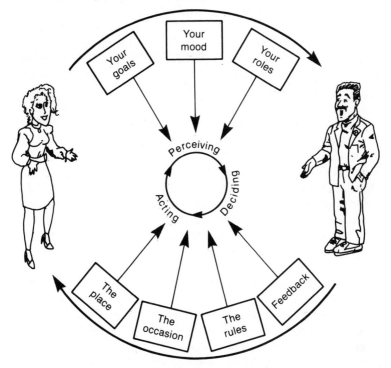

ding, funeral, sports event) limits the goals you can pursue. There are *social rules*, both general and specific to the occasion and setting, that influence your behavior. Finally, there is the *feedback* you receive as other people react to what you say and do in the situation. On the basis of the feedback, you adjust your goals, reinterpret your roles, and refine your understanding of the rules.

INTERPERSONAL RELATIONSHIPS AND PERSONAL WELL-BEING

A real friend is one who walks in
when the rest of the world walks out.

Walter Winchell

Life without friends is not much of a life. Loneliness stunts growth, sparks failure, makes life meaningless, kills, creates anxiety and depression, and makes one more fragile, lost in the past, and inhumane. *Loneli-*

ness is a state of dejection or grief caused by feeling alone. Within any given period of several weeks, many American adults feel painfully lonely. The incidence of loneliness is considerably higher among adolescents. Loneliness can result from the *social isolation* of not having a network of friends who share your interests and concerns and help provide a sense of community or from the *emotional isolation* of not having deep relationships, as between lovers, married couples, parents, and children, that provide a sense of attachment. Physical isolation does not create loneliness, and being near others does not end loneliness. It is a need for companionship and social support, not being alone, that causes loneliness. It is the absence of an intimate, satisfying relationship that makes loneliness an intensely unpleasant experience.

Relationships are not a luxury. They are a necessity. We have to reach out to others. Relationships are the key to our personal development and identity, productivity and career success, meaning in and quality of life, physical health, psychological health, coping with stress, self-actualization, and humaneness (Johnson & Johnson, 1991).

Personal Development and Identity

Interpersonal relationships are essential for our personal well-being in many ways, helping us to grow and develop cognitively and socially, to build a positive and coherent personal identity, and to feel we are firmly in touch with reality. *Human development* follows a pattern of expansion of interdependence with other people. As growing children, we are impelled to become aware of and interact with a widening social circle. From having to relate to members of the family, we move on to interaction with peers and other people in the neighborhood. Our social world is expanded dramatically when we begin formal schooling. When, as young adults, we enter a career organization and become members of a community, we must build and maintain relationships with a larger and larger number of people. And it is from our family, peers, friends, colleagues, and teachers that we learn new skills and competencies and acquire knowledge, attitudes, and values. As we grow and develop there is an ever-expanding number of people with whom we must build and maintain relationships. We are required to cooperate with others in family, school, career, community, and societal settings. We learn how to do so from the people with whom we interact. Both our social and our intellectual growth and development are determined by the quality and nature of our relationships with other people.

Our *identity* is built out of our relationships with other people. As we interact with others we note their responses to us, we seek feedback as to how they perceive us, and we learn how to view ourselves as they view us. From the reflections of others, we develop a clear and accurate picture of ourselves. When others view us as worthwhile, we tend to view ourselves similarly. We try to incorporate into ourselves character-istics that we admire in other people. In our relationships with other people we adopt social roles such as "student" or "engineer" that be-come part of our self-definition. It is within our relationships that we discover who we are as persons.

As we strive to make sense of the world around us, to determine what is real and what is illusory, we depend on other people to validate our perceptions and impressions. This is called *social comparison*. Many questions concerning reality cannot be answered by our physical senses. Although we can touch a leaf or smell a flower we cannot tell for sure what is fair or unfair, whether we are fast or slow, what is good or bad, or whether something is beautiful or ugly, without checking our opin-ions against the opinions of others. In order to make sense of the world, we need to share our perceptions and reactions with other people and find out whether or not other people perceive and react similarly.

We need to be *confirmed* as a person by other people. Confirmation consists of responses from other people in ways that indicate we are nor-mal, healthy, and worthwhile. Other people *disconfirm* us when they suggest we are ignorant, inept, unhealthy, unimportant, or of no value, and, at worst, that we do not exist. In most interpersonal interactions, we implicitly request, "Please validate me as a person." In our relation-ships we need to give and receive such confirmations.

Career Productivity and Success

Roger is an excellent computer programmer. He likes computers, and computers seem to like him. He turns out high-quality work very fast, is knowledgeable, and is motivated to do well at his job. At his last job, he never missed a day of work in 6 months and was always on time. But he could not get along with his fellow employees. He argued, com-plained, fought, criticized, and generally upset everyone he interacted with. After 6 months with the company, Roger was fired. He did not survive on the job because he could not work effectively with other people.

Whether you have just graduated from high school and are taking your first college class, or are a senior looking towards being graduated, or a person starting or returning to college after raising a family or changing a career, you are likely to realize that a college education or vocational training will help improve your career life. *You may be less aware that interpersonal skills may be the most important set of skills to your employability, productivity, and career success.* A recent national survey found that employers of liberal arts graduates value five types of skills: verbal communication skills, responsibility, interpersonal skills, initiative, and decision-making skills. The question all employers have in mind when they interview each job applicant is, Can this person get along with other people? Having a high degree of technical competence is not enough to ensure a successful career. You also have to have a high degree of interpersonal competence.

In 1982, for example, the Center of Public Resources published *Basic Skills in the U.S. Workforce*, a nationwide survey of businesses, labor unions, and educational institutions that found that 90 percent of the people fired from their jobs were fired for poor job attitudes, poor interpersonal relationships, inappropriate behavior, and inappropriate dress. Being fired for lack of basic and technical skills was infrequent. Even in high-tech careers, the ability to work effectively with other high-tech personnel is essential, and so is the ability to communicate and work with people from other professions to solve interdisciplinary problems.

In the real world of work, the heart of most jobs, especially the higher-paying, more interesting jobs, is getting others to cooperate, leading others, coping with complex power and influence issues, and helping to solve people's problems in working with each other. Millions of technical, professional, and managerial jobs today require much more than technical competence and professional expertise. They also require leadership. That is, you will be asked to get things done by influencing a large and diverse group of people (bosses, subordinates, peers, customers, and others) despite lacking much or any formal control over them and despite their general disinterest in cooperating. To learn to be a leader you need to acquire the interpersonal skills that enable you to motivate others to achieve goals, negotiate and mediate, get decisions implemented, exercise authority, and develop credibility. If you want to be a leader in business, industry, government, education, or any other field, the interpersonal skills covered in this book are prerequisites to success.

Quality of Life

> From the standpoint of everyday life . . .
> there is one thing we do know:
> that man is here for the sake of other men—
> above all, for those upon whose smile
> and well-being our own happiness depends,
> and also for the countless unknown souls
> with whose fate we are connected
> by a bond of sympathy.
> Many times a day I realize how much

*my own outer and inner life is built upon
the labors of my fellow men,
both living and dead,
and how earnestly I must exert myself
in order to give in return as much
as I have received.*

Albert Einstein

Life is a search for daily meaning as well as for daily bread. And the primary determinant of meaning is other people. When a national sample of people was asked, "What is it that makes your life meaningful?" almost all respondents named friends, parents, siblings, spouses, lovers, children, and the feeling of being loved and wanted by others. The primary determinant of happiness is other people. When asked, "What makes your life happy?" the most common answer was "intimate relationships." In a number of national surveys most people considered it very important to have "a happy marriage, a good family, and good friends." Less importance was given to work, housing, beliefs, and financial security. There is no simple recipe for producing happiness, but all of the research indicates that for almost everyone a necessary ingredient is some kind of satisfying, close, personal, intimate relationship.

Personal relationships have effects that extend far beyond those directly experienced by the individuals themselves. Our lives are shaped not only by our own relationships, but also by the relationships of thousands of other people. The social and economic costs of divorce, abuse, and isolation, for example, affect the entire society. The consequences of premarital sex and teenage pregnancy influence not only the adolescent parents and their children, but also social welfare programs, the level of taxation, and the community at large. The personal relations among workers influence the quality of products and, consequently, the quality of life of those who buy the products. All members of our society have a stake in each other's personal relationships. We all benefit from the existence of successful relationships and share, at least indirectly, the costs of deficit relationships.

Physical Health

We must love another or die.

W. H. Auden

Loneliness kills. Relationships create and extend life. Positive, supportive relationships have been found to be related to living longer lives, recovering from illness and injury faster and more completely, and experiencing less severe illnesses. People who are connected with others live longer than isolated people in every age and ethnic and racial group, and across all diseases.

Interpersonal skills help. Recent studies in Europe have found that heart-disease-prone individuals are characterized by anger, hostility, and aggression, whereas cancer-prone individuals are characterized by (a) the inability to express emotions such as anger, fear, and anxiety; (b) the inability to cope with stress; and (c) a tendency to develop feelings of hopelessness, helplessness, and finally depression. A key change for cancer-prone individuals is to stop being overly passive and to take more initiative in their relationships. The key change for heart-disease-prone individuals is to abandon their tendencies toward hostility and aggression and become more constructive in the way they deal with conflict. The interpersonal skills required by both can be taught.

Psychological Health and Adjustment

Loneliness and emotional isolation create psychological illness. There are few feelings more distressful than feeling unloved, abandoned, alienated from others, isolated, lonely, and unknown. *Psychological health* is the ability to build and maintain cooperative, interdependent relationships with other people. It depends almost entirely on the quality of your relationships with other people. People who, for one reason or another, are unable to establish acceptable relationships often develop considerable anxiety, depression, frustration, and alienation. They tend to be afraid and to feel inadequate, helpless, and alone. They often cling to unproductive and unskilled ways of reaching out to others, and they seem unable to change to more successful methods of building and maintaining relationships. Having poor interpersonal skills seems to be a major cause of psychological pathology.

Positive, supportive relationships, on the other hand, are related to psychological health and adjustment, lack of neuroticism and psychopathology, reduction of psychological distress and effective coping with stressful situations, resilience in stressful situations, self-reliance and autonomy, a coherent and integrated self-identity, greater psychological safety, higher self-esteem, increased general happiness, and increased interpersonal skills.

Constructively Coping With Stress

It is during major life transitions that stress tends to be highest and social support may be most needed. When you move from school to a job, when you lose or change jobs, when you get married or divorced, when your spouse or parents die, or when you move from one part of the country to another, stress is high and social support is an important resource for coping. Positive and supportive relationships provide the caring, information, resources, and feedback you need to cope with stress and flourish physically and psychologically. They decrease the number and severity of stressful events in your life. They reduce your anxiety and help you appraise the nature of the stress and your ability to deal with it constructively. Discussions with supportive peers help you perceive the meaning of the stressful event, regain mastery over your life, and enhance your self-esteem. Such discussions have helped such diverse populations as runaways, addicted individuals, unmarried mothers, cancer patients, first-time parents, the bereaved, rape victims, step-parents, parents of acting-out teenagers, teenage children of acting-out parents, and many other individuals experiencing adversity, challenges, and stress.

Self-Actualization

It is through our relationships that we actualize our personal resources and find joy and a sense of fulfillment. There is in all of us a drive to actualize our potential. We do so by being time competent and autonomous. *Time competent* is tying the past and the future to living fully in the present. The self-actualized person appears to be less burdened by guilts, regrets, and resentments from the past than is the non-self-actualized person, and the self-actualized person's aspirations are tied realistically to present goals.

Self-actualization is also dependent on being autonomous. *Autonomous* people have internalized the love, support, and acceptance of others so that they can apply values and principles flexibly in order to act in ways that are appropriate to the current situation. They are controlled neither by a small number of values and principles set early in life that are rigidly adhered to, no matter what the situation (*inner-directed*), nor by others' expectations and pressure to conform (*outer-directed*).

The time competence and the autonomy of the self-actualizing person are related qualities, in the sense that a person who lives primarily in the present relies more on his or her own support and expressiveness than does a person living primarily in the past or in the future. To live fully in the present means that you must be autonomous, free not only from rigid inner values but also from the excessive need to conform to social prescriptions in order to get approval from other people. *It is within our most meaningful relationships that we autonomously live in the present to actualize the person we have the potential to be.*

Being Human

What makes us human is the way we interact with other people. To the extent that our relationships reflect kindness, mercy, consideration, tenderness, love, concern, compassion, cooperation, responsiveness, and caring, we are becoming more human. In *humanizing* relationships, individuals are sympathetic and responsive to human needs. They invest each other with the character of humanity, and they treat and regard each other as human. It is the positive involvement with other people that we label as humane. In a *dehumanizing* relationship, people are divested of those qualities that are uniquely human and are turned into machines and objects, in the sense that they are treated in impersonal ways that reflect unconcern with human values. To be inhumane is to be unmoved by the suffering of others, to be unkind, even cruel and brutal. In a deep sense, the way we relate to others and the nature

TABLE 1.1:   FRIENDSHIPS

Ingredients of friendship

A recent *Psychology Today* survey of friendship revealed how important the following qualities are in a friend. The percentages represent the number of people who said that particular quality was "important" or "very important."

	Percent		Percent
Keeps confidences	89	Similar occupation	3
Loyalty	88	Similar income	4
Warmth, affection	82	Job accomplishments	8
Supportiveness	76	Physical attractiveness	9
Frankness	75	About my age	10
Sense of humor	74	Similar education	17

What friends do together

According to *Psychology Today*, here is what friends did together within the past month.

Women Percent	Men Percent	
90	78	Had an intimate talk.
84	80	Was asked by a friend to do something for him or her.
84	77	Went to dinner in a restaurant.
80	75	Asked a friend to do a favor.
75	70	Had a meal at home or at a friend's home.
67	64	Went to a movie, play, or concert.
62	64	Went drinking together.
62	49	Went shopping.
45	55	Participated in sports.
41	53	Watched a sporting event.

of the relationships we build and maintain determine what kind of people we become.

THE DIFFICULTY OF FORMING RELATIONSHIPS

A friend is one before whom I may think aloud.

Ralph Waldo Emerson

It is not easy to initiate, develop, and maintain positive relationships. It takes work and considerable skill. Interacting with others, for example, is a dynamic process. The interaction is constantly shifting and changing as you and the other person respond and react to each other. Sometimes communication will be clear; other times you may misunderstand each other. Sometimes you will have common goals and needs; other times your goals and needs will conflict. Everything you do will affect the relationship to some degree. Everything the other person does will affect your perceptions and feelings about the other person and the relationship.

There is a general rule that positive perceptions of and feelings toward another person are hard to acquire but easy to lose; however, negative perceptions of and feelings toward another person are easy to acquire and hard to lose. A perception of another person as kind, for example, may develop as you see the person act in sympathetic and generous ways towards others. But one instance of deliberate cruelty can change your perception of the person dramatically. On the other hand, the sight of a person kicking a dog on a single occasion would probably stick in your memory, and repeated evidence of kindness would not wipe out the impression that the person can be cruel.

The complex and constantly changing nature of relationships, the slowness with which positive feelings and impressions are built, and the fragileness of relationships all point to the difficulty in developing friendships. Loneliness, however, pushes most people into the effort to do so. The experience of feeling lonely is a central fact of human existence.

Roots of Loneliness

Loneliness has been aggravated by a number of contemporary developments. One is our *nomadic life style*. The average American moves 14 times in a lifetime. About 40 million Americans change their home addresses at least once every year. The extended family (in which children, parents, and grandparents live in the same household, or at least within short walking distance of one another) has almost disappeared in modern America. The people we know and love today may be hundreds of miles away tomorrow. Several times during our lives we may be faced with beginning anew with people we do not know. Very few adults today retain friendships formed during their childhoods. The dramatic change in mobility has had a profound effect on friendship patterns, on the family, and on the whole fabric of human interaction.

In addition to increased mobility, the *impersonality of city life* has radically changed friendship patterns. In large cities, people often do not know the names of those in the next apartment. They know little about the personal lives of business associates, the doorman, or the checkout clerk at the supermarket. People such as checkout clerks are often not seen as individuals but, rather, as an extension of the ''machine'' that provides our groceries.

Third, *relationships are limited* in terms of the energy one's friends are willing to commit to the relationship and the context within which the relationship occurs. Many people are overcommitted and busy without a great deal of flexible time to spend with a friend. Relationships at work, furthermore, may be quite positive without extending into leisure activities. The limited nature of relationships contributes to feelings of social and emotional isolation. Many people feel isolated from others and believe that even their friends do not know them well and do not care for them intensely.

Destructive and Abusive Relationships

Relationships are not always positive. There are many examples of human indifference to the suffering and problems of others. Individuals have watched someone being killed without attempting to help; heard a woman in the next room fall off a stepladder and injure herself without asking if she needed assistance; walked casually by, around, and over a woman with a broken leg lying on a sidewalk; administered in blind obedience to an authority painful electric shocks to another human being even after the person screamed in pain, pounded on the door, begged to be released, and then fell into ominous silence; physically and psychologically abused spouses and children; and through fear, hate, and prejudice deprived other people of their civil rights, robbed them of their freedom, and even killed them.

Relationships and Problems in Living

Many if not most of life's problems have their origins in interpersonal relationships. Abuse of drugs, criminal acts such as shoplifting, and unwanted sexual activity often begin from having poor models from which to pattern personal behavior and from conforming too much to peer influences. Individuals, for example, who believe that they will lose their best friend or will miss their last chance to be loved and accepted unless they take drugs will tend to do so, especially if they have observed their parents and other adults use drugs. Abusing drugs, having a criminal record, or being involved in an unwanted pregnancy can result in the loss of long-term goals and opportunities such as attending college, getting a desired job, or even finding the right person to fall in love with. Such problem behaviors are avoided when you have high quality relationships with parents and peers, are part of groups who frown on the problem behaviors, and are committed to a set of values based on caring about oneself and others. Individuals who plan to continue their education or who have other long-term goals tend to avoid problem behaviors that will block the accomplishment of their long-term goals.

Interpersonal Skills Required

Connecting with others is hard work. First you have to build a friendship. Then you have to maintain it. Friendships are like money—easier made than kept. Overcoming the nomadic life style, impersonality of city life, and limited nature of relationships in order to build and maintain caring and committed friendships is not easy. It takes interpersonal skills to build and maintain a positive relationship. Despite their value, interpersonal skills are taken for granted by most people. Mastering the skills required to build and maintain positive relationships is not automatic or easy. It takes training and it takes practice. You must reach out with sensitivity and grace.

FORMING AND MAINTAINING POSITIVE RELATIONSHIPS

Don't walk in front of me
I may not follow
Don't walk behind me
I may not lead
Walk beside me
And just be my friend.

      Albert Camus

The hardest part about having friends is being a friend. Being a friend takes time, effort, and skill. Time is a problem for most relationships. You have to plan to spend quality time with your friends, in activities both of you consider enjoyable, such as exercise, games, meals, sports events, musical concerts, and so forth. You have to have intimate conversations with each other, share your feelings, reactions, thoughts, values, perceptions, and plans. You have to work constantly on the interpersonal skills required to be a friend and to relate effectively to others.

There are three ways to find the positive relationships you need. The first way is the easiest. You simply *wait* until someone finds you and wants to be your friend. The second way is harder. You simply *ask* other people to be your friends. Unfortunately, many of us are afraid to ask. We do not want to risk the rejection; we feel embarrassed; we see asking as a weakness to be ashamed of; or we are too shy. The third way to find a positive relationship is to *give* your friendship to others. In the long run, this is the surest way to build positive relationships. You get what you give in life. If you want friends, be a friend. If you want others to care about you, care about them. If you want others to comfort you, comfort them. Being a friend or giving your friendship to others requires interpersonal skills.

Interpersonal skills are the sum total of your ability to interact effectively with other people. Whenever you interact with other people, whether they are friends, family members, acquaintances, business associates, or store clerks, interpersonal skills are a must. Your social skills allow you to take appropriate social initiatives, understand people's reactions to them, and respond accordingly. Your interpersonal skills determine your ability to initiate, develop, and maintain caring and productive relationships. Interpersonal skills generally fall into four areas:

1. Knowing and trusting each other
2. Communicating with each other accurately and unambiguously
3. Accepting and supporting each other
4. Resolving conflicts and relationship problems constructively

By letting others know you, you create the potential for trust, caring, commitment, growth, self-understanding, and friendship. How can other people care about you if they do not know you? You let people know you when you disclose to them how you are reacting to what is currently taking place. Such openness depends on your self-awareness and self-acceptance. If you are unaware of your reactions, you cannot communicate them to another person. If you cannot accept your perceptions and feelings, you will try to hide them. To let them know you, you must first be aware of who you are and accept yourself. When you let others know you, trust is built if they react positively, and trust is destroyed if they reactive negatively. (Chapters 2 and 3 deal with the skills involved in appropriate self-disclosure and trust building.)

If you are alive, you are communicating. Some people communicate well, some communicate poorly. Ideas, perceptions, feelings, and attitudes all have to be communicated accurately and unambiguously. Especially important is communicating warmth and liking. Unless you believe the other person likes you and the other person believes that you like him or her, a relationship will not develop. Communication skills begin with sending messages that are phrased so that the other person can easily understand them. They also include listening in ways that ensure you have fully understood the other person. It is through sending and receiving messages that all relationships are initiated, developed, and stabilized (chapters 4, 5, and 6 cover these skills).

When a friend asks you for help, what is the best way to respond? When someone you know is going through a personal or family crisis and needs your personal support, what is the best way to express your concern? The third area of interpersonal skills development concerns mutual acceptance and support. Responding in helpful ways to another person's problems and concerns, communicating acceptance and support, using modeling to increase the constructiveness of another person's behavior are all important relationship skills (see chapter 7).

A conflict is a "moment of truth" within a relationship. The more two people interact and the more two people care about each other, the more conflicts they will have. We fight with people we care about, not with strangers. Conflicts will arise no matter how much two people care about each other and work together. How conflicts are managed determines whether two people become emotionally closer and more able to work together effectively, or whether they like each other less and are less committed to working together well. Whether relationships grow and develop or wither on the vine is largely determined by how conflicts are managed. Important aspects of conflict management include being aware of your usual strategies for managing conflicts, defining conflicts in ways that facilitate or help bring about a constructive resolution, being able to negotiate resolutions that are beneficial both to you and to the other person, and being able to manage your feelings (such as anger) constructively. Conflicts are inevitable, even among the best of friends, and ensuring that conflicts deepen rather than weaken a relationship involves a vital set of interpersonal skills. (This material is covered in chapters 8, 9, and 10.) The barriers to increasing your interpersonal skills are discussed in chapter 11.

THE APPLICATION OF SOCIAL SCIENCE RESEARCH TO INTERPERSONAL SKILLS

A friend is a present you give yourself.

Robert Louis Stevenson

We have at our disposal a vast amount of social science research on interpersonal interaction, yet this knowledge has not been translated into a form useful to individuals who wish to apply it to increase their interpersonal skills. This book attempts to fill the gap between the findings of the research on interpersonal attraction and the application of this knowledge to the development of interpersonal skills.

To make this book as readable as possible, a minimum of footnotes and references to research and theory are included. This does not mean that there is no empirical support for the behaviors recommended. The basic skills that determine a person's interpersonal effectiveness have been identified from the results of the author's research, from the results of the research on effective therapeutic relationships, and from the results of the social-psychological research on interpersonal relationships. In addition, much of the material in this book has been used in a variety of training programs aimed at increasing interpersonal skills. The evaluation of these programs indicates that the material in this book is effective in increasing the interpersonal skills of readers.

Any person concerned with increasing his or her interpersonal skills and any practitioners who work with people will find this book helpful. It is not a review of theory and research for scholars; it translates theory and research findings into a program for developing the skills necessary to form productive and fulfilling relationships with other people. Anyone, young or old, will be able to understand and use the material in this book.

CO-ORIENTATION

In building a relationship, two individuals must be *co-oriented*; that is, they must operate under the same norms and adhere to the same values. The co-orientation does not have to be perfect; rewarding relationships are quite common between individuals from different backgrounds and even different cultures. But in order to develop a relationship, you must agree on the norms and values that will determine your behavior in that relationship.

Norms refer to common expectations about the behavior that is appropriate for you and the other person in the relationship: Do you ask each other to do favors? How personal are your discussions? What types of things can you depend on each other for? Norms depend to a large extent on the values two individuals agree to adhere to in a relationship. The skills emphasized in this book will establish norms about expected behaviors in a relationship (to self-disclose, build trust, be supportive and accepting, face conflicts, and so forth). These norms are based on a set of humanistic values (to assume responsibility for your behavior, strive to build caring and committed relationships, be empathetic and kind, provide caring support to those in need, and so forth). If you use the skills presented in this book, your interactions with other people will promote norms that will help you develop fulfilling and meaningful relationships.

Often, establishing mutual norms and values for how you and the other person are going to relate is more important than the actual level of interpersonal skills you and the other person possess. Being mutually committed to facing conflicts and resolving them constructively, for example, may be more important than the actual level of your conflict-management skills. Your mutual commitment to be self-disclosing and genuine with each other may be more important in creating comradeship and intimacy than the actual skill with which you disclose your feelings and reactions. This book emphasizes developing your interpersonal skills. It should be remembered, however, that whenever you apply the skills discussed in this book, you are also promoting a set of norms and values for your relationships.

LEARNING FROM EXPERIENCE

We all learn from our experiences. From touching a hot stove we learn to avoid heated objects. From dating we learn about male-female relationships. Every day we have experiences from which we learn. Many things about relating to other people can be learned only by experience. Seeing a movie about love is not the same as experiencing love. Hearing a lecture on friendship is not the same as having a friend. It takes more than explanations to teach interpersonal skills.

To learn interpersonal skills, you first need to understand what the skills are and when they should be used, and second, you need the opportunity to actually practice the skills. The best way to learn about the skills and to master them is through structured exercises. The plan in this book is for you to learn interpersonal skills through experiences as well as through reading. Each chapter has a series of exercises that provide opportunities to experience and master the interpersonal skills after reading about them. To learn skills you must understand them conceptually as well as behaviorally, and experiential learning is the best way to do this.

Experiential learning is based on three assumptions: (1) people learn best when they are personally involved in the learning experience; (2) knowledge has to be discovered if it is to mean anything or make a difference in behavior; and (3) commitment to learning is highest when people are free to set their own learning goals and actively pursue them within a given framework. Learning by experience is a process of making generalizations and conclusions about your own direct experiences. It emphasizes experiencing directly what you are studying, building a personal commitment to learn, and being responsible for organizing the conclusions you draw from your experiences.

The process of experiential learning is shown in Figure 1.3. The learner reflects on his or her concrete personal experiences and examines their meaning in order to formulate a set of concepts or principles to help understand such experiences. The sequence is (1) concrete personal experiences followed by (2) observation of, reflection on, and examination of one's experiences; this leads to (3) the formulation of abstract concepts and generalizations, which leads to (4) hypotheses to be tested in future action. Experiential learning results in personal theories about effective behavior and continuously recurs as these theories are tested out and confirmed or modified.

Learning from your experiences is especially useful when you want to learn skills. No one wants to ride in an airplane with a pilot who has read a book on how to fly but has never actually flown a plane. Reading about how to communicate is not enough to make you skillful in communicating with others; you need practice and experience in

FIGURE 1.3:   Experiential Learning Cycle

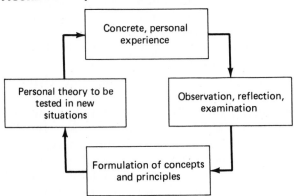

good communication skills. The next section examines skill learning in greater depth.

LEARNING INTERPERSONAL SKILLS

No one can make you a skillful person but yourself. Reading a book on physical conditioning exercises will not make you fit. Studying books on golf, swimming, or horseback riding will not make you an expert golfer, swimmer, or horseback rider. Learning interpersonal skills is no different. You are not born with interpersonal skills nor do they appear magically when you need them. You have to learn them. Socially skilled individuals are not born, they are made.

To learn an interpersonal skill you must first *see the need* for the interpersonal skill, then *understand* what the skill and its component parts are, and finally *practice, practice, practice* until the skill is an automatic reflex that does not require conscious thought or practice. It helps to see other people model the skill and to have others give you feedback as to how well you are engaging in the skill.

With most skills there is a period of slow learning, then a period of rapid improvement, then a period when performance remains the same, and then another period of rapid improvement, and then another plateau, and so forth. Individuals have to practice the interpersonal skills long enough to make it through the first few plateaus and integrate the skills into their behavioral repertoires. To become skillful in interacting with others, you must practice, practice, practice. Once learned, social skills are automatic. We do not need to rethink consciously how to carry out a greeting every time we see a person. It has been estimated that some 80 percent or more of our behavior is automatic, though we constantly monitor and adjust it, depending on the response we are given. But we constantly learn new skills, giving conscious attention to what we only later use automatically.

Most skill development goes through the following stages:

1. Awareness that the skill is needed.
2. Understanding of what the skill is and the component behaviors required to perform the skill. To learn a skill, you must have a clear idea of what the skill is, and you must know how to perform it. Often it is helpful to have someone who has already mastered the skill go through it several times while describing it step by step. We need models to imitate. The skill is easier to recognize and its effects are much easier to judge when it is performed by another person.

3. Practicing the skill while receiving feedback and encouragement. We practice the skill and receive feedback on how well we perform it. We often practice skills by performing them in our imagination first. After visualizing how the skill is used, we try it out in real life. The more immediate and specific the feedback we receive, the more able we are to modify our performance. Coaching, feedback, and reinforcement during and after rehearsal of the skill and detailed observations of how you are doing will help you to monitor, adjust, and improve your performance. We also need encouragement to keep practicing.

First, there is self-conscious, *awkward* engagement in the skill. Practicing any new skill feels awkward. The first few times you throw a football, play a piano, or paraphrase, it feels strange. Second, there are feelings of *phoniness* while engaging in the skill. After a while the awkwardness passes and enacting the skill becomes more smooth. You may next, however, feel unauthentic or phony when performing the skill. Encouragement is often needed to move you through this stage.

While you are learning interpersonal skills you may feel that the process is somewhat *mechanical* and unreal. This is true of every kind of skill development. Learning how to play the piano, for example, involves the mechanical practice of specific behaviors, which seem unreal compared with the performance of a beautiful piano concerto. It is when you apply your interpersonal skills to real situations that they will gain the fire and life that may sometimes be lacking in practice. Automatic, *routine* use is achieved when the skill is fully integrated into your behavioral repertoire and seems like a natural action.

You learn any skill (tennis or managing conflict) by following these steps:

1. Taking a risk by engaging in a challenging action, that is, experimenting to increase your competence
2. Assessing and obtaining feedback on the success or failure of your efforts
3. Engaging in self-reflection and analysis of the effectiveness of the actions taken
4. Modifying your actions, and trying again
5. Recycling to step 2 and repeating the process over and over again

In learning any skill it is helpful to remember the following advice: You have to sweat on the practice field before you perform on the playing field! You must study the lessons before you get the grades! You have to make the call before you get the sale!

As you read this book you will be asked to participate in skill-building exercises and practice activities. You will be asked to support and encourage the efforts of other readers to do likewise. Improving your interpersonal competence is an exciting and exhilarating experience, but in doing so it is often helpful to remember the stages of skill learning involved. Do not worry about feeling awkward the first time you implement a skill. Persevere and practice and soon the awkwardness will pass.

How well you master interpersonal skills depends on how frequently you practice them. If you isolate yourself you will have little opportunity to consolidate your skills. Isolated individuals are more likely to fail to learn interpersonal skills than those who have friends and acquaintances with whom to interact.

SUMMARY

To live is to reach out to others. We all need other people. We engage in relationships because we have goals we wish to pursue that require the participation of other people as well as ourselves. Relationships are profoundly cooperative in that they are built on shared goals and joint activities. Relationships begin with an initiative that begins a cycle of social interaction that includes perceiving what the other person is doing, deciding how to respond, taking action, and then perceiving the other person's response. When both persons are involved in the cycle, they spontaneously coordinate their behavior to build a relationship. This repeating cycle is influenced by their goals, their roles, their moods, the physical setting, the nature of the occasion, relevant social rules, and the feedback they receive from others.

Life without friends is not much of a life. Relationships are a necessity, not a luxury. Relationships are the key to our development cognitively and socially, to forming an identity, to achieving career success, to finding a meaning to our lives, to maintaining our physical health, to maintaining our psychological health, to coping with adversity and stress, to actualizing our potential, and to becoming humane. Forming and maintaining relationships, however, is not easy. With every interaction the relationships change. Many people do not have the interpersonal skills, the opportunities, and the will to create close relationships.

They may be lonely, be involved in indifferent or abusive relationships, and engage in problem behaviors. To form caring and committed relationships individuals need the interpersonal skills to get to know and trust each other, communicate accurately and unambiguously, accept and support each other, and resolve conflicts constructively. These interpersonal skills are covered in this book. This book is constructed to facilitate your mastery of the essential interpersonal skills by providing discussions of the skills and exercises that will enable you to practice and perfect the skills.

Exercise 1.1: Your Relationships

Make new friends
And keep the old.
One is silver,
The other gold.

   Children's song

The purpose of this exercise is to reflect on your current relationships. The procedure is as follows:

1. On a piece of paper draw a circle in the center about the size of a 50-cent piece. Write your name inside this circle.

2. Draw a number of smaller circles (25-, 5-, 10-cent sizes) around the big circle. These circles represent our relationships.

3. Think about the persons with whom you have the strongest and closest bonds. Fill in the various circles with their names. List the people you care for, have warm feelings for, and are comfortable with. List the people you would like to talk with if you were having a hard time. Think of who you would like to share a meal with or receive a letter from. The more personal the relationship, the larger the circle the name should appear in. Keep these points in mind:

    a. Draw the circles and jot down names quickly, just as they come to mind.

    b. Include the people who have been supportive and personally close to you all through your life as well as those who are supportive and personally close to you now.

    c. Do not worry about being "fair" or reasonable or logical. This exercise is for you alone.

4. You may wish to jog your memory by referring to your address book. Think of places you have lived and the friends you had there. Think of friends from work, old school buddies, and neighborhood friends. Think of the social, reli-

gious, and political groups you belong to and the people you have grown close to in those associations.

5. As you list friends' names, you may find yourself wishing to be in closer touch with some of them. There may be others that you find yourself wanting to call or write to or even for whom you want to buy a small present. There may be people you feel deeply for but have been unable to let them know how you feel. There may be people with whom you would like to initiate deeper and more meaningful relationships. If so, list those names on a second sheet of paper.

6. When you have finished, review each name and remember the experiences you have had with that person.

Relationships Assessment 1

FIGURE 1.4: Sample Relationships Diagram

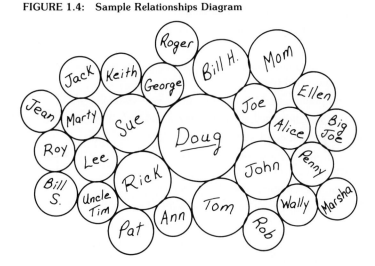

Relationships Assessment 2

SAMPLE RELATIONSHIPS LISTS

People I would like to see, call, or write	People I would like to deepen a relationship with	People I would like to begin a relationship with
1.		
2.		
3.		
4.		
5.		
6.		

Exercise 1.2: Keeping Friends

Friendship is like money—easier made than kept. You may meet many people in your lifetime and make many acquaintances, but true friends are rare. Friends are earned, and once found, they must be treasured. This requires as much care as tending a garden. The following questions may help you consider whether you are increasing or decreasing the quality of your friendships.

1. Do you enjoy doing favors for people you care about?
2. Do you publicly find fault with other people?
3. Can you keep a secret?
4. When a friend receives public recognition for his or her efforts, do you secretly wish it was you being recognized?
5. Are you generally cheerful and happy?
6. Do you see friends only if they will do things you like to do?
7. Do you feel free to share your reactions and feelings with your friends?
8. When a friend hurts your feelings, do you decide the person is not really your friend and avoid him or her?
9. Do you promise to do things and then forget about them?
10. Do you sometimes tell others things a friend told to you in confidence?
11. Is it easy to see good qualities in others?
12. Do you seek out activities and projects that you and your friends can do together?
13. Are you often depressed and negative?
14. Do you feel genuinely happy when a friend succeeds?
15. Do you hide your "true self" from your friends?
16. When you are angry with a friend, do you sit down with him or her and try to solve the problem?

Answers

1. Yes	5. Yes	9. No	13. No
2. No	6. No	10. No	14. Yes
3. Yes	7. Yes	11. Yes	15. No
4. No	8. No	12. Yes	16. Yes

Analysis

14-16 correct answers: You have friends because you are a friend to others. You are open, trustworthy, reliable, supportive, cooperative, committed, and caring, each a true art.

10-13 correct answers: You have friends, but some of them stick with you despite your faults.

5-9 correct answers: You find yourself looking for friends, but unable to find them. Look at yourself carefully and plan some changes.

2 *Self-Disclosure*

INTRODUCTION

By letting you know me, I allow you to like me. By disclosing myself to you, I create the potential for trust, caring, commitment, growth, self-understanding, and friendship. How can you care for me if you do not know me? How can you trust me if I do not demonstrate my trust in you by disclosing myself to you? How can you be committed to me if you know little or nothing about me? How can I know and understand myself if I do not disclose myself to friends? To like me, to trust me, to be committed to our relationship, to facilitate my personal growth and self-understanding, and to be my friend you must know me.

I let you know me when I disclose to you how I am reacting to what is currently taking place. Such openness depends on my self-awareness and self-acceptance. In order for me to feel free to disclose myself to you, I must accept and appreciate myself. If I am unaware of my reactions, I cannot communicate them to you. If I cannot accept my perceptions and feelings, I will try to hide them. When I let you know me, trust is built if you react positively, and trust is destroyed if you react negatively. This chapter will focus on self-awareness and the disclosure of oneself to other people. A later chapter will focus on self-acceptance.

BEING OPEN WITH AND TO OTHER PEOPLE

Relationships begin when two people reach out to each other and identify common goals, interests, activities, and values. In order to do so they must be open with and open to each other. You are *open with* other persons when you disclose yourself to them, sharing your ideas and feelings and letting them know who you are as a person. You are *open to* other persons when you are interested in their ideas and feelings and want to know who they are as individuals. To be open with another person you must be aware of who you are, accept yourself, and take the risk of trusting him or her to be accepting of you. To be open to another person you must be aware of who he or she is, accept him or her, and be trustworthy in your interactions with him or her. Your relationship grows and deepens as you and the other person are more and more open with and to each other. Your awareness of the other person increases your self-awareness and vice versa. Your acceptance of yourself increases your acceptance of the other person and vice versa. Being trusting of the other person increases your trustworthiness and vice versa.

A relationship grows and develops as two people become more open about themselves to each other. *If you cannot reveal yourself, you cannot become close to others, and you cannot be valued by others for who you are.* Two people who let each other know how they are reacting to situations and to each other are pulled together; two people who stay silent about their reactions and feelings stay strangers.

SELF-DISCLOSURE

Self-disclosure may be defined as the act of revealing how you are reacting to the present situation and of giving any information about the past that is relevant to an understanding of your reactions to the present. Reactions to people and events are not facts as much as they are feelings. To be self-disclosing means to share with another person how you feel about events that have just occurred. Self-disclosure does not mean revealing intimate details of your past life. Making highly personal confessions about your past may lead to a temporary feeling of intimacy, but a relationship is built by disclosing your reactions to events you both

FIGURE 2.1: Being Open With You + Being Open To You = An Open Relationship

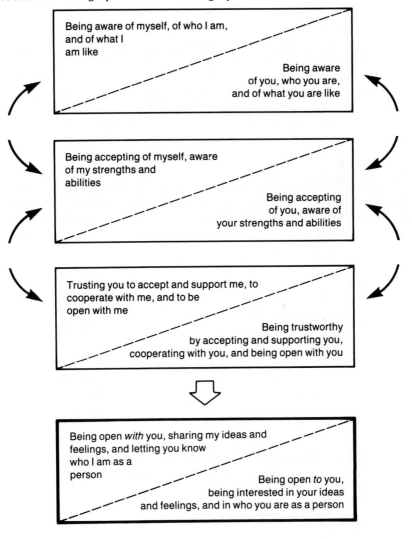

Being aware of myself, of who I am, and of what I am like

Being aware of you, who you are, and of what you are like

Being accepting of myself, aware of my strengths and abilities

Being accepting of you, aware of your strengths and abilities

Trusting you to accept and support me, to cooperate with me, and to be open with me

Being trustworthy by accepting and supporting you, cooperating with you, and being open with you

Being open *with* you, sharing my ideas and feelings, and letting you know who I am as a person

Being open *to* you, being interested in your ideas and feelings, and in who you are as a person

Being open with you + Being open to you = An open relationship

experience or to what the other person says or does. A person comes to know and understand you not through knowing your past history but through knowing how you react. Past history is helpful only if it clarifies why you are reacting in a certain way.

Self-disclosure enables other people to get to know you. Usually, the more that people know about you, the more likely they are to like you. Yet self-disclosure does carry a degree of risk. For just as knowing you better is likely to result in a closer relationship, learning too much about you may result in alienation. "Familiarity breeds contempt" means that some people may learn something about you that detracts from the relationship. Because disclosing is risky, some people prefer to hide themselves from others in the belief that no reaction is better than a possible negative reaction. "Nothing offered, nothing gained," on the other hand, means that some risk is vital to achieving any worthwhile goal. To build a meaningful relationship you have to disclose yourself to the other person and take the risk that the other person may reject rather than like you.

There is always some risk involved in disclosing, but as you gain trust in another person, you perceive that the disclosure of more revealing information is "safe." Sometimes people do not trust their spouses, siblings, and friends, and disclose to strangers (such as a bartender or people they meet in travel) instead. Strangers are seen as safe because they are in no position to use the information against them.

The amount of self-disclosure you engage in will influence the amount of self-disclosure the other person engages in. The more you self-disclose, the more the other person will tend to self-disclose. Your response to others' self-disclosures, however, does matter. In addition to being open *with* other people, you must be open *to* others to build good relationships. Being open to another person means showing that you are interested in how he or she feels and thinks. This does not mean prying into the intimate areas of another's life. It means being willing to listen to his or her reactions to the present situation and to what you are doing and saying. Being accepting and supportive will increase the other person's tendency to be open with you. It will strengthen the relationship and help it grow. Even when a person's behavior offends you, it is possible for you to express acceptance of the person and disagreement with the way he or she behaves.

Impact of Self-Disclosure on Relationships

Healthy relationships are built on self-disclosure. Self-disclosure allows individuals to identify common goals and overlapping needs, interests, activities, and values. It allows individuals to validate their perception of reality. It opens the relationship to growth and development. It frequently results in increased liking and commitment among the individuals involved. The more self-disclosing you are to another person, the more likely it will be that that person will like you. It fulfills a human need to be known intimately and forms the basis for support and caring during crises.

Relationships are built on common goals, interests, activities, and values. In order to know whether a relationship with another person is desirable, you have to know what the other person wants from the relationship, what the other person is interested in, what joint activities might be available, and what the other person values. If such information is not disclosed, the relationship may end before it has a chance to begin.

The events taking place around us and the meaning of other people's behavior are often ambiguous, open to many different interpretations. In such cases, we compare our perceptions and reactions with the reactions and perceptions of others. This is called *consensual validation*. If others have similar interpretations, we consider our perceptions validated. Without self-disclosure, consensual validation could not take place.

If you hide how you are reacting to the other person, your concealment can sicken the relationship. The energy you pour into hiding adds to the stress of the relationship and dulls your awareness of your own inner experience, thus decreasing your ability to disclose your reactions even when it is perfectly safe and appropriate to do so. Hiding your reactions from others through fear of rejection and conflict or through feelings of shame and guilt leads to loneliness. Being silent is not being strong; to be strong is to be willing to take risks in a relationship, to disclose yourself with the intention of building a better relationship.

Communicating intimately with another person, especially in times of stress, seems to be a basic human need. Disclosing yourself to another person builds a relationship that allows for such intimate communication, both by yourself and by the other. If neither you nor the other person feels free to engage in self-disclosure, you can be of little or no help to each other during periods of stress.

Finally, self-disclosure increases your self-awareness and understanding of yourself through gaining a more objective perspective on your experiences and through provoking feedback from others.

Appropriateness of Self-Disclosure

Self-disclosure must be relevant to your relationship with the other person and appropriate to the situation you are in. You can be too self-disclosing. A person who reveals too many of his or her reactions too fast may scare others away; a relationship is built gradually, except in rare and special cases. Being too self-disclosing will create as many relationship problems as disclosing too little. Although you should sometimes take risks with your disclosure to others, you should not be blind to the appropriateness of your behavior to the situation. Self-disclosure is appropriate when:

1. It is not a random or isolated act but, rather, a part of an ongoing relationship.

2. It is reciprocated. Intimate self-disclosure should continue only if it is reciprocated. When people disclose, they expect disclosure in return. When it is apparent that self-disclosure will not be reciprocated, you should limit the amount of disclosure you make.

3. It concerns what is going on within and between persons in the present.

4. It creates a reasonable chance of improving the relationship.

5. It takes account of the effect it will have upon the other person. Some disclosures may upset or cause considerable distress to the other person. Individual attitudes about disclosure vary considerably, and what you consider appropriate may not be so to someone else.

6. It speeds up when a crisis develops in the relationship.

7. It moves gradually to a deeper level. Self-disclosures may begin with the information that acquaintances commonly disclose (such as talking about hobbies, sports, school, and current events) and gradually move to more intimate information. Most people become uncomfortable when the level of self-disclosure exceeds their expectations, since receiving self-disclosure can be as threatening as giving it. As a friendship develops, the depth of disclosure increases as well. Intimate or very personal self-disclosure is most appropriate in ongoing close relationships. Disclosures about deep feelings, fears, loves, and concerns are most appropriate in close, well-established relationships.

Although relationships are built through self-disclosure, there are times when you will want to hide your reactions to a particular situation from another person. If a person has been clearly shown to be untrustworthy, it is foolish to be self-disclosing with him or her. If you know from past experience that the other person will misinterpret or overreact to your self-disclosure, you may wish to keep silent.

Self-Disclosure and Self-Awareness

Being open with another person begins with being aware of who you are and what you are like. Self-awareness arises from experiences and interactions with other people. Your awareness of who other people are and your awareness of who you are go hand-in-hand. One cannot be separated from the other. You do not get to know yourself by hiding in a closet and avoiding others. You get to know yourself by getting out and having a wide variety of experiences with many different people.

You cannot disclose your feelings and reactions if you do not know what they are. Unless you are aware of your reactions and feelings, you cannot consciously communicate them to others. Being aware of how you react to various situations and what you like and dislike as a person is the first step in being self-disclosing with other people and building strong relationships with them. Self-awareness is also the first step toward understanding yourself and making a choice as to whether or not you wish to change current patterns of behavior to more effective ones.

There are a number of ways of becoming more self-aware. *The first involves "watching" yourself in order to understand how you are feeling and reacting and what is causing your feelings and reactions.* This is called *self-perception* theory. We understand our attitudes and emotions partly by inferring them from observations of our behavior or the circumstances in which our behavior occurs. By "watching" what you do, you become aware of what you are like as a person, much as outside observers form judgments of us on the basis of what they see. When you become more self-aware, you usually focus on one facet of yourself. Asking you to look in a mirror physically focuses you on your appearance, whereas playing a tape recording of you speaking focuses you on your voice. This is called *objective self-awareness.* When you become aware of some aspect of yourself you typically evaluate it, considering how this aspect of you measures up to some internal rule or standard.

Second, when you explain your feelings, perceptions, reactions, and experiences in words, they become clearer, better organized, and take on new meanings. Explaining your reactions and disclosing your feelings to persons you trust can lead to new insights into yourself and your experiences. Most types of psychotherapy and many new classroom learning procedures are based on the premise that oral explanation results in higher-level reasoning and deeper-level understanding.

A third way of becoming more self-aware is to compare yourself to others. Social comparison is looking to other people as a way of gauging your own attitudes, emotions, attributes, and abilities. Some comparisons are easy to make. There is little room for error in deciding whether your hair is blonde or brunette or how old or tall you are. There are no objective standards, however, for determining how kind, considerate, insightful, intelligent, extroverted, or socially astute a person you are. To make such judgments, you must compare yourself to other people. In the absence of objective measures of evaluation, comparing yourself to others provides a subjective measuring tool. By comparing yourself with others, especially with reference groups that include people who are similar to you in certain key ways, you form an impression of what you are like. Through social comparison you discover your similarities and your uniqueness. From knowing others you learn to know yourself.

A fourth way of becoming more self-aware is to request feedback from other people as to how they see you and how they are reacting to your behavior. This is such an important aspect of becoming more self-aware that it is discussed in detail in the next section.

SELF-AWARENESS THROUGH FEEDBACK FROM OTHERS

Feedback from people you trust can confirm your view of yourself or reveal to you aspects of yourself and consequences of your behavior you never knew. It is through feedback from other people that you increase your self-awareness. Before considering feedback, however, it may be helpful to examine Figures 2.2, 2.3, and 2.4 (Luft 1969). Figure 2.2 is known as the Johari Window, after its two originators, Joe Luft and Harry Ingham. It illustrates their point that there are certain things you know about yourself and certain things you do not know about yourself as well as certain things other people know about you and certain things they do not know. It assumes that it takes energy to hide information from yourself and others and that the more information that is known, the clearer communication will be. Building a relationship, therefore, often involves working to enlarge your free area while decreasing your blind and hidden areas (See Figures 2.3 and 2.4). As you become more self-disclosing, you reduce the hidden area. As you encourage others to

FIGURE 2.2:   Identification of Areas of the Self

	Known to Self	Unknown to Self
Known to Others	1. Free to Self and Others	2. Blind to Self, Seen by Others
Unknown to Others	3. Hidden Area: Self Hidden from Others	4. Unknown Self

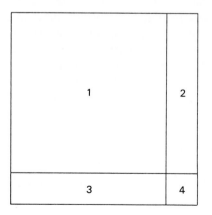

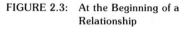

FIGURE 2.3:   At the Beginning of a
Relationship

be self-disclosing with you, your blind area is reduced. Through reducing your hidden area you give other people information to react to, thus enabling them to help you reduce your blind area. Through reducing your blind area, you increase your self-awareness; this helps you to be even more self-disclosing with others.

When other people disclose how they are reacting to your behavior, they are giving you *feedback*. The purpose of feedback is to provide constructive information to help you become aware of how your behavior affects others and is perceived by others. The key benefit of feedback is that it tells you when you are off course with respect to your desired objectives. Often the most helpful feedback is that which tells you that your behavior is not being as effective as you want it to be and, therefore, helps you modify your actions so that they become more productive. People generally like interacting with others who give a lot of feedback because they appear interested and interesting. Feedback can be

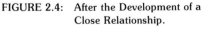

FIGURE 2.4:   After the Development of a
Close Relationship.

head nodding, focused attention, "uh-huhs," or smiles. All show that the other person is listening and interested.

When you disclose how you are reacting to the actions of another person, you are providing the other person with feedback. Helpful feedback tells the other person what effect her actions are having on you. The person receiving feedback, furthermore, is always responsible for deciding whether or not her present behavior is to be continued or changed. By increasing another person's self-awareness through feedback, you provide her with a more informed choice for future behavior. It is important to give feedback in a way that will not be threatening to the receiver and make the receiver defensive. The more defensive a person is, the less likely it is that she will hear and understand your feedback correctly. Feedback should have a focus that is helpful and non-threatening:

1. *Focus your feedback on the person's behavior, not on his personality.* Refer to what the person does, not to what you imagine his or her traits to be. Thus, you might say the person "talked frequently in the meeting" rather than saying the person "is a loudmouth." The former is an observation of what you see and hear and the latter is an inference about, or interpretation of, the person's character.

2. *Focus your feedback in descriptions rather than on judgments.* Refer to what occurred, not to your judgments of right or wrong, good or bad, or nice or naughty. You might say, "You do not pronounce words clearly, and you speak too softly to be heard," rather than, "You are a terrible, rotten, lousy public speaker." Judgments arise out of a frame of reference or value system and should be avoided, whereas description represents, as much as possible, neutral reporting.

3. *Focus your feedback on a specific situation rather than on abstract behavior.* What a person does is always related to a specific time and place. Feedback that ties behavior to a specific situation and is given immediately after the behavior has occurred increases self-awareness. Instead of saying, "Sometimes your face lights up and happiness shines out of your eyes," say, "When you and John were talking just now your face lit up and you smiled in a way that made me feel warm."

4. *Focus your feedback on the "here and now" not on the "there and then."* The more immediate the feedback, the more helpful it is. Instead of saying, "Three years ago when I saw you in the hall you didn't speak to me," say, "Hey, I just said hello and you didn't reply. Is something wrong?"

5. *Focus your feedback on sharing your perceptions and feelings rather than on giving advice.* By sharing perceptions and feelings you leave other people free to decide for themselves—in the light of their own goals in a particular situation at a particular time—how to use the perceptions, reactions, and feelings. When you give advice, you tell other people what to do with the information and thereby take away their freedom to determine for themselves what is for them the most appropriate course of action. Let the other people decide for themselves what behavior they want to change. You can give feedback such as, "You look away and blush whenever John says hello to you," without giving advice such as, "You are too shy. Go ask John for a date."

6. *Do not force feedback on other people.* Feedback is given to help people become more self-aware and to improve their effectiveness in relating to other people. It is not given to make you feel better. Feedback should serve the needs of the receiver, not the needs of the giver. Giving feedback does release tension and increase the giver's energy, but help and feedback need to be given and heard as an offer, not as something being forced on the receiver. If other people do not want to hear your feedback, do not force it on them. If you do not want to hear other people's feedback to you, do not let them force it on you. Even if you are upset and want more than anything else in the world (at that moment) to give a friend some feedback, do not give it if your friend is too defensive or uninterested to understand it.

7. *Do not give people more feedback than they can understand at the time.* If you overload other people with feedback, it reduces the chances that they will use it. When you give people more feedback than they can understand, you are satisfying some need for yourself rather than helping the people become more self-aware.

8. *Focus your feedback on actions that the person can change.* It does no good to tell people that they have a lopsided head, that you do not like the color of their eyes, or that they are missing an ear. These are things the other person cannot change.

The giving and receiving of feedback requires courage, skill, understanding, and respect for yourself and others as well as involvement. Do not give feedback lightly. Make sure you are willing to be responsible for what you say and to clarify as much as the receiver wants. Be sure the timing of your feedback is appropriate. Excellent feedback presented at an inappropriate time may do more harm than good. Finally, remember that the purpose of feedback is to increase other people's self-awareness and feelings that "I am liked, I am respected, I am appreciated, I am capable, I am valued." To invest in a relationship by providing accurate and realistic feedback is a sign of caring and commitment.

SELF-PRESENTATION AND SELF-DISCLOSURE

The image of myself which I try to create in my own mind that I may love myself is very different from the image which I try to create in the minds of others in order that they may love me.

W. H. Auden

Knowing yourself is no easy task. You attempt to be more self-aware, to evaluate your worth, understand your emotions, and explain your outcomes. But you are more than a self-contained unit. You are part of an ongoing social interaction cycle between yourself and others. And in those interactions you make many choices as to how you wish to present yourself to others. One way you disclose to others who you are as a person is how you present yourself to them.

A common goal pursued in social interaction is *self-verification:* presenting yourself as you believe yourself to be. This varies with the situation and the person. The self you present to your parents is usually different from the self you present to your peers. You present yourself differently to your boss, subordinates, colleagues, customers, neighbors, same-sex friends, opposite-sex friends, and strangers. When you are playing tennis, the aspect of yourself that loves physical exercise and competition may be most evident. When you attend a concert, the aspect of yourself that responds with deep emotion to classical music may be most evident. In church, your religious side may be most evident. In a singles bar, your interest in other people may be most evident.

You have a number of selves that are tied to certain situations and certain groups of people with whom you interact. This may sound deceitful, but it is perfectly normal and all of us do it. In fact, societal norms are such that you are virtually required to engage in careful self-presentation. You are expected to address someone considerably older than you differently from the way you address your peers. You are expected to address the president of the United States differently from how you address your next-door neighbor. In formal situations you are expected to act in ways different from how you would act in informal situations. Depending on the setting, the role relationships, and your previous experience with the person, you are expected to monitor your behavior and present yourself accordingly. In all cases you will wish to present yourself to others as you really are.

Your clothes, appearance, posture, eye contact, tone of voice, manners, and gestures all communicate who you are and what you are like. They are especially important for first impressions. The same person may be perceived in quite different ways depending on style of dress, manner, and cleanliness. Clothing, for example, transmits messages about the wearer's personality, attitudes, social status, behavior, and group allegiances. People who wear clothes associated with high status tend to have more influence than those wearing low-status clothes. Somber hues (grays, dark blues, or browns) of clothing seem to communicate ambition, a taste for moderate risks and long-range planning, and a preference for tasks that have clear criteria for success and failure.

There are many complex aspects of yourself. Given this complexity, you may choose to present yourself in different ways to different people. The general process by which you behave in particular ways to create a desired social image has been called *impression management*. Social interaction requires the participants to be able to regulate their self-presentation so that it will be perceived and evaluated appropriately by others. The choice of how you present yourself is influenced by your goals. Some goals may suggest that certain attributes of the self are most important to disclose, while other goals may call for a different presentation of self. This is not manipulation. In choosing which aspect of the self to present in a particular situation, you choose among equally true selves.

INTERPERSONAL EFFECTIVENESS

The effectiveness of your behavior depends in large measure on your self-awareness; your self-awareness depends in large part upon receiving feedback from other individuals; the quality of the feedback you receive from other persons depends largely upon how much you self-disclose. In order to improve your interpersonal effectiveness, you need to be aware of the consequences of your behavior and decide whether these consequences match your intentions. *Interpersonal effectiveness* is the degree to which the consequences of your behavior match your intentions.

When you interact with another person, you have no choice but to make some impact, stimulate some ideas, arouse some impressions and observations, or trigger some feelings and reactions. Sometimes you make people react to your behavior much differently from the way you would like. An expression of warmth, for instance, may be seen as condescension; an expression of anger may be seen as a joke. Your interpersonal effectiveness depends upon your ability to communicate clearly what you want to communicate, to create the impression you wish, to influence the other person in the way you intend. You may improve your interpersonal effectiveness by disclosing your intentions, receiving feedback on your behavior, and modifying your behavior until other individuals perceive it as you mean it (that is, until it has the consequences you intend it to have).

Exercise 2.1: Initiating Relationships

The following is a simple experience in initiating relationships. The objectives of the exercise are:

1. To initiate relationships with other individuals whom you do not know.
2. To share initial feelings and thoughts with other individuals.
3. To take risks in revealing yourself to other individuals.
4. To experience a variety of ways to disclose yourself to others.
5. To encourage openness, trust, risk taking, and feedback with other individuals.

The activities are:

1. Everyone stand up and mill around the room, making sure that you pass by everyone present. Greet each person nonverbally. This greeting may be a handshake, a smile, a wink, a sock on the arm, or any other nonverbal way you may think of to say hello. After 5 minutes of milling, find a person you don't know. If you know everyone present, find the person you know least well.
2. Sit down with the person; each of you then take 2½ minutes to introduce yourself to the other. Do this by discussing the question of who you are as a person.
3. Turn around and find someone else near you whom you don't know or know least well of the other people present. Sit down with your new partner; each of you then take 2½ minutes to discuss the most significant experience you have had recently.
4. Find someone else you don't know. Sit down with your new partner and take 5 minutes (2½ minutes each) to exchange views on what you hope to accomplish by participating in this program.
5. Find another person whom you don't know. Sit down with your new partner and take 5 minutes (2½ minutes each) to share a fantasy or daydream that you

often have. It may be connected with success, such as becoming president of the United States, or it may be connected with love, such as meeting a terrific person who immediately falls in love with you, or it may be about what you would like to do with your next vacation.

6. Now form a group no larger than ten or twelve people. Try to be in a group with as many of the individuals as you have talked with in the previous activities. In the group discuss:

   a. How you feel about the different members on the basis of the previous activities, first impression, or past experience if you knew them previously.

   b. Which activity you felt was most helpful in getting to know the person you were interacting with.

   c. What you have learned from this exercise.

   d. What individuals in the group need to share if you are to get to know them during this session.

   e. Anything else that seems relevant to initiating relationships. This discussion may continue for as long as you like.

7. Alternative topics for discussion in pairs are

   a. What animal I would like to be and why.

   b. What song means the most to me and why.

   c. What it is that I like most about myself.

   d. How I would change myself if I had complete power to do so.

   e. What my most significant childhood experience was.

   f. What my immediate impressions of you are.

   g. The ways in which we are similar or different.

Exercise 2.2: Name Tagging

The purpose of this exercise is to get to know other members of your group or class while at the same time letting them know more about you. The procedure is:

1. Working alone, write your first name in the center of a three-by-five-inch index card. Write it large enough so other people can read it at some distance. In the upper left-hand corner, write the names of two places: where you were born and your favorite place. In the upper right-hand corner, write two of your favorite activities. These may be sports, hobbies, pastimes, jobs, or other ways you spend your time. In the lower left-hand corner, write three adjectives that describe you. In the lower right-hand corner, describe something you are looking forward to, something you are excited about doing in the future—for example, a vacation or a new job.

2. Pin the card on the front of your shirt or blouse.

3. Mill around, find people you don't know, and discuss each other's cards. You should try to meet as many people as possible in the time allowed (about 20 minutes).

4. Keep your name tag and wear it at subsequent sessions until you know everyone present and they all know you.

Indiana		Mountain climbing
British Columbia		Working
	DAVE	
Intense		Backpacking
Hard-working		in the Canadian
Fun-loving		Rockies

Exercise 2.3: Sharing Your Past

The purpose of this exercise is to let other people get to know you by sharing your family history with them and to get to know them by learning more about their past. The procedure is:

1. Fill in the following chart with the names (first and last) of your grandparents and parents. If you are not sure of all the names, ask your parents what they are. If you did not grow up with your parents, use whatever parent figures you have.

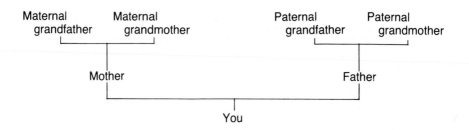

2. In small groups (from two to seven members), tell your answers to the following questions and listen carefully to the answers of the other group members.

   a. Maternal grandfather:

   1. Where was he born and raised?

   2. What was his early life like?

   3. What are (were) his outstanding characteristics?

   4. What is (was) his career?

5. Can you trace any of your characteristics or attitudes back to him?

6. Do any family traditions (activities, foods, places, etc.) come from him?

b. Maternal grandmother:

1. Where was she born and raised?

2. What was her early life like?

3. What are (were) her outstanding characteristics?

4. What is (was) her career?

5. Can you trace any of your characteristics or attitudes back to her?

6. Do any family traditions (activities, foods, places, etc.) come from her?

c. Paternal grandfather:

1. Where was he born and raised?

2. What was his early life like?

3. What are (were) his outstanding characteristics?

4. What is (was) his career?

5. Can you trace any of your characteristics or attitudes back to him?

6. Do any family traditions (activities, foods, places, etc.) come from him?

d. Paternal grandmother:

1. Where was she born and raised?

2. What was her early life like?

3. What are (were) her outstanding characteristics?

4. What is (was) her career?

5. Can you trace any of your characteristics or attitudes back to her?

6. Do any family traditions (activities, foods, places, etc.) come from her?

e. Mother:

1. Where was she born and raised?

2. What was her early life like?

3. What are (were) her outstanding characteristics?

4. What is (was) her career?

5. Can you trace any of your characteristics or attitudes back to her?

6. Do any family traditions (activities, foods, places, etc.) come from her?

f. Father:

1. Where was he born and raised?

2. What was his early life like?

3. What are (were) his outstanding characteristics?

4. What is (was) his career?

5. Can you trace any of your characteristics or attitudes back to him?

   6. Do any family traditions (activities, foods, places, etc.) come from
       him?
3. In the same small groups, discuss the following questions:
    a. How did you feel about doing this exercise?
    b. Did you learn anything new about yourself?
    c. Is it important for you to know about your family?
    d. How do you think an adopted person deals with this issue? (If you are
        adopted, how do you deal with it?)
    e. How did you react to what other members of your group said about their
        family roots?

Exercise 2.4: Self-Disclosure and Self-Awareness

The purpose of this exercise is to allow participants to focus on three of the areas
described in the Johari Window: the free area, the blind area, and the hidden area.
It is to be used with people who know each other, at least a little. Each participant
needs a number of three-by-five-inch index cards. The procedure is:

1. Working by yourself, review the material on the Johari Window. Then on a
    sheet of paper, write down several of your characteristics that you think other
    people in the room know (free area) and several of your characteristics that
    you think no one in the room knows (hidden area). Leave room on your paper
    to add characteristics in your blind area.

2. Form into groups of five. Each person then takes five three-by-five-inch index
    cards. Working by yourself, write a different group member's name on the front
    of each card (make one for yourself also). Turn the cards over and write two
    positive characteristics of the person whose name appears on the front. On
    your own card write two positive characteristics you think the other group mem-
    bers do not know about you (from your hidden area) that you are willing to
    have them know.

3. Collect all the cards, shuffle them, and place them face down in a pile in the
    center of the group. Then, one by one, take each card, read the description
    aloud, and decide by group consensus whom the card belongs to (do not look
    at the name on the front of the card). Place the card, with the name still facing
    down, in front of the person the group decides it belongs to. Repeat this proce-
    dure until all the cards have been distributed.

4. One by one, members of the group turn the cards they have been given face
    up. Each member gives his or her reactions to the cards received. If someone
    receives a card that does not belong to him, the card is given to the person it
    really belongs to. The group then discusses:
    a. Why were the cards given to the right or wrong person?

b. Are the descriptions on the cards accurate for the people for whom they are intended?

c. What has been learned from the exercise?

5. Working by yourself, take the cards you received and classify them into the free, hidden, and blind areas of the Johari Window. If your cards mention any characteristics you did not write down at the beginning of the exercise, add them to your sheet. Pay special attention to characteristics that are in your blind area.

Self-Awareness Sheet

Name _____ Date _____

Free Area

1.	6.
2.	7.
3.	8.
4.	9.
5.	10.

Hidden Area

1.	6.
2.	7.
3.	8.
4.	9.
5.	10.

Blind Area

1.	6.
2.	7.
3.	8.
4.	9.
5.	10.

Exercise 2.5: Your Unknown Area

The purpose of this exercise is to increase your awareness of aspects of yourself that may be in your unknown area. The procedure is:

1. As the instructor reads a list of topics, write down in a "free association" way the first responses that come into your mind.

2. Study your written responses. What conclusions about yourself as a person can you make from your responses? What characteristics, needs, goals, fears, or worries do your responses reflect?

3. Form into groups of five members. If you feel comfortable doing so, share your responses with the group and ask for their help in describing what you have learned about yourself. If a member of your group does not wish to report her responses, protect her right to remain silent. Be supportive of those group members who do reveal their responses to the group.

4. Working by yourself, summarize on a sheet of paper what you have learned about yourself from the exercise.

Topics

tool	musical instrument	fruit
geographic location	vacation	article of clothing
color	human	god or goddess
hero or heroine	legendary figure	piece of furniture
season of the year	food	retreat
weapon	animal	protect

Exercise 2.6: Labeling

The purpose of this exercise is to provide feedback concerning first impressions. Each participant needs ten blank name tags or labels. The procedure is:

1. The instructor gives each participant ten blank name tags or labels and a copy of the Category List.
2. Participants copy each category on a separate blank name tag or label.
3. Participants then mill around the room and choose a person who best fits each category. They then attach a category label on the clothing of the person and engage in a one-minute conversation with the person.
4. Participants form groups of five and discuss reactions to being labeled (or not labeled) by people's first impressions. Did you learn anything about yourself?

Category List

happy	warm	fun
smart	friendly	spontaneous
sincere	aloof	aggressive
mysterious		

Exercise 2.7: Interviewing

The purpose of this exercise is to get acquainted with other members of a group. Each participant needs a copy of the Interview Sheet. The procedure is:

1. Choose a partner. Make sure it is a person you would like to know better. Choose five questions from the Interview Sheet and interview your partner. He or she will then interview you by asking you five of the questions. Each of you will later introduce the other to a group, so you may want to take notes.

2. Form groups of six. Each person introduces his or her partner to the group.

3. Pick a new partner and repeat the interview and introduction procedure. The whole process may be repeated as often as there is time for.

4. Discuss in your group:
   a. How does it feel to be interviewed and introduced?
   b. Did you learn anything about yourself from the experience?

Interview Sheet

What is difficult for you to do?

What is a favorite joke of yours?

How do you define friendship?

What value is most important to you?

When do you feel most comfortable?

If you weren't what you are, what would you be?

How do you deal with your own anger?

Where do you go to be alone?

What is your favorite object?

What do you most often dream about?

Whom do you trust the most?

When do you feel most uncomfortable?

Under what circumstances would you tell a lie?

What is difficult for you to do?

Where would you most like to live?

What is your major life goal?

What is the thing your worst enemy would say about you?

What is the thing your best friend would say about you?

Exercise 2.8: Friendship Relations

The following exercise is based on the Johari Window. The objectives of the exercise are to examine your and the group's receptivity to feedback, willingness to self-disclose, and willingness to take risks in relations with friends. The procedure for the exercise is:

1. Working by yourself, complete the Friendship Relations Survey.

2. Score the results, according to the instructions on pages 53 and 54.

3. Follow the directions on the Friendship Relations Survey Summary Sheet that follows to get the final results of the survey for yourself and your group.

4. Form into groups of six. Complete a new Friendship Relations Survey Summary Sheet for the group as a whole, using the average of the members' scores. The group average is found by adding the scores of every member and dividing by the number of persons in the group.

5. Discuss the results in the group, using the following questions:

    a. What are your thoughts and feelings about when it is appropriate to receive feedback from your friends and to self-disclose to them?

    b. What are your thoughts and feelings about when you want other members of the group to give feedback to you and when you want to self-disclose to them?

    c. Do you have a conservative or a risky group?

    d. How does trust affect your receptivity to feedback and willingness to give feedback?

    e. Would you like to change the way you are now behaving?

    f. What changes in your behavior would be productive and useful in developing better relationships with your friends?

Friendship Relations Survey

This questionnaire was written to help you assess your understanding of your behavior in interpersonal relationships. There are no "right" or "wrong" answers. The best answer is the one that comes closest to representing your quest for good interpersonal relationships. In each statement, the first sentence gives a situation and the second sentence gives a reaction. For each statement indicate the number that is closest to the way you would handle the situation.

5 = You *always* would act this way.

4 = You *frequently* would act this way.

3 = You *sometimes* would act this way.

2 = You *seldom* would act this way.

1 = You *never* would act this way.

Try to relate each question to your own personal experience. Take as much time as you need to give a true and accurate answer for yourself. *There is no right or wrong answer.* Trying to give the "correct" answer will make your answer meaningless to you. *Be honest with yourself!*

1. You work with a friend, but some of her mannerisms and habits are getting on your nerves and irritating you. More and more you avoid interacting with or even seeing your friend.
   Never 1-2-3-4-5 Always

2. In a moment of weakness, you give away a friend's secret. Your friend finds out and calls you to ask about it. You admit to it and talk with your friend about how to handle secrets better in the future.
   Never 1-2-3-4-5 Always

3. You have a friend who never seems to have time for you. You ask him about it, telling him how you feel.
   Never 1-2-3-4-5 Always

4. Your friend is upset at you because you have inconvenienced him. He tells you how he feels. You tell him he is too sensitive and is overreacting.
   Never 1-2-3-4-5 Always

5. You had a disagreement with a friend and now she ignores you whenever she's around you. You decide to ignore her back.
   Never 1-2-3-4-5 Always

6. A friend has pointed out that you never seem to have time for him. You explain why you have been busy and try for a mutual understanding.
   Never 1-2-3-4-5 Always

7. At great inconvenience, you arrange to take your friend to the doctor's office. When you arrive to pick her up, you find she has decided not to go. You explain to her how you feel and try to reach an understanding about future favors.
   Never 1-2-3-4-5 Always

8. You have argued with a friend and are angry with her, ignoring her when you meet. She tells you how she feels and asks about restoring the friendship. You ignore her and walk away.
   Never 1-2-3-4-5 Always

9. You have a secret that you have told only to your best friend. The next day, an acquaintance asks you about the secret. You deny the secret and decide to break off the relationship with your best friend.
   Never 1-2-3-4-5 Always

10. A friend who works with you tells you about some of your mannerisms and habits that get on his nerves. You discuss these with your friend and look for some possible ways of dealing with the problem.
    Never 1-2-3-4-5 Always

11. Your best friend gets involved in something illegal that you believe will lead to serious trouble. You decide to tell your friend how you disapprove of his involvement in the situation.
    Never 1-2-3-4-5 Always

12. In a moment of weakness, you give away a friend's secret. Your friend finds out and calls you to ask about it. You deny it firmly.
    Never 1-2-3-4-5 Always

13. You have a friend who never seems to have time for you. You decide to forget her and to starting looking for new friends.
   Never 1-2-3-4-5 Always

14. You are involved in something illegal, and your friend tells you of her disapproval and fear that you will get in serious trouble. You discuss it with your friend.
   Never 1-2-3-4-5 Always

15. You work with a friend, but some of her mannerisms and habits are getting on your nerves and irritating you. You explain your feelings to your friend, looking for a mutual solution to the problem.
   Never 1-2-3-4-5 Always

16. A friend has pointed out that you never seem to have time for him. You walk away.
   Never 1-2-3-4-5 Always

17. Your best friend gets involved in something illegal that you believe will lead to serious trouble. You decide to mind your own business.
   Never 1-2-3-4-5 Always

18. Your friend is upset because you have inconvenienced him. He tells you how he feels. You try to understand and agree on a way to keep it from happening again.
   Never 1-2-3-4-5 Always

19. You had a disagreement with a friend, and now she ignores you whenever she's around you. You tell her how her actions make you feel and ask about restoring your friendship.
   Never 1-2-3-4-5 Always

20. A friend who works with you tells you about some of your mannerisms and habits that get on his nerves. You listen and walk away.
   Never 1-2-3-4-5 Always

21. At great inconvenience, you arrange to take your friend to the doctor's office. When you arrive to pick her up, you find she had decided not to go. You say nothing but resolve never to do any favors for that person again.
   Never 1-2-3-4-5 Always

22. You have argued with a friend and are angry with her, ignoring her when you meet. She tells you how she feels and asks about restoring the friendship. You discuss ways of maintaining your friendship, even when you disagree.
   Never 1-2-3-4-5 Always

23. You have a secret that you have told only to your best friend. The next day, an acquaintance asks you about the secret. You call your friend and ask her about it, trying to come to an understanding of how to handle secrets better in the future.
   Never 1-2-3-4-5 Always

24. You are involved in something illegal, and your friend tells you of her disapproval and fear that you will get in serious trouble. You tell your friend to mind her own business.
   Never 1-2-3-4-5 Always

Friendship Relations Survey Answer Key

In the Friendship Relations Survey there are twelve questions that deal with your willingness to self-disclose and twelve questions that are concerned with your receptivity to feedback. Transfer your scores to this answer key. Reverse the scoring for all questions that are starred; that is, if you answered 5, record the score of 1; if you answered 4, record the score of 2, if you answered 3, record the score of 3; if you answered 2, record the score of 4; and if you answered 1, record the score of 5. Then add the scores in each column.

Willingness to Self-Disclose	*Receptivity to Feedback*
*1. ____	2. ____
3. ____	*4. ____
*5. ____	6. ____
7. ____	*8. ____
*9. ____	10. ____
11. ____	*12. ____
*13. ____	14. ____
15. ____	*16. ____
*17. ____	18. ____
19. ____	*20. ____
*21. ____	22. ____
23. ____	*24. ____
Total ____	**Total** ____

On the Friendship Relations Survey Summary Sheet on page 54, add the totals for receptivity to feedback and willingness to self-disclose to arrive at an index of interpersonal risk taking which you will use in chapter 3.

Friendship Relations Survey Summary Sheet

Draw horizontal and vertical lines through your scores (Part *a*) and the group's receptivity to feedback and willingness to self-disclose (Part *b*). The results should look like the Johari Window.

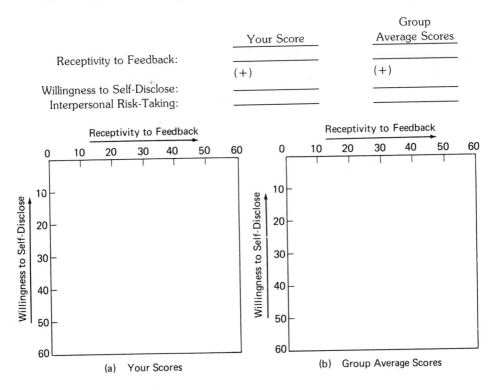

	Your Score	Group Average Scores
Receptivity to Feedback:	_____	_____
	(+)	(+)
Willingness to Self-Disclose:	_____	_____
Interpersonal Risk-Taking:	_____	_____

(a)   Your Scores

(b)   Group Average Scores

Exercise 2.9: Adjective Checklist

The following exercise is aimed at providing an opportunity for participants to disclose their view of themselves to the other members of their group and to receive feedback on how the other group members perceive them. The activities are:

1. Members should each go through the list of adjectives and circle the six adjectives they think are most descriptive of themselves.

2. Each member of the group then tells the group which adjectives he circled. Members of the group then tell the person what adjectives they would have checked if they were to describe him. Do not spend more than 5 to 10 minutes on each person in the group.

able	annoying	bold	caring
accepting	anxious	brave	certain
adaptable	authoritative	calm	cheerful
aggressive	belligerent	carefree	clever
ambitious	bitter	careless	cold

complex	impressionable	overconforming	rigid
confident	inconsiderate	overemotional	sarcastic
conforming	independent	overprotecting	satisfied
controlled	ingenious	passive	scientific
courageous	innovative	paternal	searching
cranky	insensitive	patient	self-accepting
critical	insincere	perceptive	self-actualizing
cynical	intelligent	perfectionist	self-assertive
demanding	introverted	persuasive	self-aware
dependable	intuitive	petty	self-conscious
dependent	irresponsible	playful	self-effacing
derogatory	irritable	pleasant	self-indulgent
determined	jealous	pompous	selfish
dignified	jovial	powerful	self-righteous
disciplined	juvenile	pragmatic	sensible
docile	kind	precise	sensitive
dogged	knowledgeable	pretending	sentimental
domineering	lazy	pretentious	serious
dreamy	learned	principled	shy
dutiful	lewd	progressive	silly
effervescent	liberal	protective	simple
efficient	lively	proud	sinful
elusive	logical	quarrelsome	skillful
energetic	loving	questioning	sly
extroverted	malicious	quiet	sociable
fair	manipulative	radical	spontaneous
fearful	materialistic	rational	stable
foolish	maternal	rationalizing	strained
frank	mature	reactionary	strong
free	merry	realistic	stubborn
friendly	modest	reasonable	sympathetic
genial	mystical	reassuring	taciturn
gentle	naive	rebellious	tactful
giving	narcissistic	reflective	temperamental
greedy	negative	regretful	tenacious
gruff	nervous	rejecting	tender
guilty	neurotic	relaxed	tense
gullible	noisy	reliable	thoughtful
happy	normal	religious	tough
hard	oblivious	remote	trusting
helpful	objective	resentful	trustworthy
helpless	observant	reserved	unassuming
honorable	obsessive	resolute	unaware
hostile	organized	respectful	uncertain
idealistic	original	responsible	unconcerned
imaginative	overburdened	responsive	uncontrolled
immature	overconfident	retentive	understanding

unpredictable	vapid	willful	witty
unreasonable	visionary	wise	worried
unstructured	vulnerable	wishful	youthful
useful	warm	withdrawn	zestful
vain			

Exercise 2.10: Fantasy Situations

Self-disclosure is most clearly accomplished when you tell others directly how you are reacting to the present situation. Yet many times we reveal ourselves in indirect ways, for example, by the jokes we tell, the things we find funny, the books we are interested in, or the movies we see. All these actions and attitudes tell other people something about ourselves. Often we may learn something about ourselves we were not fully aware of by analyzing our dreams, our daydreams, our interests, our values, or our humor. The following exercise lets you use your imagination in ways that may lead to a greater awareness of yourself and also may help you get to know others in a different and interesting way.

The following are a series of fantasy situations. They deal with initiating relationships with lonely people or giving help to individuals who seem to need it. The procedure for the exercise is:

1. Divide into groups of three.
2. The leader presents an unfinished fantasy situation.
3. Each member of the triad thinks about his or her ending to the fantasy situation. If you want to, write out your ending.
4. In the triad each person tells her ending to the fantasy situation.
5. Each person tells the other members of the triad what she has learned from the endings given to the fantasy situation about herself and about the other two members.
6. Switch partners and repeat steps 2, 3, 4, and 5. Do this for a series of situations, switching partners after each situation.
7. In the group as a whole, discuss what you have learned about yourself and the other members.

The fantasy situations are:

1. You are walking down a dark street. Up ahead you see a streetlight. You walk nearer and nearer to the streetlight. Underneath the streetlight is a girl crying. What do you do? What happens?
2. You are eating lunch in a school cafeteria. You get your lunch and walk into the lunchroom. The lunchroom is crowded and noisy with lots of people laughing and shouting and having a good time. Off in a corner is a boy sitting all alone at a table. What do you do? What happens?

3. You are going to a party. You enter the party, take off your coat, find something to drink, and talk to a couple of friends. Standing all by himself in the middle of the room is a person you don't know. After 10 minutes the person is still standing by himself. What do you do? What happens?

4. You are at a basketball game. It is half-time. You are talking with several of your friends. A person whom you casually met the week before is nearby. He is making obnoxious and embarrassing remarks to the people he is with. They all leave. You walk over to him and he insults you. What do you do? What happens?

5. You are sitting in class. Several persons in the class are making belittling comments about another student. The student is obviously having his feelings hurt. He catches your eye and looks at you. What do you do? What happens?

6. You are watching a group of friends talking in front of a restaurant. A person whom they consider odd and strange walks up to them and tries to join in the conversation. They ignore him. Finally one of your friends says, "Why don't you get lost?" The person turns away. What do you do? What happens?

7. You are sitting in a classroom. A student you don't know has constantly bugged the teacher and caused trouble ever since the class began several months ago. Although he is often funny, everyone is fed up with his behavior. He comes into the room and takes a seat next to you. What do you do? What happens?

8. There is a new student in the school. You have often heard her say that your school is not nearly as good as the school she previously attended and that the students at your school are "really just unreal" and "really think they're cool!" while she praises the students at her previous school. You meet her walking out of the school door. What do you do? What happens?

Exercise 2.11: Bag Exercise

This exercise is to be used in connection with the presentation of the Johari Window. The exercise focuses on the thinking through of the things about yourself that you commonly share with other individuals (your free areas) and the things that you do not commonly share with other individuals (your hidden areas). In addition, it opens up the opportunity for each group member to receive feedback on how the others see him. The materials needed for the exercise are:

1. A ten-pound paper bag for each person

2. One or two popular magazines, such as *Life*, for each person

3. Construction paper of several different colors

4. Yarn, string, and some small toys or any other objects that will help in constructing the bags

5. Crayons, paints, or pencils for drawing

6. Tape, paste, or glue

The procedure for the exercise is:

1. Each person in the group gets a paper bag. Various materials described above are scattered around the room.

2. Each person spends half an hour building his or her bag. On the outside of the bag you should attach things that represent aspects of yourself that you commonly share with other people. On the inside of the bag you should place things that represent aspects of yourself that you do not commonly share with others. You may cut pictures, words, phrases, or slogans out of the magazines, draw designs or pictures, make objects out of the construction paper, or use anything else that seems relevant in portraying the free and hidden aspects of yourself.

3. After everyone has finished, a group meeting is begun in which anyone may volunteer to talk about his bag. You may want to talk just about the outside of the bag, or you may feel like talking about part or all of what you have inside your bag. Everyone should feel free to share as much or as little as he would like to. You may want to keep working on your bag for a few days, adding things to the outside and inside, and then share it with the group at a later date.

4. After a person has shared part or all of his bag, the other members of the group may wish to comment on how their perceptions of the person match what they have heard. You may feel that the person left out qualities that you appreciate in him or perceive him as having. You may be surprised by finding that something the person felt was in his free area you have never seen in his behavior. Whatever your impressions of the person and your reactions to his bag, you should feel free to share them with him, using the characteristics of good feedback.

5. So that everyone who wants to may share her bag, you may want to put a time limit on how long the group may focus upon one person. Try to ensure that everyone who wants to share part or all of her bag has the opportunity to do so within the time limit set for the session.

Exercise 2.12: Feedback

Many of the exercises described in this chapter involve giving and receiving feedback. Feedback from others is the primary means by which you can increase your self-awareness. Since your ability to self-disclose depends upon your awareness of what you are like, it is important for you to receive as much feedback as possible from others on their impressions of you and how they are reacting to your behavior in the group. If not much feedback has been given and received during the other exercises, the group may wish to spend some time sharing their impressions of, and reactions to, each other. This can be done simply by stating, "My impression of you is . . . ," or "My reactions to your behavior are . . . ," or "The way I feel about you is. . . ." Be sure to observe the rules for constructive feedback.

Sometimes you may be unsure of what your impressions are of another person or of how you are reacting to her behavior. One way to clarify your impressions of, and reactions to, a person is to associate some animal, bird, song, color, weather, movie, book, food, or fantasy with the person. You may want to ask yourself, "What animal do I associate with this person: a puppy, a fox, a rabbit?" Or you may wish to ask yourself, "What books do I associate with this person; what songs do I associate with this person?" Finally, you may wish to ask yourself, "What fantasies do I associate with this person? Is he a knight in shining armor, an innkeeper in medieval England, a French chef, a conforming business executive, a professional singer?" Through telling that person what animal, song, color, weather, movie, food, book, or fantasy you associate with her you may clarify your impressions and reactions and provide her with some interesting, entertaining, and helpful feedback.

Exercise 2.13: Interpersonal Patterns

The following exercise focuses upon your interaction with other individuals. It may help you think about how you behave when you initiate a relationship with another person or how you act in a group. The procedure for the exercise is:

1. Divide into groups of three. Each person fills out the adjective checklist.
2. Analyze the meaning of the adjectives you checked by following the instructions that follow the checklist.
3. Share with the other two members of your triad the results of the exercise and ask for their comments on whether they perceive you in the same way as or differently than the results of this exercise indicate.

The twenty verbs listed below describe some of the ways people feel and act from time to time. Think of your behavior in interaction with other people. How do you feel and act with other people? Check the five verbs that best describe your behavior in interaction with others as you see it.

_____ acquiesces	_____ disapproves
_____ advises	_____ evades
_____ agrees	_____ initiates
_____ analyzes	_____ judges
_____ assists	_____ leads
_____ concedes	_____ obliges
_____ complies	_____ relinquishes
_____ coordinates	_____ resists
_____ criticizes	_____ retreats
_____ directs	_____ withdraws

There are two underlying factors or traits involved in the list of adjectives: *dominance* (authority or control) and *sociability* (intimacy or friendliness). Most people tend to like to control things (high dominance) or to let others control things (low dominance). Similarly most people tend to be very warm and personal (high sociability) or to be somewhat cold and impersonal (low sociability). In the following boxes circle the five adjectives you used to describe yourself in group activity. The set in which three or more adjectives are circled out of the five represents your interpersonal-pattern tendency in that group.

	HIGH DOMINANCE	LOW DOMINANCE
HIGH SOCIABILITY	advises coordinates directs initiates leads	acquiesces agrees assists complies obliges
LOW SOCIABILITY	analyzes criticizes disapproves judges resists	concedes evades relinquishes retreats withdraws

Exercise 2.14: Open and Closed Relationships

Are most of your relationships open or closed? Read through Table 2.1 carefully and classify yourself on each dimension. Do you have relationships you wish to make more open? Do you have relationships you wish to make more closed? What actions are needed to make a relationship more open? What acts are needed to make a relationship more closed? Discuss your conclusions with another member of your group.

Each of the aspects of open and closed relationships summarized in Table 2.1 will be discussed in this book.

Exercise 2.15: Self-Description

Who am I? What am I like? How do others perceive me? What are my strengths as a person? In what areas do I want to develop greater skills? At this point you have participated in a series of exercises aimed at increasing your self-awareness and your skills in self-disclosing. You should now sit down and try to summarize what you have

TABLE 2.1: Open and Closed Relationships

Closed ◄ - ► Open

Content being discussed	The content is of concern to no one (weather talk).	The content consists of technical aspects of work.	The content consists of the ideas and feelings of one person.	The content consists of the relationship between the two persons.
Time reference	No time reference (jokes and generalizations).	Distant past or future being discussed.	Recent past or future being discussed.	The immediate "here and now" being discussed.
Awareness of your sensing, interpreting, feeling, intending	You never listen to yourself and try to ignore, repress, and deny feelings and reactions.		You are constantly aware of what you are sensing, the interpretations you are making, your feelings, and your intentions about acting on your feelings.	
Openness with own ideas, feelings, reactions	Your statements are generalizations, abstract ideas, intellectualizations; feelings are excluded as irrelevant and inappropriate and nonexistent.		Your personal reactions such as attitudes, values, preferences, feelings, experiences, and observations of the present are stated and focused upon; feelings are included as helpful information about the present.	
Feedback from other people	Feedback from others is avoided, ignored, not listened to, and perceived as being hostile attacks on your personality.		Feedback from others is asked for, sought out, listened to, and used to increase your self-awareness; it is perceived as being a helpful attempt to add to your growth and effectiveness.	
Acceptance of yourself	You believe that once you are known you will be disliked and rejected and, therefore, you hide your "real" self and try to make the impression you think will be most appreciated by other people.		You express confidence in your abilities and skills; can discuss your positive qualities without bragging and without false modesty; you understand how you have used your strengths in the past to achieve your goals and are confident you will do so again in the future.	
Openness to others' ideas, feelings, reactions	You avoid and disregard others' reactions, ideas, and feelings; you are embarrassed and put off by others' expressions of feelings; you reject other people and try to one-up and better them; you refuse to hear their feedback on their reactions to your behavior.		You listen to and solicit others' reactions, ideas, and feelings; you are interested and receptive to what others are saying and feeling; you express a desire to cooperate fully with them; you make it clear that you see their value and strengths even when you disagree with them; you ask others for feedback on their perceptions of your behavior.	
Acceptance of other people	You evaluate the other person's actions, communicate that the other is unacceptable, show disregard for the other as a person.		You react without evaluation to the other's actions, communicate that the other is acceptable, value the other as a person.	

learned about yourself. Take a sheet of paper and write a description of what you are like. Use the five questions stated at the beginning of this paragraph as a guide.

CHAPTER REVIEW

Test your understanding of this chapter by answering true or false to the following statements. Answers are at the end of the chapter.

True	False	1. Self-disclosure should be aimed at making the other person improve his or her behavior.
True	False	2. Self-disclosure should be a two-way street, a shared understanding of how each person is reacting to the present situation.
True	False	3. Self-disclosure involves risk taking.
True	False	4. Statements are more helpful if they are tentative, specific, and informing.
True	False	5. Wait to discuss disturbing situations until after your feelings have built up for a while.
True	False	6. It is often helpful to describe your reactions to the other person's behavior.
True	False	7. It is often helpful to disclose full details of your past life.
True	False	8. An example of constructive self-disclosure is when Edye says to Dave, "Stop bothering me!"
True	False	9. An example of constructive self-disclosure is when Dave says to Edye, "You look angry. Are you?"
True	False	10. An example of constructive self-disclosure is when Edye says to Dave, "I feel hurt and rejected by your failure to answer my questions."
True	False	11. Self-acceptance means that you regard yourself highly and are aware of your strengths.
True	False	12. Because self-acceptance gives you the confidence to be self-disclosing, it leads to your being accepted by others, which further increases your self-acceptance.
True	False	13. It is not necessary, psychologically to be self-accepting.
True	False	14. The more self-accepting you are, the less you will be accepting of others.

True   False   **15.** The best feeling about your self-worth is an unconditional basic self-acceptance.

In this chapter we have focused on being self-disclosing, increasing self-awareness, and giving and receiving feedback. Which of these skills have you mastered and which ones do you need further work on?

1. I have mastered the following:
   ____ Self-disclosing appropriately
   ____ Giving feedback constructively
   ____ Receiving feedback constructively
   ____ Using my experiences, self-disclosures, and feedback to increase my self-awareness
   ____ Awareness of my strengths
   ____ Sharing of my strengths
   ____ Using my strengths to build relationships
   ____ Expressing acceptance nonverbally

2. I need more work on:
   ____ Self-disclosing appropriately
   ____ Giving feedback constructively
   ____ Receiving feedback constructively
   ____ Using my experiences, self-disclosures, and feedback to increase my self-awareness
   ____ Awareness of my strengths
   ____ Sharing of my strengths
   ____ Using my strengths to build relationships
   ____ Expressing acceptance nonverbally

At this point, you should have an understanding of self-disclosure and know how to self-disclose appropriately. You should also understand how to give and receive constructive feedback, and you should have increased your self-awareness. The next chapter will build on these skills by showing you how to build and maintain trust in a relationship.

ANSWERS

Chapter Review: 1. false; 2. true; 3. true; 4. true; 5. false; 6. false; 7. false; 8. false; 9. true; 10. true; 11. true; 12. true; 13. false; 14. false; 15. true.

3 *Developing and Maintaining Trust*

INTRODUCTION

I am afraid to tell you who I am, because, if I tell you who I am, you may not like who I am, and it's all that I have.

John Powell

To build a relationship with another person, you must let the other person get to know you. To disclose yourself to others, you must be aware of who you are and accept yourself enough to let others know you. In addition, you must have the skills to cope with rejection. Disclosing yourself to others involves risking rejection and ridicule. You must risk being rejected in order to build a closer relationship. To build a relationship with another person, that is, getting to know the other person and helping him or her get to know you, you must trust the other person to respond in a way that will *not* hurt your feelings and make you feel rejected. Thus, a third element in your building a relationship with another person is trust.

In studying this chapter you should seek to (1) arrive at an understanding of what trust is and what it is not; (2) understand how trust is developed and maintained in a relationship; (3) know the difference between appropriate and inappropriate trust; (4) experience a situation in which trust is either developed or destroyed; and (5) diagnose your level of skill in building and maintaining trust in a relationship. Achieving these goals will not be easy, as trust is one of the hardest social skills to understand and implement.

DEVELOPING AND MAINTAINING TRUST

Aristotle once said, "A true friend is one soul in two bodies." In order for two people to get to know each other that well, they must trust each other. Trust is essential for relationships to grow and develop. The first crisis most relationships face involves the ability of two individuals to trust each other. In order to build a relationship, you must learn to create a climate of trust that reduces your own and the other person's fears of betrayal and rejection and promotes the hope of acceptance, support, and confirmation. Trust is not a stable and unchanging personality trait. Trust is an aspect of relationships that constantly changes and varies. Everything individuals do increases or decreases the trust level in their relationship. The actions of both people are important in establishing and maintaining trust in their relationship.

What is trust and how do you create it? Trust is a word everyone uses, yet it is a complex concept and difficult to define. Perhaps the best definition is Deutsch's (1962), which proposed that trust includes the following elements:

1. You are in a situation where a choice to trust another person can lead to either beneficial or harmful consequences for your needs and goals. Thus, you realize there is a risk involved in trusting.
2. You realize that whether beneficial consequences or harmful consequences result depends on the actions of another person.
3. You expect to suffer more if the harmful consequences result than you will gain if the beneficial consequences result.
4. You feel relatively confident that the other person will behave in such a way that the beneficial consequences will result.

Making a choice to trust another person involves the perception that the choice can lead to gains or losses, that whether you will gain or lose depends upon the behavior of the other person, that the loss will be greater than the gain, and that the other person will probably behave in such a way that you will gain rather than lose. Sounds complicated, doesn't it? In fact, there is nothing simple about trust; it is a complex concept and difficult to explain. An example may help. Imagine you are a part of a learning group analyzing *Hamlet*. You begin to contribute to the discussion, knowing you will gain if you contribute good ideas that other members accept but lose if your ideas are laughed at and belittled.

Helpful Hints About Trust

1. *Trust is a very complex concept to understand.* It may take a while before you fully understand it.
2. *Trust exists in relationships, not in someone's personality.* While some people are more naturally trusting than others, and it is easier for some people to be trustworthy than others, trust is something that occurs *between* people, not *within* people.
3. *Trust is constantly changing as two people interact.* Everything you do affects the trust level between you and the other person to some extent.
4. *Trust is hard to build and easy to destroy.* It may take years to build up a high level of trust in a relationship, then one destructive act can destroy it all.
5. *The key to building and maintaining trust is being trustworthy.* The more accepting and supportive you are of others, the more likely it is that they will disclose their thoughts, ideas, theories, conclusions, feelings, and reactions to you. The more trustworthy you are in response to such disclosures, the deeper and more personal will be the thoughts a person will share with you. When you want to increase trust, increase your trustworthiness.
6. *Trust needs to be appropriate. Never* trusting and *always* trusting are inappropriate.
7. *Cooperation increases trust, competition decreases trust.* Trust generally is higher among collaborators than among competitors.
8. *Initial trusting and trustworthy actions within a relationship can create a self-fulfilling prophecy.* The expectations you project about trust often influence the actions of other people toward you.

Whether you gain or lose depends on the behavior of other group members. You will feel more hurt if you are laughed at than you will feel satisfaction if your ideas are appreciated. Yet you expect the other group members to consider your ideas and accept them. The issue of trust is captured in the question every group member asks: "If I openly express myself, will what I say be used against me?"

Another example may help. Trust is involved when you lend your older brother your bicycle. You can gain his appreciation or lose your bike; which one happens depends on him. You will suffer more if your bike is wrecked than you will gain by his appreciation, yet you really expect him to take care of your bike. (Sad experience has led an unnamed person to recommend that you never lend your bike to your older brother!)

BEING TRUSTING AND TRUSTWORTHY

You can bring your credibility down in a second. It takes a million acts to build it up, but one act can bring it down. . . . People are suspicious because for several thousand years that suspicion was warranted . . . we try very hard not to do things that will create distrust.

Howard K. Sperlich, President, Chrysler Corporation

The level of trust within a relationship is constantly changing according to individuals' ability and willingness to be trusting and trustworthy. You are *trusting* when you are willing to risk beneficial or harmful consequences by making yourself vulnerable to other people. More specifically, you are trusting when you are self-disclosing and willing to be openly accepting and supportive of others. *Openness* is the sharing of information, ideas, thoughts, feelings, and reactions to the issue being discussed. *Sharing* is the offering of your resources to other people in order to help them achieve their goals.

You are *trustworthy* when you are willing to respond to another person's risk taking in a way that ensures that the other person will experience beneficial consequences. More specifically, you are trustworthy when you express acceptance of, support for, and cooperativeness towards the other person, as when you reciprocate his or her disclosures. *Acceptance* is the communication of high regard for another person and his or her statements. *Support* is the communication to another person that you recognize he or she has the strengths and capabilities needed to manage productively the situation in which he or she is. *Coop-

erative intentions express that you want to work together to achieve a mutual goal. There is considerable evidence that the expression of warmth, accurate understanding, and cooperative intentions increases trust in a relationship, even when there are unresolved conflicts between the individuals involved (Johnson, 1971; Johnson & Matross, 1977; Johnson & Noonan, 1972). *Reciprocating the other person's self-disclosures* occurs when you share something about yourself in response to the other person's disclosures to you. Appropriate reciprocation increases trust and influences the other person to be even more self-disclosing (Johnson & Noonan, 1972).

Acceptance is probably the first and deepest concern to arise in a relationship. *Acceptance is the key to reducing anxiety and fears about being vulnerable.* Defensive feelings of fear and distrust are common blocks to the functioning of a person and to the development of constructive relationships. Certainly, if a person does not feel accepted, the frequency

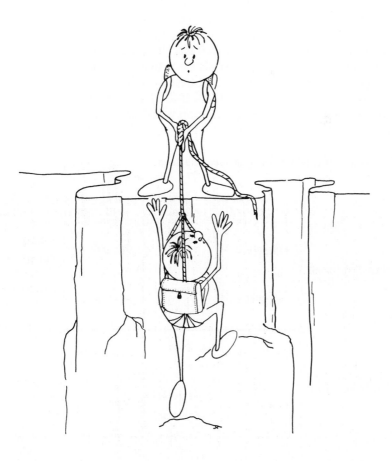

and depth of disclosures to another person will decrease. Accepting another person's disclosures and supporting his or her willingness to trust you does not mean that you agree with everything he or she says. You can express acceptance and support and, at the same time, express different ideas and opposing points of view.

The key to building and maintaining trust is being trustworthy. The more accepting and supportive you are of others, the more likely it is that they will disclose their thoughts, ideas, theories, conclusions, feelings, and reactions to you. The more trustworthy you are in response to such disclosures, the deeper and more personal will be the thoughts a person will share with you. When you want to increase trust, increase your trustworthiness.

BUILDING INTERPERSONAL TRUST

Ralph Waldo Emerson once said, "The only way to have a friend is to be one." He was calling attention to the fact that a relationship consists of two parts, how you behave toward the other person and how that person acts towards you. Trust also has two sides. Trust is established through a sequence of trusting and trustworthy actions (see Figure 3.1). If person A takes the risk of being self-disclosing, he may be either confirmed or disconfirmed, depending on whether Person B responds with acceptance or rejection. If Person B takes the risk of being accepting,

FIGURE 3.1:   The Dynamics of Interpersonal Trust

PERSON B

	HIGH ACCEPTANCE, SUPPORT, AND COOPERATIVENESS	LOW ACCEPTANCE, SUPPORT, AND COOPERATIVENESS
HIGH OPENNESS AND SHARING	PERSON A { Trusting / Confirmed PERSON B { Trustworthy / Confirmed	PERSON A { Trusting / Disconfirmed PERSON B { Untrustworthy / No risk
LOW OPENNESS AND SHARING	PERSON A { Distrusting / No risk PERSON B { Trustworthy / Disconfirmed	PERSON A { Distrusting / No risk PERSON B { Untrustworthy / No risk

PERSON A

supportive, and cooperative, she may be confirmed or disconfirmed, depending on whether Person A is disclosing or nondisclosing.

Interpersonal trust is *built* through risk and confirmation and is *destroyed* through risk and disconfirmation. Without risk there is no trust, and the relationship cannot move forward. The steps in building trust are:

1. Person A takes a risk by disclosing his thoughts, information, conclusions, feelings, and reactions to the immediate situation and to Person B.

2. Person B responds with acceptance, support, and cooperativeness and reciprocates Person A's openness by disclosing her own thoughts, information, conclusions, feelings, and reactions to the immediate situation and to Person A.

An alternative way in which trust is built is:

1. Person B communicates acceptance, support, and cooperativeness toward Person A.

2. Person A responds by disclosing his thoughts, information, conclusions, feelings, and reactions to the immediate situation and to Person B.

DESTROYING TRUST

George Elliot stated, "Friendship is the inexpressible comfort of feeling safe with a person having neither to weigh thoughts nor measure words." In other words, friendships require high trust. For trust to develop, one person has to let down his or her guard and become vulnerable to see whether the other person abuses that vulnerability. Many such tests are necessary before the trust level between two people becomes very high. *Just one betrayal, however, may create distrust and, once established, distrust is extremely resistive to change.* Distrust is difficult to change because it leads to the perception that despite the other person's attempts to "make up," betrayal will recur in the future.

There are three types of behavior that will decrease trust in a relationship. The *first* is the use of rejection, ridicule, or disrespect as a response to the other's openness. Making a joke at the expense of the other person, laughing at his disclosures, moralizing about her behavior, being evaluative in your response, or being silent and poker-faced, all communicate rejection and will effectively silence the other person and destroy some of the trust in the relationship. The *second* is the nonreciprocation of openness. To the extent that you are closed and the other person is open, he will not trust you and will feel overexposed and vulnerable. The *third* type of behavior that will decrease trust in a relationship is the refusal to disclose your thoughts, information, conclusions, feelings, and reactions after the other person has indicated considerable acceptance, support, and cooperativeness. If a person indicates acceptance and you are closed and guarded in response, he will feel discounted and rejected.

REESTABLISHING TRUST AFTER IT HAS BEEN BROKEN

How can trust, once lost, be regained? The following guidelines may help. To reestablish trust, you should:

1. Increase positive outcome interdependence by establishing cooperative goals that are so compelling that everyone will join in to achieve them. Such goals are often referred to as superordinate goals.

2. Increase resource interdependence so that it is clear that no one person has a chance for succeeding on his or her own.

3. Openly and consistently express cooperative intentions.

4. Reestablish credibility by making certain that your actions match your announced intentions. You must always keep your word.

5. Be absolutely and consistently trustworthy in your dealing with others. Acceptance and support of others are critical.

6. Periodically "test the waters" by engaging in trusting actions and making yourself vulnerable to the other persons.

7. Apologize sincerely and immediately when you inadvertently engage in untrustworthy actions.

8. Strive to build a "tough but fair" reputation by:
    a. Initially and periodically responding cooperatively to others who act competitively (even when you know in advance that the others plan to compete).
    b. Using a *tit-for-tat* strategy that matches the other person's behavior if the others continue to compete. When the competitors realize that their competitiveness is self-defeating and the best they can hope for is mutual failure, they may start cooperating.

TRUSTING APPROPRIATELY

Trust is not always appropriate. There are times when you will think it inadvisable to disclose your thoughts, feelings, or reactions to another person. There are people you undoubtedly know who would behave in very untrustworthy ways if you made yourself vulnerable to them. To master the skills in building and maintaining trust, therefore, you need to be able to tell when it is appropriate to be trusting and when it is not. You must develop the capacity to size up situations and make an enlightened decision about when, whom, and how much to trust others. Remember not to reveal yourself so fast to another person that he is overpowered and bewildered. And remember there are situations in which trust is inappropriate and destructive to your interests.

Never trusting and *always* trusting are inappropriate. Trust is appropriate only when you are relatively confident that the other person will behave in such a way that you will benefit rather than be harmed by your risk, or when you are relatively sure that the other person will not exploit your vulnerability. In some situations, such as competitive ones, trust is not appropriate. Similarly, when you have a mean, vicious, hostile boss who has taken advantage of your openness in the past, it is inappropriate to engage in trusting behavior in the present.

TRUSTING AS A SELF-FULFILLING PROPHECY

Tom joins a new group expecting the members to dislike and reject him. He behaves, therefore, in a very guarded and suspicious way toward the other group members. His actions cause them to withdraw and look elsewhere for a friendly companion. "See," he then says, "I was right. I knew they would reject me." Sue, who joins the same group at the same time Tom does, expects the members to be congenial, friendly, and trustworthy. She exudes warmth and friendliness, openly discloses her thoughts and feelings, and generally is accepting and supportive of the other members. Consequently, she finds her fellow members to be all that she expected. Both Tom and Sue have made a self-fulfilling prophecy.

A *self-fulfilling prophecy* is, in the beginning, a false definition of a situation that evokes a new behavior, one that makes it possible for the originally false impression to come true. The assumptions you make about other people and the way in which you then behave often influence how other people respond to you, thus creating self-fulfilling prophecies in your relationships. People usually conform to the expectations others have for them. If other people feel that you do not trust them and expect them to violate your trust, they will often do so. If they believe that you trust them and expect them to be trustworthy, they will often behave that way. The perceptions of others as untrustworthy is probably a major source of tensions leading to conflict. The history of labor/management strife, interracial violence, war, and revolution demonstrates the power of distrust. The lack of trust helps create conflict, and conflict leads to increased distrust. There is often a vicious circle of distrust causing conflict, which increases distrust, which increases conflict.

In building trust in a relationship, your expectations about the other person may influence how you act toward that person, thus setting up the possibility of a self-fulfilling prophecy. There is a lot to be said for assuming that other people are trustworthy.

PERSONAL PROCLIVITY TO TRUST

While trust exists in relationships, not in people, there has been some attempt to measure individual differences in willingness to trust others. Rotter (1971) developed the *Interpersonal Trust Scale* to distinguish between people who have a tendency to trust others and those who tend to distrust. A high truster tends to say, "I will trust a person until I have clear evidence that he or she cannot be trusted." A low truster tends to say, "I will not trust a person until there is clear evidence that he or she can be trusted." High trusters tend to be more trustworthy than do low trusters. High trusters, compared with low trusters, are (a) more likely to give others a second chance, respect the rights of others, and be liked and sought out as friends (by both low- and high-trust people), and (b) less likely to lie and be unhappy, conflicted, or maladjusted.

TRUST IN GROUPS

An essential aspect of group effectiveness is developing and maintaining a high level of trust among group members. The more members trust each other, the more effectively they will work together (Deutsch, 1962, 1973; Johnson, 1974). To complete tasks and achieve goals, group members are required to disclose more and more of their ideas, thoughts, conclusions, feelings, and reactions concerning immediate situations to each other. Once they do, other group members are required to respond, ideally with acceptance, support, and cooperativeness. If group members express an opinion and do not get the acceptance they need, they may withdraw from the group. If they are accepted, they will continue to risk disclosing their thoughts and observations and continue to develop their relationships with other members. Group members will more openly express their thoughts, feelings, reactions, opinions, information, and ideas when the trust level is high. When the trust level is low, group members will be evasive, dishonest, and inconsiderate in their communications.

Creating distrust within a group is not a good idea for several reasons. *First,* when group members distrust other members to do their share of the work, for example, they will loaf themselves rather than risk looking like a "sucker" who does the bulk of the work (Kerr, 1983). *Second,* when group members cannot trust each other, they often compete simply to defend their own best interests. Such competition is self-defeating in the long run, for it initiates a negative cycle. Distrust creates competition, which creates greater distrust, which creates greater competition. *Third,* distrust creates destructive conflict among group members.

COMPREHENSION TEST A

Join another individual. Take Comprehension Test A, discussing each question and arriving at one answer that both individuals agree is most correct. Then combine with another pair and repeat the procedure, making sure that all four individuals agree on the answer to each question.

Test your understanding of building trust by answering *true* or *false* to the following statements.

True	False	
True	False	1. Trust involves a risk that can lead to either harmful or beneficial consequences.
True	False	2. Your own behavior determines whether there are beneficial or harmful consequences from your trusting actions.
True	False	3. When you trust another person, you will gain more from the beneficial consequences than you will suffer from the harmful ones.
True	False	4. When you engage in trusting behavior, you are relatively confident that the other person will be accepting.
True	False	5. In responding to another person's self-disclosures, you should be noncommittal and nonjudgmental.
True	False	6. It does not matter if the other person reciprocates your self-disclosures or not.
True	False	7. When someone self-discloses, he or she will feel disconfirmed if the other person is not accepting.
True	False	8. When people communicate acceptance, then you can risk trusting them.
True	False	9. An example of trusting behavior would be Jane telling Frank about a personal problem.
True	False	10. An example of trustworthy behavior would be Frank listening noncommittally to Jane.
True	False	11. Trust is necessary for stable cooperation.
True	False	12. An ingredient of trust is the awareness that you are taking a chance of gaining or losing by it.

Match the following elements of trust with their definitions:

a. Openness
b. Sharing
c. Acceptance
d. Support
e. Cooperative intentions

f. Trusting behavior

g. Trustworthy behavior

13. The communication of high regard for another person and his contributions to the joint effort

14. Offering your materials and resources to others to help obtain the goal

15. The expectation that you and the other person will help each other

16. Sharing information, ideas, thoughts, feelings, and reactions to the issue

17. Openness and sharing with others

18. Expressing acceptance, support, and cooperative intentions

19. Communicating that you recognize another person's strengths and believe she is capable

Exercise 3.1: How Trusting and Trustworthy Am I?

There is always a risk that someone will be rejecting and competitive when you attempt to build a relationship. In order for two people to trust each other, each has to expect the other to be trustworthy, and each has to engage in trusting behavior. This exercise allows you to compare the way you see your trust-building behavior in the group with the way other people see your trust-building behavior. The procedure for this exercise is:

1. Complete the questionnaire "Understanding Your Trust Actions." Score your responses.

2. Take out a slip of paper for each member of your group. Write the name of one of the members on each slip of paper. Write (1) "openness and sharing" and (2) "acceptance, support, and cooperativeness" on each slip of paper. Then rate the members of your group from 1 to 7 (Low 1-2-3-4-5-6-7 High) on how open and accepting you perceive each to be. An example of a completed slip is shown below.

Member receiving feedback:	Edythe
1. Openness and sharing:	3
2. Acceptance, support, and cooperativeness:	6

Rate group members individually on the basis of how you think they have behaved during the entire time your group has met together.

3. Hand each member his or her slip. If there are six members in your group, you should have five ratings of yourself, and each of the other members should end

up with five slips. Compute an average of how the other members see your behavior by adding all your ratings for openness and dividing by the number of slips and adding all your ratings for acceptance and dividing by the number of slips.

4. Record in Figure 3.2 your average openness and acceptance by (1) drawing a dotted line for the results of the feedback slips you received and (2) drawing a solid line for the results of your questionnaire. Both the questionnaire and the feedback results should be recorded in Figure 3.2.

5. Discuss in the group how similar your self-perception and the perceptions of other group members are of your openness and acceptance. If there is a difference between the two, ask the group to give more specific feedback about your behavior and how it relates to trust in the group. Then discuss how to build trust with people in situations outside of the group.

FIGURE 3.2:   Johnson Trust Diagram

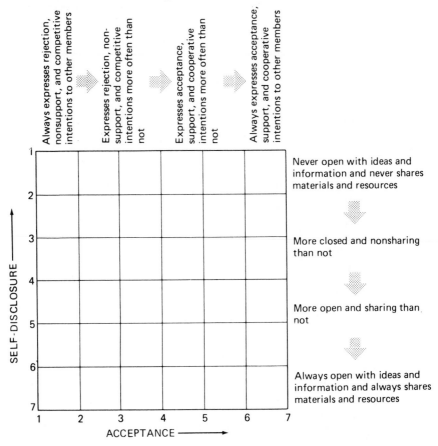

Understanding Your Trust Actions

The following is a series of questions about your behavior in your group. Answer each question as honestly as you can. There are no right or wrong answers. It is important for you to describe your behavior as accurately as possible. Answers should range between 1 (not true of me) and 7 (very true of me).

1. I offer facts, give my opinions and ideas, provide suggestions and relevant information to help the group discussion.
   Never 1—2—3—4—5—6—7 Always

2. I express my willingness to cooperate with other group members and my expectations that they will also be cooperative.
   Never 1—2—3—4—5—6—7 Always

3. I am open and candid with my dealings with the entire group.
   Never 1—2—3—4—5—6—7 Always

4. I give support to group members who are on the spot and struggling to express themselves intellectually or emotionally.
   Never 1—2—3—4—5—6—7 Always

5. I keep my thoughts, ideas, feelings, and reactions to myself during group discussions.
   Never 1—2—3—4—5—6—7 Always

6. I evaluate the contributions of other group members in terms of whether their contributions are useful to me and whether they are right or wrong.
   Never 1—2—3—4—5—6—7 Always

7. I take risks in expressing new ideas and current feelings during a group discussion.
   Never 1—2—3—4—5—6—7 Always

8. I communicate to other group members that I am aware of, and appreciate, their abilities, talents, capabilities, skills, and resources.
   Never 1—2—3—4—5—6—7 Always

9. I offer help and assistance to anyone in the group in order to bring up the performance of everyone.
   Never 1—2—3—4—5—6—7 Always

10. I accept and support the openness of other group members, supporting them for taking risks and encouraging individuality in group members.
    Never 1—2—3—4—5—6—7 Always

11. I share any materials, books, sources of information, or other resources I have with the other group members in order to promote the success of individual members and the group as a whole.
    Never 1—2—3—4—5—6—7 Always

12. I often paraphrase or summarize what other members have said before I respond or comment.
    Never 1—2—3—4—5—6—7 Always

13. I level with other group members.
        Never 1—2—3—4—5—6—7 Always

14. I warmly encourage all members to participate, giving them recognition for their contributions, demonstrating acceptance and openness to their ideas, and generally being friendly and responsive to them.
        Never 1—2—3—4—5—6—7 Always

Your Trust Behavior

In order to get a total score, write the number you circled for each question in the following tables. Reverse the scoring for the starred questions. (If you circled 2, write 6; if you circled 1, write 7; 4 remains the same.)

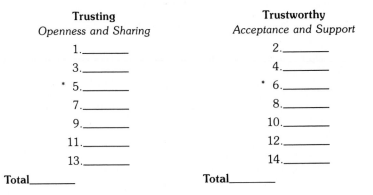

Trusting	Trustworthy
Openness and Sharing	*Acceptance and Support*
1._____	2._____
3._____	4._____
* 5._____	* 6._____
7._____	8._____
9._____	10._____
11._____	12._____
13._____	14._____
Total_____	Total_____

If a person has a score of 35 or over, classify him/her as being trusting or trustworthy, whichever most applies. If someone has a score of under 35, classify him/her as being distrustful or untrustworthy, whichever most applies.

Exercise 3.2: Practicing Trust-Building Skills

This exercise is aimed at providing you with an opportunity to practice the trust-building skills needed for relationships to grow and develop. The procedure for the exercise is:

1. Form groups of six members and choose one member to observe, using the observation sheet shown below.

2. Complete the Genetic Traits task.

3. Discuss the following questions in your group:

   a. Who engaged in what types of trust-building behaviors?

   b. What feelings do members of the group have about their participation in the group?

   c. Was trust increased or decreased by participating in this exercise?

OBSERVATION SHEET

1. Contributes ideas				
2. Describes feelings				
3. Paraphrases				
4. Expresses acceptance and support				
5. Expresses warmth and liking				

Trusting behaviors = 1 and 2
Trustworthy behaviors = 3, 4, and 5

Genetic Traits Task

Working as a group, estimate the number of people in your city (or school) who possess each of the following genetic traits. Establish the frequency of occurrence of each genetic trait, first in your group, then in the entire room. On the percentage of occurrence in your group and the room, estimate the number of people in your city (or school) who possess each trait.

1. Dimples in the cheeks versus no dimples.
2. Brown (or hazel) eyes versus blue, gray, or green eyes.
3. Attached versus free earlobes (an earlobe is free if it dips below the point where it is attached).
4. Little-finger bend versus no bend (place your little fingers together with your palms toward you—if your little fingers bend away from each other at the tips, you have the famous "little finger bend").
5. Tongue roll versus no tongue roll (if you can curl up both sides of your tongue to make a trough, you have it, and it's not contagious).
6. Hairy versus nonhairy middle fingers (examine the backs of the middle two fingers on your hands and look for hair between the first and second knuckle).
7. Widow's peak versus straight or curved hairline (examine the hairline across your forehead and look for a definite dip or point of hair extending down toward your nose).

Exercise 3.3: Prisoner's Dilemma Game

The game you are about to play is called the Prisoner's Dilemma game. It is a game in which a player has to choose between increasing his own immediate gain or increasing the total gain of both players. It derives its name from the following situation:

Two suspects are taken into custody and separated. The District Attorney is certain that they are guilty of a specific crime, but he does not have adequate evidence to convict them at a trial. He points out each prisoner's alternatives to him: to confess to the crime that the police are sure they have committed, or not to confess. If they both do not confess, then the District Attorney states he will book them on some very minor but trumped-up charge such as petty larceny and illegal possession of a weapon for which they would both receive minor punishments; if they both confess they will be prosecuted, but he will recommend less than the most severe sentence; but if one confesses and the other does not, then the confessor will receive lenient treatment for turning state's evidence, whereas the latter will get "the book" slapped at him.

[Luce and Raiffa 1957, p. 95]

Neither prisoner is aware of the other prisoner's decision. The decision of each will be very much affected by his prediction of what the other prisoner will do. Both decisions will be very much affected by the extent to which each trusts the other not to confess. The important properties of this dilemma appear in the Prisoner's Dilemma Matrix.

Prisoner's Dilemma Matrix

In the matrix it is clear that the number of points a person receives from a choice depends not only upon his own choice, but upon what the choice of the other person is. If Person I chooses A, how many points he receives depends upon whether Person II chooses C or D. If Person I chooses A, and Person II chooses C, each will receive 10 points. If Person I chooses A, and Person II choses D, Person I will lose 25 points and Person II will gain 25 points. If Person I chooses B, and Person II chooses C, Person I will gain 25 points and Person II will lose 25 points. And if Person I chooses

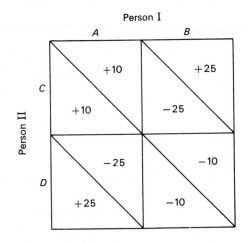

B and Person II chooses *D*, both will lose 10 points. Study this matrix until you are sure you understand it. Then answer the following questions. Answers are at the end of the chapter.

1. If Person II chooses *C* and Person I chooses *A*, Person I receives _____ points and Person II receives _____ points.

2. If Person II chooses *C* and Person I chooses *B*, Person I receives _____ points and Person II receives _____ points.

3. If Person II chooses *D* and Person I chooses *A*, Person I receives _____ points and Person II receives _____ points.

4. If Person II chooses *D* and Person I chooses *B*, Person I receives _____ points and Person II receives _____ points.

When you understand the matrix, you are ready to play the Prisoner's Dilemma game. The objective of the game is to provide an experience in which trust is either built and maintained or violated and diminished. To play the game each person needs a small pad of paper and a pencil. The procedure for the game is:

1. Pair up with another person in the group. Sit back-to-back so that you cannot see the other player. Each person should have a pencil and a small pad of paper. One person is designated as Person I and the other as Person II.

2. When the leader gives the signal, each person should make her choice (Person I chooses between *A* and *B*, Person II chooses between *C* and *D*). Next, when the leader gives the signal, each person passes a slip of paper with her choice written on it over her shoulder to the other player. You may not speak; no communication to the other player other than the choice you make is allowed.

3. This is repeated ten times. Each player should keep track of the number of points she has on the record sheet.

4. At the end of the tenth choice, the two players can discuss anything they want to with each other for 10 minutes.

5. Ten more choices are made, following the procedure outlined in step 2.

6. At the end of the twentieth choice, total your gains and losses. Then fill out the questionnaire "Impressions of Other's Behavior."

7. In the group as a whole, discuss the following questions:

   a. What were your feelings and reactions about yourself and the other player during the game?

   b. How many points did you make during the game? How many did the other player make?

   c. How did you describe the other player's behavior during the game? How did he or she describe your behavior during the game?

   d. Did the two of you trust each other? Were the two of you trustworthy?

   e. How did it feel to have your trust violated (if that happened to you)? How did it feel to violate the other player's trust?

    f. How was trust built during the game (if it was)?

    g. What effect did the period of communication have upon the way you played the game? Did it affect the way you felt about the other player's behavior?

The essential psychological feature of the Prisoner's Dilemma game is that there is no possibility for "rational" individual behavior in it unless the conditions for mutual trust exist. If each player chooses B and D to obtain either maximum gain or minimum loss for himself, each will lose. But it makes no sense to choose the other alternative, A and C, which could result in maximum loss, unless you can trust the other player. If you have to play the game, you either develop mutual trust or resign yourself to a loss by choosing competitively (that is, choosing B and D) in order to minimize your loss.

There has been a great deal of research on trust using the Prisoner's Dilemma game. Some of the conclusions from that research are:

1. Trust is often difficult to build but very easy to destroy. It may take two players a long time to arrive at a point where both consistently choose A and C, and any deviation to B and D may destroy all possibility of a cooperative solution to the dilemma.

2. Inappropriate trust may be just as dysfunctional as no trust at all; when a person consistently makes a trusting choice (A or C) and the other player consistently chooses B or D, the player exploiting the first person's trust will often feel little or no guilt, rationalizing that anyone who keeps making herself vulnerable deserves to be taken advantage of.

3. How the situation is defined will affect how easily trust may be built. If the game is defined as a problem-solving situation that the two individuals must solve, trust is relatively easy to build. If the game is defined as a competitive situation in which you must win more points than the other player, trust is very difficult to build.

RECORD SHEET: PRISONER'S DILEMMA GAME

	Your choice	Other's choice	Your gain or loss	Your total	Other's gain or loss	Other's total
1.						
2.						
3.						
4.						
5.						
6.						

	Your choice	Other's choice	Your gain or loss	Your total	Other's gain or loss	Other's total
7.						
8.						
9.						
10.						
11.						
12.						
13.						
14.						
15.						
16.						
17.						
18.						
19.						
20.						

Thus in a situation in which you are attempting to increase trust, you may want to avoid violating the other person's trust, avoid trusting the other person if he or she consistently behaves in untrustworthy ways, and ensure that the situation is defined as a problem-solving situation, not a competitive one.

Impressions of Other's Behavior

Indicate, by checking the appropriate adjectives below, your impression of the other player's behavior during the game. You may know the other player; if so, ignore everything you have felt about the person in the past and rate *only* your impressions of his or her behavior during the game.

_____ warm	_____ cold
_____ trustworthy	_____ untrustworthy
_____ fair	_____ unfair
_____ generous	_____ selfish
_____ congenial	_____ uncongenial
_____ cooperative	_____ competitive
_____ kind	_____ unkind
_____ trustful	_____ untrustful

Exercise 3.4: Trust Level Disclosures

The purpose of this exercise is for members of the group to disclose to one another their perceptions of the depth of the trust level in their relationship. Once this information is out in the open, the members of the group can discuss how trust could be increased in their relationship. Openly discussing issues concerning one's relationships is perhaps the most effective way to increase the closeness of the relationship. The procedure for the exercise is:

1. Pick the individual whom you trust least in the group and pair off with him.

2. For 15 minutes, share your perceptions of why the trust level is low in your relationship. Try to avoid being defensive or hostile. Try to understand as fully as possible why the other person feels the way he does.

3. For the next 10 minutes, share your impressions of how the trust level in the relationship can be increased. This may involve stating how you are going to behave differently or how you would like the other to behave differently. Be as specific as possible.

4. Answer the following questions with your partner:

    a. To what extent is the lack of self-disclosure by one or both persons contributing to the relatively low level of trust in the relationship?

    b. To what extent is the lack of communicated support and acceptance by one or both persons contributing to the relatively low level of trust in the relationship.

5. Now find the person in the group whom you trust the most. Pair up with her.

6. For 15 minutes, share your understanding of why the trust level is high in your relationship. Try to understand as fully as possible why each of you feel the way you do.

7. For 10 minutes, share your impressions of how the trust level in the relationship can be increased even more. This may involve stating how you are going to behave differently or how you would like the other to behave differently. Be as specific as possible.

8. Answer the following questions with your partner:

    a. To what extent is the level of self-disclosure by one or both persons contributing to the relatively high level of trust in the relationship?

    b. To what extent is the communication of acceptance and support by one or both persons contributing to the relatively high level of trust in the relationship?

In this exercise it is possible to focus on two important aspects of building and maintaining trust in a relationship. The first is the risk you and your partners took in self-disclosure. The second is the response you and your partners made to the other person's risk taking. Both the risks and the responses are crucial elements in building trust in a relationship.

How do you self-disclose your perceptions of, and your feelings about, your relationship with another person in ways that will result in a closer relationship? This question will be answered in depth in the next chapter, which focuses on communication. But if your self-disclosures include the following four elements, you have a good chance of successfully moving the relationship closer:

1. *Statement of your intentions:* For example, "I'm worried about our relationship. I want to do something that will help us become better friends."

2. *Statement of your expectations about how the other person may respond:* For example, "I think you may be uncomfortable about my bringing this up but I hope that you will listen and try to understand what I am saying."

3. *Statement of what you will do if the other person violates your expectations:* For example "If you shut me off, I will be hurt and will become defensive."

4. *Statement of how trust will be reestablished if he violates your expectations and you make your response:* For example, "If you cut me off and I become defensive, then we'll have to spend an evening talking about old times to get ourselves back together again."

To the extent that these four points become clear in the conversation in which you take a risk, you may feel more confident that the relationship will not be damaged even if the risk turns out badly.

The response you make to another person's risk taking is crucial for building trust in the relationship. The other person will feel it is safe to take risks in self-disclosure to the extent that she feels she will receive support when necessary and acceptance rather than rejection. To ensure that the relationship grows you should do the following:

1. Make sure the other person feels supported for taking the risk.

2. If you disagree with what he is saying, make sure that it is clear that it is his ideas you are rejecting, not him as a person.

3. Make sure you disclose your perceptions and feelings about the relationship. Always reward openness with openness when you are dealing with friends or individuals with whom you wish to develop a closer relationship.

Exercise 3.5: Nonverbal Trust

Taking a risk that makes you vulnerable to another person and receiving support can take place in a variety of nonverbal as well as verbal ways. One of the interesting aspects of the development of trust in a relationship is that sometimes the sense of physical support can be as powerful a developer of trust as can a sense of emotional support. Your group may like to try some of the following nonverbal exercises. Each of them is related to the development of trust. Before you attempt the exercises, however, you should carefully consider the following points:

1. No one with a bad back or another physical condition that might be adversely affected should participate in an exercise in which participants might be handled roughly.

2. Although these nonverbal exercises can be used as a form of play, they should be used only for educational purposes. That is, they should be done for a specific learning purpose, such as learning more about the development of trust, and they should be discussed thoroughly after they have been done.

3. Do not enter into an exercise unless you plan to behave in a trustworthy manner. If you cannot be trusted to support another person, do not enter into an exercise in which you are responsible for physically supporting someone. No one should be allowed to fall or to suffer any injury.

4. No group pressure should be exerted upon individuals to participate. Participation should be strictly voluntary. If you do not feel like volunteering, however, you may find it interesting to analyze why. You may learn something about yourself and your relationships with the other members of the group from such an analysis. A lack of trust in the group or in other individuals might lead you to refuse to participate; on the other hand, a sense of adventure and fun might lead you to volunteer even though you do not trust the group or other individuals.

Trust Circle

The group stands facing into a closed circle. A volunteer, perhaps a person who wishes to develop more trust in the group, is handed around the inside of the circle by the shoulders and upper torso. He should stand with his feet in the center of the circle, close his eyes, and let the group pass him around or across their circle. His feet should not move from the center of the circle. After as many people who want to try it have been passed around the circle, discuss the following questions:

1. How did it feel to be on the inside of the circle? What were you thinking about; what was the experience like?

2. How did it feel to be a part of the circle, passing others around? What were you thinking about; what were you experiencing? Did you feel differently with different people in the center? Did the group behave differently when different people were in the center?

3. Some of the groups take a great deal of care in passing a person around and are very gentle; other groups engage in aggressive play and toss the person from side to side. What did your group do? What does it signify about the group and members?

Trust Walk

Each member of the group pairs up with another person. One person is designated as the guide, the other as a blind person. The blind person should close her eyes and the guide will lead her around the room. The guide should grasp the wrists of the blind person and, either from the side or from behind, guide the blind person around the room, planning as "rich" an experience as possible for the blind person using all the senses other than sight. Various touching experiences such as feeling the wall, the covering of a chair, the hair or face of another person are all interesting. If you can go outdoors, standing in the sun or the wind is enjoyable. In a large room, trust in the guide can be tested by running across the room, the blind person keeping her eyes shut. After 15 minutes, reverse roles and repeat. After everyone has been both a guide and a blind person, discuss the following questions in the group as a whole:

1. How did it feel to be the blind person?
2. What were some of the best experiences your guide gave you?
3. What did you learn about the guide?
4. What did you learn about the blind person?
5. How did it feel to be the guide?
6. At this point, how do the two of you feel about each other?

Trust Cradle

The group forms two lines by the side of a volunteer. The volunteer leans back and the group picks him up, someone supporting his head. The volunteer should close his eyes and relax as much as possible. The group rocks him forward and backward. Slowly the group raises the person up, rocking him all the time, until he is as high as they can lift him. The group then slowly lowers the person to the floor, rocking him back and forth all the time. This can be repeated with several or all of the members of the group, depending upon the amount of time available. Afterwards, the group as a whole should discuss the following questions:

1. How did it feel to be cradled? What were you thinking of while the group was cradling you? What were you experiencing?
2. How did it feel to cradle the different members of the group? Did you have different feelings with different people?
3. How has trust in the group been affected by the experience?

Trust Fall

Partners stand, one with his back turned to the other's front. With his arms extended sideways, he falls backwards and is caught by his partner. Reverse roles and repeat.

You may like to try the exercise with several different group partners. Then discuss in the group as a whole the following questions:

1. How did it feel to fall? Did you doubt that the other would really catch you?
2. How did it feel to catch your partner? Did you doubt that you would be able to catch him?
3. How has trust in the individuals who caught you been affected?

Elevated Trust Passing

The group lines up in a straight line, each person facing the back of the person in front of him. The person at the beginning of the line is lifted high and is passed over the top of the others to the end of the line, where she is slowly brought down. The person now at the head of the line is lifted high and is passed over the top of the others to the end of the line. If a group member does not wish to be passed, she moves to the end of the line when she finds herself at the head of the line. The exercise continues until all members who want to have been lifted and passed.

1. How did it feel to be passed?
2. What were you thinking; what were you experiencing?
3. How did it feel to pass the other members of the group?
4. How has trust in the group been affected by the exercise?

Exercise 3.6: Developing Trust

The objectives for this exercise are for the members of the group to arrive at a summary statement concerning the ways in which trust can be built in a relationship. The procedure for the exercise is:

1. Divide into groups of four.
2. Arrive at the ten most important things a person can do to develop trust in a relationship. Take 20 minutes for this.
3. Share the results across the group.
4. As a whole, rank the ten most important aspects of developing trust from the most important to the least important.

Did your list include any of the following: progressively disclosing oneself to the other person; making sure your behavior regarding the other person is consistent; following through on your commitments to the other person; expressing warmth and acceptance to the other person; avoiding being judgmental of the other person; being trustworthy; being honest?

CHAPTER REVIEW

Test your understanding of this chapter by taking the following quiz. Answers are at the end of the chapter.

True   False   **1.** In a trust situation, you can be either accepted or rejected.

True   False   **2.** In a trust situation, you should prepare for rejection in order to keep from getting hurt.

True   False   **3.** Once you develop trust in a situation, you will not have to work on the relationship anymore.

True   False   **4.** What you expect from a situation can determine what you will get.

True   False   **5.** Risk trusting in every situation.

True   False   **6.** Your response to another person's self-disclosure determines your trustworthiness.

True   False   **7.** An example of good risk taking is when Helen tells Roger how she expects him to respond to her self-disclosure.

True   False   **8.** A good response to risk taking is when Roger interrupts Helen to make his own self-disclosures.

9. What four elements should you have in a conversation when you are taking a risk in self-disclosure in a relationship?
   a. An initial statement of neutral interest
   b. A statement of your intentions
   c. A statement of your expectations and how the other person may respond
   d. A comment about how good the other person looks
   e. A statement of what you will do if the other person violates your expectation
   f. A statement of how the other person bothers you
   g. A statement of how trust will be reestablished

10. When the other person takes a risk in self-disclosure, what three things should you work into the conversation?

a. Support of the other person for taking the risk

b. Complete acceptance of the other person's ideas

c. Your nervousness in self-disclosing

d. If you disagree, your rejection of the person's ideas but not of the person

e. Your own openness in response to the other person's openness

f. How much you've learned from reading this book

In this chapter we have focused on the skills involved in engaging in trusting and trustworthy behavior. Which of these skills have you mastered, and which ones do you need further work on?

1. I have mastered the following:

_____ Expression of warmth and cooperative intentions

_____ Taking appropriate risks with self-disclosure

_____ Responding to another person's self-disclosures with acceptance and support

_____ Reciprocating another person's self-disclosures

2. I need more work on:

_____ Expression of warmth and cooperative intentions

_____ Taking appropriate risks with self-disclosure

_____ Responding to another person's self-disclosures with acceptance and support

_____ Reciprocating another person's self-disclosures

At this point, you should understand what trust is and when it is appropriate to engage in trusting and trustworthy actions. You should also have an understanding of how to develop and maintain trust in a relationship. However, in order for you to self-disclose appropriately and effectively, you need to communicate effectively. The next chapter deals with increasing your communication skills.

ANSWERS

Comprehension Test A: 1. true; 2. true; 3. false; 4. true; 5. true; 6. false; 7. false; 8. true; 9. false; 10. false; 11. true; 12. true; 13. c; 14. b; 15. e; 16. a; 17. f; 18. g; 19. e.

Prisoner's Dilemma: 1. +10, +10; 2. +25, −25; 3. −25, +25; 4. −10, −10.

Chapter Review: 1. true; 2. false; 3. false; 4. true; 5. false; 6. true; 7. true; 8. false; 9. b, c, e, g; 10. a, d, e.

4 *Increasing Your Communication Skills*

To live is to communicate! All life communicates in some way. Living cells communicate by means of hormones and nerve fibers. Animals and insects communicate by means of chemicals, movements, and sounds. Humans use all of these to communicate, but they add words: a unique system based on symbols that stand for the objects and/or ideas to which humans refer. The importance of communication cannot be overemphasized. Communication is the foundation for all interpersonal relationships, and our daily lives are filled with one communication experience after another. Through communication we reach some understanding of each other, learn to like, influence, and trust each other, begin and end relationships, and learn more about ourselves and how others perceive us. Through communication we learn to understand others as individuals and we help others to understand us. Any discussion of interpersonal skills must emphasize the skills of communicating effectively.

WHAT IS COMMUNICATION?

Our basic social nature demands that we seek out communication with other people. We *have* to communicate with others. All of us have personal needs that can be satisfied only by relating to others. Interpersonal communication reflects our mutual need to establish contact and join our efforts to achieve mutual goals. The very process of communication—exchanging messages to achieve understanding of each other's perceptions, ideas, and experiences—makes people interdependent. It takes two to communicate, and through the very act of communicating with another person we begin or maintain a relationship. What prompts communication is our desire for someone else to know what we know, to value what we value, to feel what we feel, and to decide what we decide.

Two people sensing each other through sight, sound, touch, or smell will have a continuous effect on each other's perceptions and expectations of what the other is going to do. Interpersonal communication can be broadly defined as any verbal or nonverbal behavior that is perceived by another person. In other words, communication is much more than the exchange of words; all behavior conveys some message and is, therefore, a form of communication. *Interpersonal communication* is more commonly defined as a message sent by a person to a receiver (or receivers) with a conscious intent of affecting the receiver's behavior. Communication is initiated in order to change the other person in some way. A person sends the message "How are you?" to evoke the response "Fine." A teacher shakes his head to get two students to stop throwing erasers at him. Under this more limited definition, any signal aimed at influencing the receiver's behavior in any way is a communication.

The definition of communication does not mean that an orderly sequence of events in time always exists in which a person thinks up a message and sends it, and someone else receives it. Communication among people is a process in which everyone receives, sends, interprets, and infers all at the same time, and there is no beginning and no end. All communication involves people sending one another symbols to which certain meanings are attached. These symbols can be either verbal (all words are symbols) or nonverbal (all expressions and gestures are symbols). The exchange of ideas and experiences between two people is possible only when both have adopted the same ways of relating a particular nonverbal, spoken, written, or pictorial symbol to a particular experience. And all communication affects the relationship between two people, one way or the other.

Figure 4.1 represents a model of the process of communication be-

FIGURE 4.1: The Interpersonal Communication Process

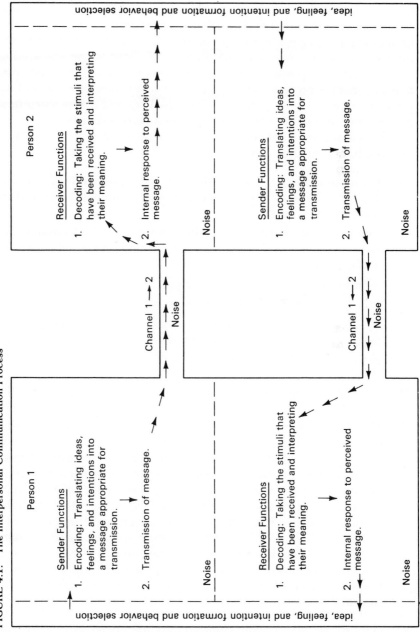

tween two individuals. In this model the communicator is referred to as the *sender* and the person at whom the message is aimed is the *receiver.* The *message* is any verbal or nonverbal symbol that one person transmits to another. The *channel* is the means of conveying the message to the receiver; the sound waves of the voice or the light waves involved in seeing words on a printed page are examples of channels. Because communication is a process, sending and receiving messages often take place simultaneously; a person can be speaking and at the same time paying close attention to the receiver's nonverbal responses.

Communication between two people may be viewed as consisting of seven basic elements (see Figure 4.1):

1. The intentions, ideas, and feelings of the sender and the way she decides to behave, all of which lead to her sending a message that carries some content.

2. The encoding of the message by the sender—she translates her ideas, feelings, and intentions into a message appropriate for sending.

3. Sending the message to the receiver.

4. The channel through which the message is translated.

5. The decoding of the message by the receiver—he interprets its meaning. The receiver's interpretation depends on how well the receiver understands the content of the message and the intentions of the sender.

6. An internal response by the receiver to this interpretation of the message.

7. The amount of *noise* in the above steps. Noise is any element that interferes with the communication process. In the sender, noise refers to such things as the attitudes, prejudices, frame of reference of the sender, and the appropriateness of her language or other expression of the message. In the receiver, noise refers to such things as his attitudes, background, and experiences that affect the decoding process. In the channel, noise refers to (1) environmental sounds, such as static or traffic, (2) speech problems, such as stammering, and (3) annoying or distracting mannerisms, such as a tendency to mumble. To a large extent, the success of communication is determined by the degree to which noise is overcome or controlled.

How do you tell whether communication is effective? *Effective communication* exists between two people when the receiver interprets the sender's message the way the sender intended it. If John tries to communicate to Jane that it is a wonderful day and he is feeling great by saying "Hi" with a warm smile, and if Jane interprets John's "Hi" as meaning John thinks it is a beautiful day and is feeling well, then effective communication has taken place. If Jane interprets John's "Hi" as meaning he wants to stop and talk with her, then ineffective communication has taken place.

Why is it so common for two individuals not to understand each other? Perhaps the most recurring and basic source of misunderstandings between two people is a communication failure resulting from the receiver's understanding the meaning of a message differently from what was intended. We do not always communicate what we mean to. Since intentions are private and known directly only to the person who experiences them, a sender's intentions are not always clear to the receiver. I know my intentions, but I must make inferences about yours. You know your intentions, but you must infer mine. Because of the private nature of intentions, difficulties in communication often result from the failure of the receiver to understand correctly the intentions of the sender.

The communication failures arising from the gap between what the sender meant and what the receiver thought the sender meant do not usually arise from word usage, grammatical form, or lack of verbal ability. Rather, they are created by emotional and social sources of noise. People, for example, are often so preoccupied that they just do not listen to what others are saying. Or they can be so interested in what they have to say that they listen to others only to find an opening to get the floor to say what they want to say. Sometimes individuals are so sure that they know what the other person is going to say that they distort his statements to match their expectations—for example, when a man who has a very low opinion of himself asks a woman for a date and takes her statement "Let me think for a minute" as a refusal.

Sometimes individuals listen in order to evaluate and make judgments about the speaker, which in turn makes the speaker guarded and defensive in what he is trying to say. An example of this occurs when a person is presenting an argument and the receiver is constantly saying, "That's stupid; that's wrong." The speaker then becomes very careful about what he is saying.

At times individuals do fully understand the words a communicator is using without understanding the real underlying meaning of what he is trying to say. For example, a person may say, "It's a nice day," in an attempt to change the subject, and the receiver may think the speaker is really interested in the weather. All of these problems in communication will be discussed more fully later in the chapter.

Finally, a lack of trust seems to act as a principal cause of communication distortion. Distrust can cause a reduction of the information shared and a suspiciousness of what little information is communicated. To a certain extent, increasing the communication between two individuals results in greater accuracy of understanding only when trust is high.

When you stop to think of how many ways individuals can misunderstand each other, it seems at times a wonder that any effective communication can take place at all. But in the exercises in this chapter we will examine and practice communication skills that promote effective, accurate understanding of each other's communications.

COMPREHENSION TEST A

Test your understanding of what communication is by taking the following quiz. Answers are at the end of the chapter.

True   False   **1.** If you are alive, you have to communicate something.

True   False   **2.** It takes two to communicate.

True   False   **3.** In interpersonal communication, the sender wants to affect the receiver's behavior in some way.

True   False   **4.** Communication is an orderly sequence of events in which a person thinks up a message and sends it, and the message is received.

True   False   **5.** A person's attitude can be noise that interferes with communication.

True   False   **6.** Effective communication exists when the receiver gets the message that was sent.

True   False   **7.** Effective communication is a little old lady hitting a burglar over the head with her umbrella.

True   False   **8.** Effective communication is your reading this book and trying to answer this question.

9. What are the seven basic elements of communication?

    a. The subject of the conversation, around which all communication occurs

    b. The intentions of the communicator

    c. The receiver's reactions to the sender

    d. Encoding

    e. Transmission of the message

    f. The receiver's understanding of the content of the message and the intention of the sender

    g. The preferred style of thinking of the sender

    h. The channel through which the message is sent

    i. The internal response of the receiver

    j. Noise

    k. The categories of response the receiver has in mind

    l. Expressing acceptance and support

10. What are three common communication faults of the receiver?

    a. Not giving the sender undivided attention

    b. Turning off the sender's hearing aid

    c. Relating the conversation to something the speaker does not know about

    d. Thinking about her replies instead of paying attention to the sender

    e. Listening for details rather than the essential message

    f. Listening to the essential but missing details

SENDING MESSAGES EFFECTIVELY

How can you send messages effectively? What can you do to ensure effective communication of your ideas and feelings? In this and the following three chapters we discuss the answer to these questions. There are several ways senders of a message can increase the likelihood that they will be understood. The three basic requirements are: understandable messages, credibility of the sender, and optimal feedback on how the message is affecting the receiver.

Research supports the conclusion that the skills of sending messages include the following:

1. *Clearly "own" your messages by using first person singular pronouns: I, my.* Personal ownership includes clearly taking responsibility for the ideas and feelings that are expressed. People disown their messages when they use terms like "most people," "some of our friends," and "our group." Such terms make it difficult to tell whether the people really think and feel what they are saying or whether they are repeating the thoughts and feelings of others.

2. *Make your messages complete and specific.* Include clear statements of all necessary information the receiver needs in order to comprehend the message. Being complete and specific seems so obvious, but often people do not communicate the frame of reference they are using, the assumptions they are making, the intentions they have in communicating, or the leaps in thinking they are making.

3. *Make your verbal and nonverbal messages congruent.* Every face-to-face communication involves both verbal and nonverbal messages. Usually these messages are congruent, so if a person is saying that he has appreciated your help, he is smiling and expressing warmth nonverbally. Communication problems arise when a person's verbal and nonverbal messages are contradictory. If a person says, "Here is some information that may be of help to you" with a sneer on his face and a mocking tone of voice, the meaning you receive is confused by the two different messages being sent.

4. *Be redundant.* Repeating your messages more than once and using more than one channel of communication (such as pictures and written messages as well as verbal and nonverbal cues) will help the receiver understand your messages.

5. *Ask for feedback concerning the way your messages are being received.* In order to communicate effectively you must be aware of how the receiver is interpreting and processing your messages. The only way to be sure is to continually seek feedback as to what meanings the receiver is attaching to your messages.

6. *Make the message appropriate to the receiver's frame of reference.* The same information will be explained differently to an expert in the

field than to a novice, to a child than to an adult, or to your boss than to a co-worker.

7. *Describe your feelings by name, action, or figure of speech.* When communicating your feelings, it is especially important to be descriptive. You may describe your feelings by name ("I feel sad"), by actions ("I feel like crying"), or by figures of speech ("I feel down in the dumps"). The description will help communicate your feelings clearly and unambiguously.

8. *Describe other people's behavior without evaluating or interpreting.* When reacting to the behavior of other people, be sure to describe their behavior ("You keep interrupting me") rather than evaluating it ("You're a rotten, self-centered egotist who won't listen to anyone else's ideas").

One of the most important elements in interpersonal communication is the credibility of the sender. *Sender credibility* refers to the attitude the receiver has toward the trustworthiness of the sender's statements. Several dimensions affect the credibility of the sender:

1. The reliability of the sender as an information source—the sender's dependability, predictability, and consistency.

2. The intentions of the sender or the sender's motives. The sender should be open as to the effect she wants her message to have upon the receiver.

3. The expression of warmth and friendliness.

4. The majority opinion of other people concerning the trustworthiness of the sender. If all our friends tell us the sender is trustworthy, we tend to believe it.

5. The sender's relevant expertise on the topic under discussion.

6. The dynamism of the sender. A dynamic sender is seen as aggressive, emphatic, and forceful and tends to be viewed as more credible than a more passive sender.

There is little evidence available from the studies on sender credibility to suggest which of the above dimensions is the most important. It seems that a highly credible sender is one who is perceived in a favorable light on *all* of these dimensions. A source low in credibility, on the other hand, is one who is perceived in a negative light on *any one* of the dimensions. Unless we appear credible to the receiver, he will discount our message and we will not be able to communicate effectively with him. Sender credibility is often discussed as the perceived trustworthiness of the sender, and therefore credibility relates to the discussion of trust in chapter 3.

> *Each individual in a relationship is constantly commenting on his definition of the relationship implicitly or explicitly. Every message exchange (including silence) defines the relationship implicitly since it expresses the idea "this is the sort of relationship where this sort of message may be given."*
>
> *Donald Jackson*

COMPREHENSION TEST B

Test your understanding of sending understandable messages and having good credibility by marking the following questions true or false. The answers are given at the end of the chapter.

True   False   1. It is important to express what you think, not what other people think.

True   False   2. It is important that your verbal and nonverbal messages go together.

True   False   3. If you express yourself clearly, you will not need to repeat your message.

True   False   4. Evaluating and interpreting other people's behavior is a necessary part of effective communication.

True   False   5. As long as you express yourself clearly, you need not check on how your message is being received.

True   False   6. You must be seen as high on all the credibility dimensions in order to have high credibility.

True   False   7. The opinions of other people can influence how trustworthy the receiver sees the sender.

True   False   8. A passive sender is more credible than an aggressive one.

True   False   9. An example of good communication is Frank calling Edye a pig after she eats all the Christmas cookies.

True   False   10. An example of good credibility is a happily married psychiatrist giving his sister careful, loving advice on how to improve her marriage.

Exercise 4.1: One- and Two-Way Communication*

One of the best ways a sender can make sure messages are received correctly is to obtain optimal feedback on the effects his message is having on the receiver. Feedback is the process through which the sender finds out how his message is being decoded and received. The response the receiver makes to the sender's message can subsequently cause the sender to modify his messages to communicate more accurately with the receiver. If the sender is not able to obtain information on how his message is being decoded, inaccuracies in communication may occur and never be uncovered. Open two-way communication facilitates understanding in communication, which in turn helps such things as developing a fulfilling relationship and being able to work together effectively.

One-way communication occurs when the sender is not able to determine how the receiver is decoding the sender's message. Two-way communication occurs when the sender is able to obtain feedback concerning how the receiver is decoding the sender's message. In this exercise we will compare one- and two-way communication. The objective is to demonstrate the differences between a situation in which two-way communication exists and ones in which communication goes only one way. For this exercise each participant needs two pieces of paper and a pencil. The leader needs copies of Square Arrangement I and Square Arrangement II, which are given in the Appendix. The leader should copy Tables 4.1A–C onto a blackboard or a large sheet of paper.

The procedure for this exercise is:

1. The leader selects a sender and two observers (if the group has fewer than seven members, select only one observer). The sender should be a person who communicates well and who speaks clearly and loudly enough to be heard.

2. The sender is seated either with her back to the group or behind a screen. She is given Square Arrangement I. The leader should be careful that the group members do not see the diagram of squares that the sender will describe. The sender is told to study the first arrangement carefully for 2 minutes in order to be prepared to instruct the group members on how to draw a similar set of squares on their paper.

3. The first observer is asked to note the behavior and reactions of the sender during the exercise and to make notes for later comment. The second observer is asked to make notes on the behavior and reactions of the group members.

*This exercise is adapted from an exercise in Harold J. Leavitt, *Managerial Psychology* (University of Chicago Press, 1958), pp. 118–28.

TABLE 4.1A: MEDIANS FOR TRIALS I AND II

Medians	I	II
Time elapsed:	————	————
Guess accuracy:	————	————
Actual accuracy:	————	————

TABLE 4.1B: FIRST TRIAL

Number correct	Guess	Actual
5	————	————
4	————	————
3	————	————
2	————	————
1	————	————
0	————	————

TABLE 4.1C: SECOND TRIAL

Number correct	Guess	Actual
5	————	————
4	————	————
3	————	————
2	————	————
1	————	————
0	————	————

Facial reactions, gestures, posture, and other nonverbal behaviors may be observed.

4. The group is given these instructions: "The sender is going to describe a drawing to you. You are to listen carefully to her instructions and draw what she describes as accurately as you can. You will be timed, but there is no time limit. *You may ask no questions of the sender and give no audible response.* You are asked to work independently."

5. Tables 4.1A–C are shown in the front of the room. The sender is then told to proceed to give the instructions for drawing the first figure of squares as quickly and accurately as she can. The leader should ensure that there are no questions or audible reactions from the group members.

6. When the sender has completed giving the instructions for Square Arrangement I, the leader records the time it took to do so in the proper space in the first table. Each member of the group is asked to write down on his paper the number of squares he thinks he has drawn correctly in relation to the preceding one.

7. The leader instructs the sender to face the group members. She gives the sender Square Arrangement II and tells her to study the relationship of the squares in this new diagram for 2 minutes in preparation for instructing the group members on how to draw it.

8. The group is then given these instructions: "The sender is going to describe another drawing to you. This time she will be in full view of you and you may ask as many questions as you wish. She is free to reply to your questions or amplify her statements as she sees fit. She is not, however, allowed to make any hand signals while describing the drawing. You will be timed, but there is no time limit. Work as accurately and rapidly as you can."

9. The sender is told to proceed.

10. When the sender has completed giving instructions for the second figure, the time is again recorded in the appropriate space of Table 4.1A. The group members are asked to guess the number of squares they have drawn correctly and to record the number on their papers.

11. A median for guessed accuracy on the first drawing is obtained by recording the number of group members who guessed zero, the number who guessed one, and so on in Table 4.1B. The median guessed number is found by counting from zero the number of group members guessing each number until you reach half the members of the group. The median is then recorded in Table 4.1A.

12. The method is repeated to get the median of accurate guesses for the second drawing.

13. Members are shown the master drawing for the first set of squares, and the relationship of each square to the preceding one is pointed out. Each square must be in the exact relationship to the preceding one as it appears on the master drawing to be counted as correct. When this step has been completed, the members are asked to count and record the actual number right. A similar count is taken for the second chart.

14. The median for accuracy for the first and second drawings is obtained and placed in Table 4.1A.

15. The following questions are discussed.

    a. What may be concluded from the results in terms of time, accuracy, and level of confidence?

    b. What did the observers record during the exercise? How did the behavior of the sender and the group members vary from one situation to the other? The group members and the sender should comment on what they were feeling during the two situations.

    c. How does this exercise compare with situations you find yourself in at work, school, or home? How might you change your behavior in relating to your friends and acquaintances as a result of what you have experienced during this exercise?

The typical result of this exercise is that one-way communication is quicker and less accurate, and the level of confidence of the receiver is lower. Two-way communication takes more time, but it is also likely to be more accurate, and the level of confidence of the receiver is higher. Two-way communication promotes more accurate understanding between the sender and the receiver and builds a more cooperative relationship between the two. The sender, however, usually is more disturbed and frustrated during the two-way communication process.

Just as the sender can increase the accuracy of communication by transmitting his message through a variety of channels, it is also an aid to accuracy if feedback is available in a variety of channels. Feedback does not have to be only verbal; the nonverbal cues such as facial expression, posture, gestures, sighs, and tone of voice when asking questions are often indications of how your message is being interpreted by the receiver.

COMPREHENSION TEST C

Test your understanding of one- and two-way communication by answering true or false to the following statements. Answers are at the end of the chapter.

True   False   **1.** Feedback is the process by which the receiver tells the sender how the message is being received.

True   False   **2.** Feedback is the primary process for clearing up misunderstandings in communication.

True   False   **3.** Feedback is not given in one-way communication.

True   False   **4.** One-way communication is quicker than two-way communication.

True   False   **5.** One-way communication is more frustrating to the sender than two-way communication.

True   False   **6.** Two-way communication is usually more accurate than one-way communication.

True   False   **7.** The confidence level of the receiver is higher in two-way communication.

True   False   **8.** Helen is getting feedback when Edye tells her how delicious her Christmas cookies are.

True   False   **9.** Edye is getting feedback when Buddy makes a face after taking a bite of her cookies.

True   False   **10.** David is getting feedback when no one buys his cookies.

PRACTICE IN COMMUNICATION SKILLS

You are about to receive instructions for a series of experiences dealing with effective and ineffective communication. These experiences will provide you with the opportunity (1) to become more aware of effective and ineffective communication procedures, (2) to become more aware of your own behavior in communicating with others, and (3) to practice effective communication procedures in order to develop increased skills. Such practice will increase your ability to develop and maintain effective interpersonal skills.

The suggested procedures at first may seem deceptively simple. Once you attempt them, however, you may find them more difficult than you expected. You will also find that they are very powerful when skillfully used. If you become involved in the exercise and consciously attempt both to learn as much as possible and to enjoy yourself, you will develop considerably better communication skills. If you try the activities willingly and with enthusiasm, you can have a lot of fun while learning.

The steps of the following exercise are designed to lead you from a situation in which you conduct an irrelevant, somewhat destructive conversation to a situation in which you use the tools of communicating effectively in building more personal relationships. The exercise serves the following purposes:

1. It allows you to experience two types of conversation that interfere with developing personal relationships and two kinds of conversation that facilitate development of personal relationships.

2. It provides skill practice in how to listen effectively and how to respond to messages sent by another person.

3. It provides skill practice in how to send effective messages that facilitate the development of close personal relationships.

4. It introduces several key concepts on communication, such as (a) listening with understanding, (b) selective perception, (c) personal statements, and (d) relationship statements.

The session consists of three steps. The first two steps will contrast effective and ineffective ways of listening and responding. The final step will permit effective listening and responding in a situation emphasizing effective ways of sending messages. In each step a combination of experience, theory, and discussion will be used. At the end, a summary will be given and further skill development will be discussed.

All communication affects the relationship between the sender and the receiver. It moves the relationship forward or backward, or keeps it the same. Communication can deepen a relationship, or it can make the relationship more distant and impersonal. Many problems found in close relationships stem from failures to communicate effectively. The following activities will illustrate the skills involved in deepening relationships through communication.

You will need a partner and two more people to make groups of two and four. Communication is not a solitary activity, so find three other individuals and proceed.

Exercise 4.2A: Increasing Communication Skills

Step One: Not Listening Versus Closely Listening; Irrelevant Response Versus Relevant Response

Part 1: Discussion on Listening. What types of problems make it difficult for two persons to understand each other? What failures in sending, listening, and responding cause communication gaps? List below at least four reasons why two persons may fail to communicate with each other.

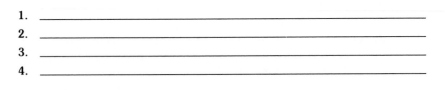

1. _____
2. _____
3. _____
4. _____

Do your suggestions include the following?

1. Inaccurate expression of one's thoughts
2. Failing to listen to all that is being said
3. Trying to say too much in one statement
4. Two individuals not talking about the same thing while they are in a conversation with each other

Part 2: Not Listening and Irrelevant Response. Divide into groups of four.

1. Conduct a discussion on establishing close friendships or on relating to others. Allow 5 minutes of discussion. During the discussion, you must talk about the assigned topic, and what you say must be *unrelated* to what others in the group say. It is as though you did not hear them.

2. After the discussion, jot down answers to the following questions to use later.

    a. How did it feel to make a statement and have no one respond to it?

    _____

    _____

    _____

    b. How did it feel to ignore a statement made by others in the group?

    _____

    _____

    _____

Part 3: Close Listening and Relevant Response. Within the group of four divide into pairs. Designate one member of each pair *A*, the other *B*.

1. *A* makes a statement to *B* either about himself, about *B*, or about the relationship between them. Try not to make bland statements, but say something that you have some feelings about and that can have real meaning for both of you.

2. *B* paraphrases *A*'s statement, stating in his own words what *A*'s remark meant to him. There is to be no discussion of the statements. *A* simply makes the statement; *B* paraphrases it back. Some general rules for paraphrasing response are

    a. Restate the other person's expressed feelings and ideas in your own words; don't mimic or parrot the exact words of the other person.

    b. Preface reflected remarks with "You feel . . . ," "You think . . . ," "It seems to you that . . . ," "It sometimes appears to you that . . . ," and so on.

    c. In paraphrasing another person's statements, avoid any indication of approval or disapproval. Refrain from blaming, interpreting, giving advice, or persuading.

3. *A* makes a second statement to *B*, *B* paraphrases it.

4. *A* makes a third statement to *B*, *B* paraphrases it.

5. Reverse the process. *B* makes three statements to *A*; after each one *A* paraphrases it back.

6. Jot down answers to the following questions to use later:

    a. How did it feel to make a statement and have your partner paraphrase it?

    _____

    _____

    _____

b. How did it feel to paraphrase a statement made by your partner?

_____

_____

_____

7. Discuss your experiences in the group of four. Some questions you may use in the discussion are

   a. Did you find that you had difficulty in listening to others during the exercise? Why?

   b. Did you find that you were not getting across what you wanted to say?

   c. What was your reaction to the paraphrasing of your partner? Was he receiving what you intended to send?

   d. Was the manner of presentation by your partner affecting your listening ability? In what way?

   e. What were the differences in your feelings during the two types of experiences?

THEORY ON LISTENING AND RESPONDING

Give every man thine ear, but few thy voice.

Polonius (Hamlet)

To speak precisely and to listen carefully presents a challenge. You have just been through an exercise in which you both sent and received messages. There are several common faults that people often make when they communicate. Were you guilty of any of these mistakes in communicating?

_____ Not organizing your thoughts before speaking

_____ Including too many (and sometimes unrelated) ideas in your messages

_____ Making short statements that did not include enough information and repetition to be understood

_____ Ignoring the amount of information the receiver already had about the subject

_____ Not making your message appropriate to the receiver's point of view

_____ Not giving your undivided attention to the sender

_____ Thinking about your reply before listening to everything the sender had to say

_____ Listening for details rather than for the entire message

_____ Evaluating whether the sender was right or wrong before you fully understood the message

These are not the only mistakes you can make in communicating, but they all need to be avoided if you are to be effective in communicating with other people.

The way you listen and respond to another person is crucial for building a fulfilling relationship. You can either listen and respond in ways that make the relationship more distant and impersonal, or you can listen and respond in ways that bring you and the sender into a closer, more personal relationship. It is crucial in a close relationship for you to communicate that you have clearly heard and understood the sender. It is characteristic of impersonal relationships that the receiver communicates he has not heard and has not understood the sender. When you listen accurately and respond relevantly, you communicate to the sender, "I care about what you are saying, and I want to understand it." When you fail to listen and respond irrelevantly, you communicate to the sender, "I don't care about what you are saying, and I don't want to understand it." The previous experiences have highlighted the two different ways of listening and responding.

There are other ways of listening and responding that alienate the sender (Rogers and Roethlisberger 1952; Rogers 1965). Perhaps the major barrier to building close relationships is the very natural tendency we have to judge, evaluate, approve, or disapprove of the statements made by the sender. For instance, the sender makes a statement and you respond silently or openly with, "I think you're wrong," "I don't like what you said," "I think your views are right," or "I agree entirely."

Although the tendency to give evaluative responses is common in almost all conversations, it is heightened in situations where feelings and emotions are deeply involved. The stronger the feelings, the more likely it will be that two persons will evaluate the other's statements, each from only his own point of view.

More effective communication occurs, and this evaluative tendency is avoided, when the receiver gives understanding responses (*paraphrases*). An understanding response not only communicates desire to understand the sender without evaluating his statements; it also helps the receiver to see the expressed ideas and feelings from the sender's point of view. When paraphrasing is skillfully done, the receiver is able to achieve the sender's frame of reference in regard to the message. Although paraphrasing sounds simple, it is often very difficult to do. Yet it has powerful effects. Many counselors and psychotherapists have

found that listening intently to what a person says, understanding how it seems to him, and seeing the personal flavor it has for him is very helpful to the sender. If you paraphrase a message, the act tends to reduce the sender's fears about revealing himself to you and decreases the sender's defensiveness about what he is communicating. It facilitates psychological health and growth. There is every indication that empathetic understanding is such an effective approach to building close interpersonal relationships that it can bring about major positive changes in personality.

How do you improve your skills in listening empathetically to others? One way is simply to follow this rule the next time you get deeply involved in a conversation or argument: *Each person can speak up for himself only after he has first restated the ideas and feelings of the previous sender accurately and to the sender's satisfaction.* This means that before presenting your own point of view, it would be necessary for you to achieve the other's frame of reference, to understand his thoughts and feelings so well that you could paraphrase them for him. Sound simple? Try it. You will find that it is one of the most difficult things you ever attempted. You will also find that your arguments will become much more constructive and productive if you are able to follow the above rule successfully.

COMPREHENSION TEST D

You may wish to assess your comprehension of the above material on listening and responding by answering the following questions. Answers are at the end of the chapter.

1. What is the effect of judgmental or evaluative responses on communication?
    a. They increase the accuracy of communication.
    b. They encourage the sender to elaborate on her statements.
    c. They increase the sender's fears about disclosing her ideas and feelings to the receiver.
    d. They spice up the conversation.
    e. They increase the sender's defensiveness about what she is saying.
    f. They alienate the sender.
2. What are three rules for effective paraphrasing?
    a. Repeat the sender's words exactly and with the same inflections.

   b. Restate the sender's message in your own words.

   c. Preface your paraphrasing with such remarks as, "You feel
. . . ."

   d. Indicate whether you approve or disapprove of his message.

   e. Do not indicate any approval or disapproval of the sender's
statements.

3. How does giving an understanding response, a paraphrase, facilitate communication?

   a. It helps the receiver to see the expressed ideas and feelings
from the sender's frame of reference.

   b. It communicates to the sender that the receiver cares about the
message and wants to understand it.

   c. It increases the amount of time two individuals talk with each
other.

Exercise 4.2B: Increasing Communication Skills

**Step Two: Partial Listening versus Listening for Meaning;
Asyndetic Response versus Attending and Negotiation for
Meaning Response**

Part 1: Partial Listening and Asyndetic Responding. Divide into groups of four.

1. Conduct a discussion about establishing a close friendship, relating to others,
or some other related topic. Discuss the topic for 5 minutes.

2. This time you are to listen to what the others say but only for the purpose of
using some small part of what they say in order to change the discussion to
something more interesting to you. In other words, you acknowledge their
statement but use it only as a polite way of introducing your own ideas into the
conversation. This is called an *asyndetic response.*

3. Jot down answers to the following questions for use in a later discussion:

   a. How did it feel having others change the subject right after your statement?

   b. How did it feel changing the subject right after others had made a statement?

Part 2: Listening for Meaning, and Attending and Negotiating for Meaning Response. Divide into pairs. Designate one person *A*, and the other *B*.

1. *A* makes a statement about herself, about *B*, or about their relationship.

2. *B* responds by saying, "What I think you mean is . . ." (He then says what he
thinks *A* meant.) He does not try to speculate about why he thinks that or about

why *A* might be saying that. He simply tells *A* exactly what he thinks *A* meant by the statement, *A* and *B* then negotiate until they are in complete agreement about what *A* really meant, and *A* is able to respond to *B* with, "Yes, that is exactly what I meant." Do not add to or go beyond the original meaning, and don't try to analyze each other. Simply attempt to get at the exact meaning of what was said.

3. *A* makes a second statement. *B* responds with, "What I think you mean is . . . " The two then negotiate the exact meaning of the statement.

4. *A* makes a third statement. *B* responds as before.

5. Reverse the process. *B* makes three statements and *A* responds.

6. Answer these questions:

    a. How did it feel to make a statement and have my partner reply with what he thought it meant, then for us to negotiate the exact meaning of the statement?

    b. How did it feel to listen to my partner's statement and respond with what I thought it meant, then for us to negotiate the exact meaning of the statement?

7. Discuss the experiences in your group of four. Some questions you may use in the discussion are:

    a. Did you always communicate what you wanted to communicate?

    b. Did you find the listener responding to only part of what you said?

    c. Was it ever unclear what the speaker had in mind? What made it unclear?

THEORY ON SELECTIVE PERCEPTION IN LISTENING AND RESPONDING

Did you notice that in responding to your partner's statement you selected part of her message to respond to and did not respond to other parts? This is very common in communication. It is based on the fact that our perceptions have to be selective. A message has too many aspects, both verbal and nonverbal, for a receiver to respond to all of them. Even when a person says, "How are you?" a receiver may ignore the tone of voice, facial expression, gestures of the sender, and the appropriateness of the message to the situation; he may respond only to the usual meaning of the words. Most communication is so complex that we have to be selective about what we perceive and what we respond to. Selective perception, however, is one of the sources of "noise" in the communication process. Some of the factors that influence what we respond to in a message are our expectations, our needs, wants, and desires, and our opinions, attitudes, and beliefs.

If you expect a person to act unfriendly, you will be sensitive to anything that can be perceived as rejection and unfriendliness. If your past experience has led you to expect certain people to be hostile, you will be sensitive to any expression that can be seen as hostile. Such sensitization may make you completely blind to friendly expressions.

If you need and want someone to give you support, on the other hand, you may be highly sensitive to any expressions that can be perceived as supportive. If you are hungry you may be sensitive to any messages about food; or if you want to go home after a long evening you may be sensitive to how tired others are. Your wants and your needs constantly affect what you perceive in interpersonal-communication situations.

Finally, there is evidence that you will be more sensitive to perceiving messages that are consistent with your opinions and attitudes. You will tend to misperceive or fail to perceive messages that are opposite to your opinions, beliefs, and attitudes. You learn and remember material that is consistent with your attitudes, beliefs, and opinions. In many ways your attitudes, beliefs, and opinions affect what you perceive in interpersonal communication.

In listening and responding appropriately to others, it is important to be aware of the likelihood of selectivity in what you perceive and to be ready to change your perceptions when it becomes evident that you have misperceived a message. Your interpretations of what messages mean will always be tentative until confirmed by the sender; that is one reason it is so important to negotiate the meaning of a message before you respond to it.

COMPREHENSION TEST E

You may wish to answer the following questions to see how well you have understood the material on selective perception. Answers are at the end of the chapter.

1. What is selective perception?
   a. Responding to all the aspects, both verbal and nonverbal, of a message
   b. Responding only to a few of the verbal and nonverbal aspects of a message
   c. The name of a famous race horse
2. Which of the following are factors that influence selective perception?
   a. Self-disclosure
   b. Expectations

    c. The weather

    d. Needs, wants, desires

    e. Opinions, attitudes, beliefs

    f. Trust

3. How can you avoid misunderstandings due to selective perception?

    a. Do not try to communicate.

    b. Keep all interpretations of messages tentative until confirmed by the sender.

    c. Do not have expectations, needs, or opinions.

Exercise 4.2C: Increasing Communication Skills

Step Three: The Use of Effective Communication Skills—Clarifying Personal Strengths and Clarifying Relationships

Part 1: Clarifying Strengths. Divide into pairs.

1. *A* takes 3 minutes to share with *B* what she considers to be his personal strengths, including things he thinks he does well, things he likes about himself, and things he thinks others like about him.

2. *B* bombards *A* with any observations he has about *A*'s strengths and personal assets. In each case, when *A* receives an item of feedback she responds (a) by paraphrasing the feedback and (b) by stating what she thinks *B* means and by negotiating the meaning. Do not take more than 5 minutes to do this.

3. Reverse roles and repeat the same process.

PERSONAL STATEMENTS

One of the most basic sending skills is speaking for oneself. When you speak for yourself, you take responsibility for and acknowledge ownership of your thoughts, opinions, observations, and feelings. You are an expert on *your* ideas, feelings, and needs, while other people are experts on *their* ideas, feelings, and needs. You speak for yourself when you use the personal pronouns, *I, me, my,* and *mine. Personal statements* are messages referring to yourself—about what you are feeling, what you are doing, what you are thinking, how you see yourself and your behavior, and so on. Whenever you refer to yourself the discussion target is "personal." You take *ownership* of your ideas, feelings, and needs when you say, "I think . . . ," "I feel . . . ," and "I want. . . ." The more you speak for yourself, the clearer your messages will be. The less you speak for yourself, the more confused your messages will be.

There are two ways you can confuse the ownership of your messages. The first is to *speak for no one*. To speak for no one you can substitute words like "it," "some people," "everyone," or "one" for a personal pronoun. Or you can use no pronoun at all. As a result, it is not clear who is the owner of the ideas or feelings. Examples are, "Most people believe that students from Southeast Central are chickens!" or "It is commonly believed that students from Southeast Central have a big yellow streak down their back!"

The second way to confuse ownership of a message is to *speak for others*. When you speak for others you substitute pronouns such as "you" or "we" (or the person's name) for a first-person-singular pronoun. Examples are, "Bill doesn't like you—he thinks you're a lousy boss," and "We are bored, bored, bored!" Speaking for other people may make them angry or, at the very least, boxed in by your statements. And other people will be confused as to what your thoughts, feelings, and needs are.

Personal statements reveal who you are to the receiver and they increase the personal quality of the relationship. They also communicate personal involvement and trust in the relationship. Not "owning" your messages is a symbol of mistrust and decreases the possibilities of a closer relationship developing between you and the person you are talking with.

Part 2: Practicing Personal Statements. With your partner, decide which of the following are personal statements *(P)*, which speak for no one *(N)*, and which speak for someone else *(O)*. Answers are at the end of the chapter.

_____ 1. Everyone here hates Bill.
_____ 2. I love you.
_____ 3. I hate you.
_____ 4. Rumor has it that you are a beautiful person.
_____ 5. We think flying is for the birds.
_____ 6. Anyone can tell from looking at your face that you feel terrible.
_____ 7. I want to find a better job.

Then discuss with your partner the following questions.

1. In making statements about your strengths, to what extent were the statements clearly personal ones?

2. What is your reaction to making personal statements and to receiving personal statements?

3. How do you think personal statements help develop a relationship and improve communication between the sender and the receiver?

Part 3: Clarifying Relationships. Divide into pairs.

1. Person A says, "One thing you could do to improve our relationship is . . . "

2. Person B (a) paraphrases the statement and (b) states what he thinks A meant by the statement; they then negotiate its meaning. Once the meaning is clearly agreed upon, B states, "My reaction to that is . . ."

3. Repeat the process.

4. Reverse roles and repeat steps 1-3.

RELATIONSHIP STATEMENTS

Happiness is having good relationships. With some people, you will automatically become friends or enemies. But most relationships do not "just happen." They have to be built and maintained. At times your relationships will be smooth and enjoyable. At other times, conflicts and problems will arise and will have to be solved. At such times, you will have to sit down with the other person and discuss the current problems in the relationship and negotiate a solution. During such a conversation, you will need to make relationship statements.

A *relationship statement* is a message describing how you view the relationship or how you view some aspect of the relationship. It focuses on the relationship, not on you or the other person, and it speaks only for yourself. An example of a relationship statement is, "I appreciate your listening to me carefully." A good relationship statement indicates clear ownership and describes the relationship. A poor relationship statement speaks for the other person and makes judgments about the relationship. Relationship statements change the relationship; they consider clearly where the relationship is and what needs to happen in order for it to develop. Making relationship statements clarifies where two individuals stand and facilitates the expression of feelings and perceptions that can lead to a deeper, more satisfying relationship. Relationship statements also decrease the possibility of faulty communication.

Part 4: Understanding Relationship Statements. With your partner, decide which of the following are good relationship statements (R) and which are poor ones (No). Then review your answers for all poor relationship statements. Decide which ones are about a person and not a relationship (P), which ones make a judgment about the relationship *(J)* rather than describing how you perceive the relationship, and which ones speak for the other person *(O)* rather than for the speaker. The answers are given below.

_____ 1. We really enjoyed ourselves last night.
_____ 2. Our relationship is really lousy!
_____ 3. For the past two days, you have not spoken to me once. Is something wrong with our relationship?
_____ 4. You look sick today.
_____ 5. You really make me feel appreciated and liked.
_____ 6. You're angry again. You're always getting angry.
_____ 7. My older brother is going to beat you up if you don't stop doing that.
_____ 8. This job stinks.
_____ 9. I'm concerned that when we go to lunch together we are often late for work in the afternoon.

Answers

1. "We really enjoyed ourselves last night." This is a poor relationship statement because it speaks for the other person as well as for oneself. It should be marked *O*.

2. "Our relationship is really lousy!" This is a poor relationship statement because it judges the quality of the relationship rather than describing some aspect of the relationship. It should be marked *J*.

3. "For the past two days you have not spoken to me once. Is something wrong with our relationship?" This is a good relationship statement because it describes how the speaker sees one aspect of the relationship. It describes the speaker's perceptions of how the two people are relating to one another. Label it *R*.

4. "You look sick today." This is a poor relationship statement because it focuses on a person, not on a relationship. It should be marked *P*. The person may look sick, but such a statement does not describe how the two people are relating to each other. It could be reworded as a good relationship statement as follows: "For the past 15 minutes you have been holding your head in your hands. Are you not feeling well or is what I'm saying giving you a headache?"

5. "You really make me feel appreciated and liked." This is a good relationship statement because the speaker is describing one aspect of how the speaker and the other person relate to each other. Label it *R*.

6. "You're angry again. You're always getting angry." This is a poor relationship statement because it speaks for the other person. It should be marked *O*. A good relationship statement would be: "You look angry. You have frequently looked angry to me during the past two days. Is there a problem about our relationship that we need to discuss?"

7. "My older brother is going to beat you up if you don't stop doing that." This statement focuses on two other people (the older brother and the receiver). It should be marked *P*.

8. "This job stinks!" Definitely a judgment *(J)*. To be a good relationship statement, it would have to be something like the following: "I get so angry and upset at the way you treat me that I dislike working here."

9. "I'm concerned that when we go to lunch together we are often late for work in the afternoon." This is a relationship statement and should be marked *R*. It describes an aspect of the relationship in that the two people manage their lunches together in such a way that they end up being late for work in the afternoon.

COMPREHENSION TEST F

Test your understanding of the previous communication skills by answering true or false to the following statements. Answers are at the end of the chapter.

True   False   1. Evaluative responses encourage the sender to elaborate on her statements.

True   False   2. Paraphrasing is restating the ideas and feelings of the sender before responding.

True   False   3. Paraphrasing shows that you care about what the other person is saying.

True   False   4. Paraphrasing helps the receiver understand the sender's message.

True   False   5. In selective perception, you respond to only part of the communication.

True   False   6. Our own needs, attitudes, and expectations can bring about selective perception.

True   False   7. The way to avoid misunderstandings due to selective perception is to avoid having any expectations, needs, or opinions.

True   False   8. The more you speak for yourself, the more confused your message will be.

True   False   9. When you make good personal statements, you talk about the other person's personal life.

True   False   10. Relationship statements focus mainly on the other individual in the relationship.

UNDERSTANDING THE OTHER'S PERSPECTIVE

Meg and Marge attend the same college. Meg is very wealthy, having inherited a great deal of money from her grandparents. Marge, whose parents are very poor, earns barely enough money to pay her tuition, buy books, and live inexpensively. They both buy tickets for the state lottery in which they could win up to $5,000. Two months later, they both receive letters. Meg reads her letter and says, "Hey, I won $5,000 in that lottery. Imagine that." Marge reads her letter, starts jumping up and down and screams, "I won! I won! I won $5,000!!! I won $5000! I won! I won!" She throws her arms around her friend, both crying and laughing at the same time. She is too excited to eat or sleep.

Why did Meg and Marge react so differently to the news that they had each won $5,000 in the state lottery?

Different people have different perspectives. You see things from your shoes, I see things from my shoes, and our perspectives will never be quite the same. Misunderstandings often occur because we assume that everyone sees things from the same perspective as we do. If we like Italian food, we assume that all our friends like Italian food. If we are interested in sports, we assume that everyone is interested in sports. If

we get angry when someone laughs at our behavior, we assume that being laughed at angers everyone. If we think a boss is stupid, we are surprised when a co-worker thinks the boss is brilliant. As children, we can see things only from our perspective. As we become adults, we learn that different people have different perspectives, and we learn how to understand other people's perspectives.

You can have two different perspectives at two different times. When you are a tired clerk who wants to go home early to get ready for an important date, a customer's behavior may seem unreasonable. When you are a manager who is trying to increase sales, the same customer behavior may seem very understandable. On Monday, if a clerk overcharges you, you may laugh it off. But on Tuesday, when you have been overcharged at the last three stores you have visited, a careless clerk may make you angry. If you have been lifting 100-pound bags of cement and someone tosses you a 40-pound bag, it will seem very light, but if you have been lifting 20-pound bags, the 40-pound bag will seem very heavy. As your experiences, assumptions, career, and values change, your perspective will change.

The same message can mean two entirely different things to two different people. If you tease a classmate, she may laugh. But if you tease a prominent professor, she may get angry and throw you out of class. *Different perspectives result in the message being given different meanings.* From one perspective, a message may be interpreted as a joke. From another perspective, the same message may be interpreted as hostile insubordination.

Perspective taking is a vital skill for communicating effectively. To phrase your messages effectively, you need to take into account the perspective of the receiver. When deciding how to phrase a message, you need to consider:

1. The receiver's perspective
2. What the receiver already knows about the issue
3. What further information the receiver needs and wants about the issue

By taking these factors into account, you can phrase the message so the receiver can easily understand it.

To be skilled in receiving messages accurately, you need to understand the sender's perspective. When deciding what a message means, you need to take into account:

1. The sender's perspective
2. The meaning of the message from the sender's perspective

By taking these factors into account, you can decide accurately what the sender wanted to communicate with the message.

There is no skill more important for effective communication than taking into consideration the other person's perspective. Try standing in someone else's shoes; it will considerably improve your communication with that person.

Exercise 4.3: From Their Shoes

The purpose of this exercise is to provide some practice in phrasing messages so they are appropriate to the receiver's perspective. The procedure is:

1. Form into groups of four and read the story entitled "The Typists," which follows below. As a group, write out what Jim might say to Sally, John Adams, and Dr. Elizabeth Smith. Then read the story entitled "The Laboratory Technicians." Write out what Edythe might say to Buddy, Helen, Dr. Smith, and Mrs. Jonathan.

2. In your group, discuss the following questions:

   a. How do your group's answers compare with the answers of the other groups?

   b. What did you learn about making messages appropriate to the perspective of the receiver?

   c. How do you find out what another person's perspective is?

The Typists

Sally and Jim are typists for a small publishing firm. Sally and Jim often tease each other about who is the faster typist. Their boss, John Adams, asks Jim to type a manuscript for one of their authors, whose name is Dr. Elizabeth Smith. Dr. Smith is a well-known authority in mathematical psychology. The manuscript is very complicated. It contains a great many mathematical equations that are hard to type. It contains a lot of psychological jargon that Jim does not understand. It has handwritten notes all over it that are impossible for him to read. Dr. Smith, for example, has written sentences filled with psychological jargon, in small and sloppy handwriting and in ink that is smeared all over the page. It takes Jim hours trying to figure out what the handwritten notes say. Since he does not know what half the words mean, he cannot be sure whether he has typed the notes correctly or not. The math included in the manuscript, furthermore, is very complicated. It all has to be double checked to make sure it is correctly typed. This has taken hours and hours of proofreading and correcting mistakes. All in all, Jim hates the manuscript. But he is working hard to finish it correctly. To top it all off, Jim is using an old typewriter that is difficult to type on. He asked his boss, John, for a new one several weeks ago, but so far John has not tried to get him one.

One morning Sally looks over at Jim, smiles, and says, "That manuscript is really taking you a long time to type. How come?" Then John walks in and asks, "Jim, I have other typing for you to do and you're still working on Dr. Smith's manuscript. Why is it taking you so long?" Then Dr. Smith phones Jim and says, "Look! I have to revise the manuscript before next month! I need a clean, typed copy immediately. Why haven't you finished it?"

If you were Jim, would you say the same thing to Sally, John, and Dr. Smith? If you phrased your answers differently, what would you take into account about the persons? In phrasing his messages to each person, Jim might take into account:

1. Who the person is

2. What his or her position in the company is

3. How much the person knows about the condition and content of the manuscript

4. What the nature of the relationship between Jim and the person is

5. How appropriate it is to be fully honest about:

   a. Jim's feelings about the manuscript

   b. The facts about why it is so hard to type

The Laboratory Technicians

Buddy and Edythe are laboratory technicians in a large hospital. They have worked with each other for just a few days and do not know each other very well. One morning their supervisor, Helen, asks them to do a rush job on a blood sample. Helen is Edythe's older sister. Helen states that Dr. Smith is very worried about the patient. The tests, therefore, have to be done perfectly. The patient's name is Mrs. Jonathan. Edythe has never met either Dr. Smith or Mrs. Jonathan.

Edythe quickly conducts a series of blood tests. The results indicate that Mrs. Jonathan has blood cancer. As she finishes writing the results of the tests, Buddy comes over and asks, "What'd you find?" Then Helen rushes in and asks, "What were the results of the blood tests for Dr. Smith?" Dr. Smith then calls on the phone for a quick report from Edythe. Finally, later in the day, Mrs. Jonathan calls up Edythe and says, "Look! I'm the person paying the bills! I want to know the results of my blood tests! And don't tell me to ask Dr. Smith! I already did and he won't tell me!"

If you were Edythe, would you say the same thing to Buddy, Helen, Dr. Smith, and Mrs. Jonathan? If the answer is no, what would you take into account in replying to each person? You might want to take the following factors into consideration:

1. Who the person is

2. What his or her position in the hospital is

3. How much the person knows about blood tests and blood cancer

4. What the nature of the relationship between Edythe and the person is

5. How appropriate it is to be fully honest about the results of the blood tests

Exercise 4.4: Observing Communication Behavior

You have just been through a series of short experiences on effective and ineffective communication behavior. You may wish to sharpen your skills in recognizing such behavior. The procedure for this exercise is:

1. Pick a group to observe, or sit down in a crowded area in which a number of conversations are going on.

2. Using the observation sheets that follow, count the number of times each type of effective or ineffective communication behavior takes place.

3. Within a week's time, discuss in the group the results of your observations. What general conclusions can you draw from what the members of your group observed?

Observation Sheet for Ineffective Communication

1. The receiver fails to listen to the message:

   _____

   _____

2. The receiver listens only to part of the message in order to say what he wants to say rather than responding fully to the message:

   _____

   _____

3. The receiver distorts the message to conform with his expectations of what he thought the sender was going to say:

   _____

   _____

4. The receiver is listening in order to make judgments and evaluations of the sender, thus making the sender defensive and guarded in formulating the message:

   _____

   _____

5. The receiver understood the words of the message but not the underlying meaning:

   _____

   _____

6. The sender uses general pronouns and nouns to refer to her own feelings and ideas:

   _____

   _____

7. Other ineffective communication behaviors:

   _____

   _____

Observation Sheet for Effective Communication

1. The receiver paraphrases the sender's remarks:

   _____

   _____

2. The receiver checks out the meaning of the sender's remarks:

   _____

   _____

3. The receiver does not give evaluations or judgments about the sender's remarks:

   _____

   _____

4. The receiver keeps his interpretation of the sender's remarks tentative until he checks it out with the sender:

   _____

   _____

5. The receiver focuses upon the meaning of the message, not the specific words:

   _____

   _____

6. The sender uses personal statements:

   _____

   _____

7. The sender uses relationship statements:

   _____

   _____

8. Other effective communication behaviors:

   _____

   _____

TOWARD IMPROVED COMMUNICATION SKILLS

The difficulties in establishing effective communication between individuals are very real. What, then, can be done to improve understanding? One thing is the development of an atmosphere of mutual confidence and trust through the use of personal and relationship statements. Secondly, the use of communication skills such as paraphrasing, negotiating meaning, and making your responses relevant to the sender's message improves understanding. You may also facilitate the development of close, personal relationships by making your messages reflect personal and relationship statements and by making your responses reflect a recognition of the other person's strengths and capabilities. Through the use of such skills, you can consciously make the most of your chances to develop close, fulfilling relationships with other people.

CHAPTER REVIEW

Test your understanding of how to increase your communication skills by answering true or false to the following statements. Answers are at the end of the chapter.

True   False   1. Interpersonal communication is a message sent with a conscious attempt to affect the receiver's behavior.

True   False   2. The factors that most interfere with communication are external, not internal.

True   False   3. In effective communication, the receiver must interpret the message the way the sender intended.

True   False   4. Sending messages effectively involves "owning" your messages.

True   False   5. If a sender is lacking in credibility, she will have trouble communicating.

True   False   6. Getting feedback from the receiver helps eliminate misunderstandings.

True   False   7. Paraphrasing involves giving your opinion of the sender's message.

True   False   **8.** Relationship statements describe how one person feels about how both people are relating.

True   False   **9.** Most people have the same perspective.

True   False   **10.** Different perspectives result in the same message having different meanings.

In this chapter a series of communication skills have been discussed. Indicate below which ones you have mastered and which ones you need more work on.

1. I have mastered the following:
   - ____ Paraphrasing response
   - ____ Negotiating for meaning response
   - ____ Making good personal statements
   - ____ Making good relationship statements
   - ____ Understanding the other person's perspective
   - ____ Recognizing when effective or ineffective communication is taking place
2. I need more work on:
   - ____ Paraphrasing response
   - ____ Negotiating for meaning response
   - ____ Making good personal statements
   - ____ Making good relationship statements
   - ____ Understanding the other person's perspective
   - ____ Recognizing when effective or ineffective communication is taking place

You now should have increased your communication skills, and you should now know how to send and receive messages accurately. These skills take continual practice to perfect. As you continue to practice communication skills, you need to be able to say what you feel. The next chapter will discuss how to become more aware of your feelings and more skillful in communicating them effectively.

ANSWERS

Comprehension Test A: 1. true; 2. true; 3. true; 4. false; 5. true; 6. true; 7. true; 8. true; 9. b, d, e, f, h, i, j; 10. a, d, e.

Comprehension Test B: 1. true, 2. true; 3. false; 4. false; 5. false; 6. true; 7. true; 8. false; 9. false; 10. true.

Comprehension Test C: 1. true; 2. true; 3. true; 4. true; 5. false; 6. true; 7. true; 8. true; 9. true; 10. true.

Comprehension Test D: 1. c, e, f; 2. b, c, e; 3. a, b.

Comprehension Test E: 1. b; 2. b, d, e; 3. b.

Practicing personal statements: 1. 0; 2. P; 3. P; 4. N; 5. O; 6. N; 7. P.

Comprehension Test F: 1. false; 2. true; 3. true; 4. true; 5. true; 6. true; 7. false; 8. false; 9. false; 10. false.

Chapter Review: 1. true; 2. false; 3. true; 4. true; 5. true; 6. true; 7. false; 8. true; 9. false; 10. true.

5 *Expressing Your Feelings Verbally*

Feeling the warmth, support, acceptance, and caring of close friendships is one of the most exciting aspects of being alive. And feelings are especially wonderful when they are shared with other people. One of the most rewarding aspects of relationships is sharing personal feelings. The more you share your feelings with other people, the happier and more meaningful your life will be. Yet one of the characteristics of our society is that we are not given much training in how to express feelings in such a way that there will be little chance of misunderstanding. Years and years of our education focus on communicating ideas clearly and unambiguously, yet relatively little education is given in communicating feelings clearly and unambiguously. And although the words that describe aspects of friendships, such as ''like,'' ''love,'' ''dislike,'' and ''hate,'' are among the most frequently used in the English language, our language has relatively few words that label feeling states. Sanskrit, for example, is reputed to have over nine hundred words describing various feeling states, but English has fewer than fifty, if one excludes slang and figures of speech.

To experience emotions and express them to another person is not only a major source of joy, but also necessary for your psychological well-being. It is natural to have feelings. The capacity to feel is as much a part of being a person as is the capacity to think and reason. A person without feelings is not a person at all; he or she is a machine. The quest of individuals who really enjoy life is to feel a greater range of emotions and to build relationships in which emotions are aroused and allowed positive expression. Feeling and expressing caring for another person, feeling and expressing love for another person, even feeling and expressing anger toward another person are all potentially highly rewarding and beautiful experiences. And it is through experiencing and sharing feelings that close friendships are built and maintained.

There is a wide variety of feelings you may have while relating to other people. Here is a partial list of the feelings you may experience:

happy	confused	cautious	proud
pleased	surprised	confident	anxious
daring	silly	glad	grieving
bored	lonely	excited	confused
satisfied	elated	delighted	overjoyed
uncomfortable	apathetic	fearful	frightened
ecstatic	hopeful	embarrassed	humiliated
angry	weary	supported	accepted
shy	scared	discontented	
loved	appreciated	sad	

Feelings are internal physiological reactions to your experiences. You may begin to tremble, sweat, or have a surge of energy. Your heart may beat faster. Tears may come. Although feelings are internal reactions, they do have outward signs. Sadness is inside you, but you cry or frown on the outside. Anger is inside you. But you may stare and shout at the person you are angry with. Feelings are always internal states, but you use overt behaviors to communicate your feelings to other people.

It is often difficult to express feelings. Whenever there is a risk of being rejected or laughed at, expressing feelings becomes very difficult. The more personal the feelings, the greater the risk you may feel. It is also sometimes difficult to control your expression of your feelings. You may cry when you don't want to, get angry when it is best not to, or even laugh at a time it disturbs others. Expressing feelings appropriately often means thinking before you communicate them.

Having feelings is a natural and joyful part of being alive and being human. Feelings provide the cement holding relations together as well as the means for deepening relationships and making them more personal. The accurate and constructive expression of feelings, furthermore, is one of the most difficult aspects of building and managing your relations with other people. The purpose of this chapter is to provide the material and experiences necessary for becoming more skillful in appropriately saying how you feel.

WHAT'S GOING ON INSIDE?

You can't enjoy your feelings if you aren't aware of them. You can't express feelings you refuse to acknowledge. You can't communicate feelings you refuse to accept as yours. To accept your feelings you have to be aware of them and accept them as yours. You have to "own" them. And you have to communicate effectively. That is what this chapter is about.

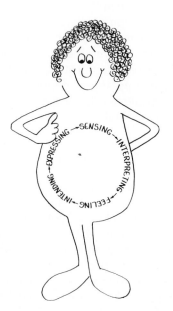

Feelings are internal reactions to your experiences. To be aware of your feelings you have to be aware of how you are reacting to what is currently taking place around you. There are five aspects of such internal reactions (Miller, Nunnally, and Wachman 1975):

1. You gather information about what is going on through your five senses (seeing, hearing, touching, tasting, smelling).

2. You decide what the information means by interpreting the meaning of the information you sense.

3. You have a feeling based on your interpretation.

4. You decide how you intend to express your feeling.

5. You express your feeling.

Here is an example. "I see you sitting in the library, a book open in front of you, but you are looking around the room (sensing). I think you must be looking for an excuse to stop studying so that you can go to lunch (interpreting). I feel sorry that you can't take a break from studying (feeling). I want to give you a chance to enjoy yourself for a few minutes (intending). So I ask you if you'd like to eat lunch with me (expressing)."

When we are relating to other people, we sense, interpret, feel, intend, and express all at the same time. It all happens faster than you can read a word. *Everything happens so fast that it seems as though it is only one step instead of five!* To become aware of the five steps you have to slow down the process. Being aware of, and understanding, the five aspects of experiencing and expressing a feeling give you the basis for skillfully and appropriately communicating your feelings and for changing negative feelings (such as anger, depression, guilt, hopelessness, frustration, and fear) to positive ones. Each of the five steps, therefore, is discussed below in more detail.

Sensing

The only way you can gather information is through your five senses: seeing, hearing, touching, tasting, and smelling. All information about the world and what is taking place in your life comes to you through one of the five senses. You look, listen, touch, taste, and smell to be aware of your immediate experiences. These senses give you *descriptive* information only. You hear a person's voice get louder. You see a person frown. You feel his fist hit your nose. You smell and taste the blood dripping from your nose. *Such sensory information only describes what is taking place. It does not place any meaning on what is happening.*

Interpreting: Deciding What It Means

After your senses make you aware of what is going on, you have to decide what the information means. *The information is neutral: You decide what it means.* Interpretations are yours; they take place inside you. They are not in another person's behavior or in the events that take place in your life. Different people, for example, interpret the same sensory information quite differently. One friend may interpret the fact that your voice is loud to mean that you are angry. Another friend may decide that your loud voice means you are nervous. The sensory information (your voice seems loud) they have is the same, but they interpret it in two different ways.

When you are interacting with your friends and acquaintances, or even with strangers, your interpretations of what the information gathered by your senses means depends on at least three things:

1. The information you receive through your senses
2. What you think is causing the other person's actions
3. The assumptions you make about what is good or bad, what you do or do not need, and what causes what in the world (your assumptions are an important part of your perspective, which was discussed in the previous chapter)

The information you receive through your senses has already been discussed, so we will now look at deciding what is causing another person's actions. When someone's voice gets louder, you look around to see what's causing it. If you see a huge dog with its teeth embedded in the person's leg, you decide that pain and fear are causing his voice to get louder. If you see someone else tickling him, you interpret the loud voice as indicating happiness. If you notice that the person has just paid $1,000 for a new stereo, and it fell apart when he picked it up to take it home, you decide his loud voice means he is angry.

What you decide is causing the person's actions will influence your interpretation of the meaning of the information you sense. Let's take another example. You feel pain on your nose. You see that a fist of another person has just landed on your nose. You then decide whether the person intended to hit you, or whether it was an accident. If it was an accident, you will be less angry than if you decide the person did it on purpose. If you decide the person intended to hit you, you decide whether he had just cause (you were kicking him at the time) or whether he did not have just cause (he is a mean, nasty person). All of this happens so fast that for the most part you are not aware that it is going on. Your interpretations follow your gathering of information much faster than a speeding bullet!

Finally, your perspective influences your interpretations. Your assumptions especially influence what you decide the sensory information means. If you *assume* that people are as mean and nasty as goblins, your interpretation of someone's fist landing on your nose may be biased. You may immediately jump to the conclusion that this is another example of how mean and nasty people are. Or, if you *assume* that people are basically gentle and harmless creatures, you may jump to the conclusion that the person hit you accidentally. Your assumptions and your overall perspective have a powerful effect on your interpretations.

First you sense, then you interpret, and finally you feel. Your interpretations determine your feelings. Every feeling you have is based on an interpretation about the meaning of the information you sense. You can, therefore, control what you feel. By changing your interpretations, you can change your feelings. This does not mean that changing your feelings is easy. Most people make interpretations so automatically that it seems difficult to change them. But it can be done if they want to work at it. Chapter 7 explains how feelings such as anger, depression, resentment, fear, frustration, and guilt can be changed and controlled.

Feeling

You sense, you interpret, then you feel. Your feelings are a spontaneous reaction to your interpretations. You may hear and see an acquaintance say, ''Hope you're feeling well this morning!'' How you feel in response to the statement is based on what you decide it means. If you think the acquaintance is being sarcastic, you may feel angry. If you think the acquaintance is expressing liking and concern for you, you will feel warmth and appreciation. All this happens immediately and automatically. The important thing to remember is that the acquaintance's actions did not cause your feeling; your feeling was caused by your interpretation of the meaning of the person's statement.

Feelings promote an urge to take action. They prepare your body for action. If you feel angry, for example, your muscles tense, adrenalin is pumped into your bloodstream, your heart begins to beat faster, all of which prepares you for either running away or physically fighting. Feelings activate the physiological systems within your body so that they are ready for action. Because of the action-urge aspect of feelings, it takes energy to hide your feelings from yourself and others. That means the more you are aware of your feelings, accept them as yours, and express them to others, the more energy you will have for enjoying yourself and your friendships. In addition, you will be able to communicate more easily and effectively.

It is unhealthy, both physically and psychologically, to avoid expressing your feelings. Yet many people do try to avoid or ignore their feelings. Some people believe that what they are not aware of does not exist and can't hurt them. Yet the repression and denial of feelings such as anger can lead to physiological damage due to the failure to take action and reestablish a homeostatic state within one's body. Ulcers and headaches are commonly thought to result from chronically repressed anger. And the repression of feelings can lead to a self-alienation that leaves a person confused as to what motivates and causes his or her behavior.

Feelings will keep trying to be expressed until you do so in a way that ends them. Sadness, for example, can be expressed by crying and talking to an understanding friend. Walking around with a smile on your face will not end the sadness inside of you. When you refuse to express your feelings, they start to control you. If you are holding sadness inside, for example, you will begin to avoid anything that makes you sad. When your friends become sad you will get angry at them. Pretty soon your whole life is organized around avoiding sadness because you are afraid that otherwise your own sadness will come out.

You *do not* control feelings by holding them inside. You *do not* control feelings by pretending they really don't exist. You *do* control feelings by accepting them as being yours and expressing them. You let them happen. Don't fight them or hold them back. Be aware of them. Take responsibility for them. They are yours. Usually things will be all right if you let your feelings take their natural course. It is even helpful to try to feel them more. If you are happy, feel happier. If you are sad, feel sadder. The important thing is to allow them to exist and to be appropriately expressed. Feelings don't have to be justified, explained, or apologized for. As you become more and more aware of your feelings, you will recognize what they are telling you about yourself and the situation you are in. *You control feelings by being aware of them, accepting them, giving them direction, and expressing them appropriately.* And if you are constantly depressed, anxious, or unhappy, you can change your feelings by changing the interpretations you are making.

Feelings activate your body physically so it is ready for action. Feelings urge you to take action to express them. What is lacking is a sense of direction. Do you run? Do you fight? Do you hug? Do you move toward another person? Do you move away? Feelings get the body ready for action. But they do not give you a sense of direction. It is your intentions that give you a sense of direction.

Intending

Your senses provide you with information about what is taking place within your environment. Your interpretations give the information meaning. Your feelings are your reactions to your interpretations. Your *intentions* are your guides to action, pointing out how the feelings can be expressed. They are your immediate goals as to what you want to have happen as a result of your feeling the way you do.

Intentions give your feelings direction. A few examples of intentions are:

to reject	to love	to play	to be caring
to cooperate	to clarify	to help	to share
to avoid	to hurt	to demand	to understand
to praise	to persuade	to accept	to defend yourself
to protest	to support	to resign	to try harder

Intentions are important because they have such power over your actions. They organize your actions in expressing your feelings. They identify what you want to do to express your feelings. They guide your actions so that your feelings are terminated through expression.

Once you decide how to express your feelings, the next step is taking action and actually expressing them.

Expressing

You say it. You act it out. You smile. You frown. You laugh. You cry. You jump up and down. You run screaming out of the building. You burn this book. Your words and nonverbal actions express your sensations, interpretations, feelings, and intentions. This chapter focuses on expressing your feelings verbally in a way that is easily understood. The next chapter deals with the nonverbal expression of feelings. Chapter 7 discusses how you can control your feelings by modifying your interpretations.

COMPREHENSION TEST A

Test your understanding of the above material by answering true or false to the following statements. Answers are at the end of the chapter.

True	False	1. Feelings are external events that force a reaction from you.
True	False	2. Feelings are internal reactions to your experiences.
True	False	3. Expressing feelings is a sign of weakness.
True	False	4. Expressing feelings is a psychological necessity and a source of joy.
True	False	5. Your senses gather information about what is happening and give meaning to it.

True	False	**6.** You interpret the information that your senses gathered and decide what it means and whether it's good or bad.
True	False	**7.** Your previous assumptions will influence your interpretations of an event.
True	False	**8.** Your feelings are caused by the event you are responding to.
True	False	**9.** Controlling feelings means that you hold them inside.
True	False	**10.** Your intentions are your guides on how to express your feelings.

WHEN FEELINGS ARE NOT EXPRESSED

One of the most frequent sources of difficulty in building and maintaining good relationships is communicating feelings. We all have feelings about the people we interact with and the experiences we share, but many times we do not communicate these feelings effectively. Problems arise in relationships not because we have feelings but because we are not effective in communicating our feelings in ways that strengthen our relationships. When we repress, deny, distort, or disguise our feelings, or when we communicate them in an ineffective way, we are asking for trouble in our relationships.

There are several difficulties that arise when feelings are not recognized, accepted, and expressed constructively.

1. Suppressing and denying your feelings can create relationship problems. If you suppress your feelings, it can result in increased conflicts and barriers that cause deterioration in the relationship. A friend's actions may be irritating, and as the irritation is suppressed, anger and withdrawal from the relationship may result.

2. Suppressing and denying your feelings can interfere with the constructive diagnosis and resolution of relationship problems. Maintaining a relationship requires an open expression of feelings so that difficulties or conflicts can be dealt with constructively. There is a common but mistaken belief that being rational, logical, and objective requires you to suppress and ignore your feelings. Nothing is further from the truth! If you want to be effective in solving interpersonal problems, you need all the relevant information (including feelings) you can get. This means that your feelings need to be conscious, discussable, and controllable.

3. Denying your feelings can result in selective perception. When feelings are unresolved, your perceptions of events and information may be affected. If you are denying your anger, you may perceive all hostile actions but be completely blind to friendly overtures. Threatening and unpleasant facts are often distorted or not perceived. Unresolved feelings tend to increase blind spots and selective perception.

4. Suppressing your feelings can bias your judgments. It is common for people to refuse to accept a good idea because someone they dislike suggested it, or to accept a poor idea because someone they like is for it. If you are aware of your feelings and manage them constructively, you will be far more unbiased and objective in your judgments.

5. Implying a demand while expressing your feelings can create a power struggle. Many times feelings are expressed in ways that demand changes in the receiver's behavior. If someone says to you, "You make me angry when you do that," she is indirectly saying, "Stop doing it." Or if a friend says, "I like you, you are a good friend," he may be indirectly demanding that you like him. When feelings imply demands, a power struggle may result over whether or not the demands are going to be met.

6. Other people often ask you to suppress or deny your feelings. A person may say, "Don't feel that way" whenever you express a feeling. If you say, "I feel depressed," he will say, "Cheer up!" If you say, "I'm angry," she will say, "Simmer down." If you say, "I feel great," she will say, "The roof will cave in any moment now." All these replies communicate: "Don't feel that way. Quick, change your feeling!"

COMPREHENSION TEST B

Test your understanding of expressing your feelings constructively by answering true or false to the following statements. Answers are at the end of the chapter.

True   False   1. Problems arise in relationships because we have feelings.

True   False   2. Feelings should be ignored when making rational decisions.

True   False   3. If feelings are communicated effectively, the relationship will be strengthened.

True	False	4. If feelings are ignored, an idea may be disliked because the person suggesting it is disliked.
True	False	5. Blind spots happen when facts are ignored or distorted on account of unresolved unpleasant feelings about them.
True	False	6. Unresolved feelings will tend to increase blind spots.
True	False	7. Expressing feelings may imply a demand for the other person to do something.
True	False	8. People often respond to expressions of feelings by telling others to deny them.
True	False	9. If someone tells you that he is sad, you should say something to make him happy.
True	False	10. If someone tells you that your actions make her unhappy, she may be asking you to change.

EXPRESSING YOUR FEELINGS VERBALLY

There are two ways of communicating feelings: verbally and nonverbally. If you want to communicate clearly, your verbal and your nonverbal expression of feelings must agree or be congruent. Many of the communication difficulties experienced in relationships spring from giving contradictory messages to others by indicating one kind of feeling with words, another with actions, and still another with nonverbal expressions. This chapter focuses on the verbal expression of feelings. The next chapter focuses on the nonverbal expression of feelings. The congruence between the verbal and nonverbal expression of feelings is emphasized in both chapters.

Communicating your feelings depends on your being aware of your feelings, accepting them, and being skillful in expressing them constructively. When you are unaware or unaccepting of your feelings, or when you lack skills in expressing them, your feelings may be communicated indirectly through:

1. *Labels:* "You are rude, hostile, and self-centered" versus "When you interrupt me I get angry."
2. *Commands:* "Shut up!" versus "I'm annoyed at what you just said."
3. *Questions:* "Are you always this crazy?" versus "You are acting strangely, and I feel worried."

4. *Accusations:* "You do not care about me!" versus "When you do not pay attention to me I feel left out."

5. *Sarcasm:* "I'm glad you are early!" versus "You are late; it has delayed our work, and that irritates me."

6. *Approval:* "You are wonderful!" versus "I like you."

7. *Disapproval:* "You are terrible!" versus "I do not like you."

8. *Name Calling:* "You are a creep!" versus "You are embarrassing me."

Such indirect ways of expressing feelings are common. But they are ineffective because they do not give a clear message to the receiver. And the receiver often will feel rejected and "put down" by the remarks. We are taught how to describe our *ideas* clearly and correctly. But we are rarely taught how to describe our *feelings* clearly and correctly. We express our feelings, but we do not usually name and describe them. Here are four ways you can describe a feeling.

1. Identify or name it: "I feel angry." "I feel embarrassed." "I like you."

2. Use sensory descriptions that capture how you feel: "I feel stepped on." "I feel as if I'm on cloud nine." "I feel as if I've just been run

over by a truck." Because we do not have enough names or labels to describe all our feelings, we make up ways to describe them.

3. Report what kind of action the feeling urges you to do: "I want to hug you." "I want to slap your face." "I want to walk on your face."
4. Use figures of speech as descriptions of feelings: "I feel like a stepped-on toad." "I feel like a pebble on the beach."

You describe your feelings by identifying them. A description of a feeling must include:

1. A personal statement—refer to *I*, *me*, *my*, or *mine*
2. A feeling name, simile, action urge, or figure of speech

Anything you say can convey feelings. Even the comment, "It's a warm day," can be said so that it expresses resentment or irritation. To build and maintain a friendship or any relationship, you must be concerned with communicating your feelings clearly and accurately, especially the feelings of warmth, affection, and caring. If you convey your feelings by commands, questions, accusations, or judgments, you will tend to confuse the person with whom you are interacting. When you want to express your feelings, your ability to describe them is essential for effective communication.

When you describe your feelings, expect at least two results. First, describing your feelings to another person often helps you to become more aware of what it is you actually do feel. Many times we have feelings that seem ambiguous or unclear to us. Explaining them to another person often clarifies our feelings to ourselves as well as to the other person. Second, describing your feelings often begins a dialogue that will improve your relationship. If other people are to respond appropriately to your feelings, they must know what the feelings are. Even if the feelings are negative, it is often worthwhile to express them. Negative feelings are signals that something may be going wrong in the relationship, and you and the other person need to examine what is going on in the relationship and figure out how it may be improved. By reporting your feelings, you provide information that is necessary if you and the other person are to understand and improve your relationship. When discussing your relationship with another person, describing your feelings conveys maximum information about what you feel in a more constructive way than giving commands, asking questions, making accusations, or offering judgments.

COMPREHENSION TEST C

Test your understanding of expressing feelings by answering true or false to the following statements. Answers are at the end of the chapter.

True   False   **1.** Indirect methods of communicating feelings are often quite effective.

True   False   **2.** Indirect methods of communicating feelings do not give a clear message to the receiver.

True   False   **3.** Eight indirect ways to communicate feelings are labels, commands, questions, accusations, sarcasm, approval, disapproval, and name calling.

True   False   **4.** Describing your feelings can help you become aware of your feelings.

True   False   **5.** Describing your feelings can begin a dialogue that will improve your relationship.

True   False   **6.** You should describe only positive feelings if you want to maintain relationships.

True   False   **7.** A feeling description must include a personal statement and the name of a feeling.

True   False   **8.** "I think you stink!" is a good feeling description.

True   False   **9.** Feeling descriptions can be figures of speech or sensory descriptions.

True   False   **10.** "I feel like a low-down toad" is a good feeling description.

Exercise 5.1: Describing Your Feelings

The objectives of this exercise are to help you recognize when you are displaying feelings without describing them, to explain how you may express your feelings verbally in a way that communicates them effectively, and to give you a chance to practice the latter. In the list below, each of the ten items consists of two or three statements. One statement is a description of a feeling; the others are expressions that do not describe the feeling involved. The procedure for the exercise is:

1. Divide into groups of three.
2. Work individually. In item 1 put a *D* before the sentence that describes the sender's feelings. Put a *No* before the sentence that conveys feeling but does

not describe what it is. Mark the answers for item 1 only; do not go on to item 2 yet.

3. Compare your answers to item 1 with those of the other two members of your triad. Discuss the reasons for any differences.

4. Turn to the answers that follow the list and read the answer for item 1. Discuss the answer in your triad until you all understand the point.

5. Repeat steps 2, 3, and 4 for item 2. Then continue the same procedure for each item until you have completed all ten.

1. _____ a. Stop driving this fast! Slow down right now!
   _____ b. Your driving this fast frightens me.

2. _____ a. Do you have to stand on my foot?
   _____ b. You are so mean and vicious. You don't care if you cripple me for life!
   _____ c. I am annoyed at you for resting your 240-pound body on my foot.

3. _____ a. I feel ecstatic about winning the Reader's Digest Sweepstakes!
   _____ b. This is a wonderful day!

4. _____ a. You're such a helpful person.
   _____ b. I really respect your ideas; you're so well informed.

5. _____ a. Everyone here likes to dance with you.
   _____ b. When I dance with you I feel graceful and relaxed.
   _____ c. We all feel you're a great dancer.

6. _____ a. If you don't start cleaning up after yourself, I'm moving out!
   _____ b. Did you ever see such a messy kitchen in your life?
   _____ c. I am afraid you will never do your share of the housework.

7. _____ a. This is a very interesting book.
   _____ b. I feel this is not a very helpful book.
   _____ c. I get very excited when I read this book.

8. _____ a. I don't feel competent enough to contribute anything of worth to this group.
   _____ b. I'm not competent enough to contribute anything worthwhile to this group.

9. _____ a. I'm a born loser; no one will ever like me!
   _____ b. Sue is a rotten creep! She laughed when I told her my score on the test!
   _____ c. I'm depressed because I flunked that test.

10. _____ a. I feel warm and comfortable in my group.
    _____ b. Someone in my group always seems to be near when I need company.
    _____ c. I feel everyone cares that I'm part of this group.

Answers

1. **a.** No   Commands like these communicate strong feelings, but they do not name the feeling that underlies the commands.

   b. D   This statement both expresses and names a feeling. The person communicates the feeling by describing himself as frightened.

2. **a.** No   A feeling is implied through a question, but the specific feeling underlying the question is not described.

   b. No   This statement communicates considerable feeling through an accusation, but it is not clear whether the accusation is based on anger, hurt, fear, or some other feeling.

   c. D   The person describes the feeling as annoyance. Note that the speaker also "owns" the feeling by using the personal pronoun "I."

3. **a.** D   The speaker describes herself as feeling ecstatic.

   b. No   This statement communicates positive feelings without describing what they are. The speaker appears to be commenting on the weather when in fact the statement is an expression of how the speaker feels. We cannot tell whether the speaker is feeling proud, happy, caring, accepted, supported, or relieved.

4. **a.** No   The speaker makes a value judgment communicating positive feelings about the other person, but the speaker does not describe the feelings. Does the speaker admire the other person or like the other person, or is the speaker only grateful?

   b. D   The speaker describes the positive feelings as respect.

5. **a.** No   This statement does name a feeling (likes) but the speaker is talking for everyone and does not make clear that the feeling is personal. A description of a feeling must contain "I," "me," "my," or "mine" to make clear that the feelings are within the speaker. Does it seem more friendly for a person to say, "I like you," or "Everybody likes you"?

   b. D   The speaker communicates clearly and specifically the feeling the speaker has when dancing with the other person.

   c. No   First, the speaker does not speak for herself, but rather hides behind the phrase "we feel." Second, "You're a great dancer" is a value judgment and does not name a feeling. Note that merely placing the word *feel* in front of a statement does not make the statement a description of feeling. People often say *feel* when they mean *think* or *believe*.

6. **a.** No   This statement communicates general and ambiguous negative feelings about the person's behavior. It refers to the condition of the apartment or house and the speaker's future behavior, but not the speaker's inner feelings.

   b. No   The speaker is trying to communicate a negative feeling through a rhetorical question and a value judgment. Although it is clear the feeling is negative, the specific feeling is not described.

c. D   The speaker describes fear as the negative feeling connected with the other person's housework.

Note: Notice that in *a* and *b* the feelings could easily have been interpreted as anger. Many times the expression of anger results from an underlying fear. Yet when the receiver tries to respond, she may understand that the other person is angry without comprehending that the basic feeling to be responded to is a feeling of fear.

7. a. No   The speaker communicates a positive value judgment that conveys feelings, but the specific feelings are not described.

b. No   The speaker uses the words "I feel" but does not then describe or name a feeling. Instead, the speaker gives a negative value judgment. What the speaker actually meant was "I believe" or "I think" the book is not very good. People commonly use the word *feel* when they mean *think* or *believe*. Consider the difference between, "I feel you don't like me" and "I believe (think) you don't like me."

c. D   The speaker describes a feeling of excitement while reading this book.

Note: Many times people who say they are unaware of what they feel—or who say they don't have any feelings about something—state value judgments about recognizing that this is the way their positive or negative feelings get expressed. Many times useless arguments can be avoided if we are careful to describe our feelings instead of expressing them through value judgments. For example, if Joe says the book is interesting and Fred says it is boring, they may argue about which it "really" is. If Joe, however, says he was excited by the book and Fred says he was frustrated by it, no argument should follow. Each person's feelings are what they are. Of course, discussing what it means for Joe and Fred to feel as they do may provide helpful information about each person and about the book.

8. a. D   Speaker communicates a feeling of incompetence.

b. No   Warning! This statement is potentially hazardous to your health! Although it sounds much the same as the previous statement, it states that the speaker actually is incompetent—not that the speaker currently feels incompetent. The speaker has passed a negative value judgment on himself and labeled himself as incompetent.

Note: Many people confuse *feeling* with *being*. A person may feel incompetent yet behave very competently or a person may feel competent and perform very incompetently. A person may feel hopeless about a situation that turns out not to be hopeless once his behavior is given an appropriate focus. *A sign of emotional maturity is that a person does not confuse feelings with the reality of the situation.* An emotionally mature person knows he can perform competently, even though he feels incompetent. He does not let his feelings keep him from doing his best because he knows the difference between feelings and performance and knows that the two do not always match.

9. **a.** No   The speaker has evaluated herself—passed a negative value judgment on herself by labeling herself a born loser.

    b. No   This statement also communicates a negative value judgment, but against another person rather than of oneself. Although the statement contains strong feelings, the feelings are not specifically named or described.

    c. D   The speaker states she feels depressed. Statements *a* and *c* highlight the important difference between passing judgment on yourself and describing your feelings.

    Note: Feelings are constantly changing and are by no means written in concrete once they occur. To say that you are now depressed does not imply that you will or must always feel the same. If you label yourself as a born loser, however, you imply a permanence to a feeling of depression by defining it as a trait rather than as a temporary affective response. You can *feel* anger without being an *angry person*. You can *feel* shy without being a *shy person*. Many people try to avoid new situations and activities by labeling themselves. "I'm not artistic," "I'm not a good public speaker," and "I can't participate in groups" are examples. If we could recognize what our feelings are beneath such statements, maybe we would be more willing to risk doing things we are somewhat fearful of.

10. **a.** D   The speaker communicates a feeling by describing it and taking ownership of it.

    b. No   The speaker communicates a positive feeling but does not take direct ownership of it and does not say whether the feeling is happiness, gratefulness, supportiveness, or what.

    c. No   Instead of "I feel" the speaker should have said "I believe." The last part of the statement really tells what the speaker believes the others feel about her. It does not tell what the speaker feels. Expressions *a* and *c* relate to each other as follows: "Because I believe that everyone cares whether I am part of this group, I feel warm and comfortable."

Exercise 5.2: Ambiguity of Expression of Feelings

The objective of this exercise is to increase your awareness of the ambiguity or unclearness in expressing feelings in ways that are not descriptive. Given below are a series of statements. Each statement presents an interpersonal situation. The procedure for the exercise is:

1. Divide into groups of three.

2. For each situation below write descriptions of *two different* feelings that might have given rise to the expression of feelings in the statement.

3. Compare your answers with the answers of the other members of your trio. Discuss them until you understand each other's answers.

4. In the group as a whole, discuss the results of ambiguity in expressing feelings in interpersonal relationships.

   a. What happens when persons make ambiguous statements of feeling? How do other persons respond? How do they feel?

   b. Why would you state feelings ambiguously? In what circumstances would you be ambiguous rather than descriptive? What would be the probable consequence?

1. A girl asks her boyfriend, "Why can't you ever be any place on time?" What might the girl have said that would have described her feelings openly?

2. You notice that a person in the group who was talking a lot has suddenly become silent. What might the person have said that would have described his feelings openly?

3. During a group meeting, you hear John tell Bill, "Bill, you're talking too much." What might John have said that would have described his feelings openly?

4. Sally abruptly changed the subject after Ann made a comment. What might Sally have said that would have described her feelings openly?

5. A boy told his girl friend, "You shouldn't have bought me such an expensive gift." What might the boy have said that would have described his feelings openly?

6. You hear a passenger say to a taxi driver, "Do we have to drive this fast?" What might the passenger have said that would have described his feelings openly?

7. Sam says to Jane, "You're really wonderful." What might Sam have said that would have described his feelings openly?

CHECKING YOUR PERCEPTION OF ANOTHER'S FEELINGS

Feelings are internal reactions, and we can tell what people are feeling only from what they tell us and from their overt actions. Overt actions include such things as smiles, frowns, shouts, whispers, tears, and laughter. When other people describe their feelings to us, we can usually accept their feelings to be what they say they are. But if other people express their feelings indirectly (such as through sarcasm) or nonverbally (such as through a frown), we often need to clarify how they actually feel. A basic rule in interpersonal communication is that before you respond to a person's feelings, you need to check to make sure you really know what the other person actually feels.

The best way to check out whether or not you accurately understand how a person is feeling is through a perception check. A *perception check* has three parts:

1. You describe what you think the other person's feelings are.
2. You ask whether or not your perception is accurate.
3. You refrain from expressing approval or disapproval of the feelings.

' You look sad. Are you?'' is an example of a perception check. It describes how you think the person is feeling, then it asks the person to agree with or correct your perception, and it does both without making a value judgment about the feeling. A perception check communicates the message, ''I want to understand your feeling; is this the way you feel?'' It is an invitation for other people to describe their feelings more directly. And it shows you care enough about the person to want to understand how the person feels. Perception checking will help you avoid actions you later regret because they are based on false assumptions about what the other person is feeling.

Checking out our impressions of how others are feeling is an important communication skill. Our impressions are often biased by our own fears, expectations, and present feelings. If we are afraid of anger and expect other people to be angry, then we may think they are angry when in fact they are not. If we feel guilty, we may think other people are about to reject us. We frequently misperceive how other people are feeling, and it is therefore essential that we check out our perceptions before taking action.

Exercise 5.3: Is This the Way You Feel?

The purpose of this exercise is to provide an opportunity to increase your understanding of perception checking by indicating which of the statements given below are perception checks and which are other types of statements. The procedure is:

1. Working by yourself, read each of the statements below. On a separate sheet of paper write your answers.

   Put a *PC* for each perception check.

   Put a *J* for each statement that makes a judgment about the other person.

Put an O for each statement that speaks for the other person rather than for yourself.

Put a Q for each question that does not include a description of your perceptions of the other person's feelings.

2. Form groups of four. Review the answers of each member for each statement. Discuss any disagreements until all members agree on the answer. Answers are at the end of the chapter.

3. Go around the group and have members check out their perceptions of how other members are feeling.

Statements

1. _____ Are you angry with me?

2. _____ You look as if you are upset about what Sally said. Are you?

3. _____ Why are you mad at me?

4. _____ You look as if you feel put down by my statement. That's stupid!

5. _____ What is it about your boss that makes you resent her so much?

6. _____ Are your feelings hurt again?

7. _____ You look unhappy. Are you?

8. _____ Am I right that you feel disappointed that nobody commented on your suggestion?

9. _____ Why on earth would you get upset about that? That's pretty crazy!

10. _____ I get the impression you are pretty happy with my work. Are you?

11. _____ Are you feeling rejected?

12. _____ If you are dumb enough to get angry about that, the hell with you!

13. _____ You're always happy!

14. _____ I'm not sure whether your expression means that I'm confusing you or hurting your feelings. Which one is it?

15. _____ Half the time you're laughing. The other half of the time you're staring off into space. What's going on?

CHAPTER REVIEW

Test your understanding of how to express your feelings verbally by answering true or false to the following statements. Answers are at the end of the chapter.

True   False   1. You become aware of your feelings by being aware of how you are reacting to what is happening around you.

True   False   **2.** You express your feelings after you have gone through the process of sending, interpreting, feeling, and intending.

True   False   **3.** The best way to express your feelings is to describe how the other person feels.

True   False   **4.** How you feel about a situation reflects how the situation really is.

True   False   **5.** "Everyone likes you!" is an example of a good feeling description.

True   False   **6.** A perception check is done to make sure a person really understands how you feel.

True   False   **7.** In a perception check, you describe what you think the other person's feelings are and ask whether you are right, without showing approval or disapproval.

True   False   **8.** A perception check will help you understand the other person's message.

True   False   **9.** We often receive an inaccurate impression of someone else's feelings because of our fears and anger.

True   False   **10.** "You look happy! Is that the way you feel?" is an example of a good perception check.

Indicate below which skills you have mastered and which you still need more work on.

1. I have mastered the following:

_____ Being aware of my feelings

_____ Describing my feelings to others in a direct way

_____ Using a perception check when it is needed

_____ Avoiding the indirect expression of feelings through commands, questions, accusations, and so on

2. I need more work on the following:

_____ Being aware of my feelings

_____ Describing my feelings to others in a direct way

_____ Using a perception check when it is needed

_____ Avoiding the indirect expression of feelings through commands, questions, accusations, and so on

By now, you should know how to get in touch with your feelings and express them verbally in constructive ways. You should also know how to check your perception of another person's feelings. The next chapter will help you learn the skills of constructively expressing your feelings nonverbally.

ANSWERS

Comprehension Test A: 1. false; 2. true; 3. false; 4. true; 5. false; 6. true; 7. true; 8. false; 9. false; 10. true.

Comprehension Test B: 1. false; 2. false; 3. true; 4. true; 5. true; 6. true; 7. true; 8. false; 9. true; 10. true.

Comprehension Test C: 1. false; 2. true; 3. true; 4. true; 5. true; 6. false; 7. true; 8. false; 9. true; 10. true.

Is This the Way You Feel?: 1. Q; 2. PC; 3. O; 4. J; 5. O; 6. Q; 7. PC; 8. PC; 9. J; 10. PC; 11. Q; 12. J; 13. O; 14. PC; 15. PC.

Chapter Review: 1. true; 2. true; 3. false; 4. false; 5. false; 6. false; 7. true; 8. true; 9. true; 10. true.

6 *Expressing Your Feelings Nonverbally*

When we talk we rarely trust the words alone to convey our messages. We shift our weight, stand close to the other person or far away, wave our arms, smile or frown, speak loudly or softly, touch or don't touch, or use other nonverbal behaviors to emphasize or clarify what our words mean. We communicate by the way we sit or stand, straighten our clothing, place our hands, manipulate a glass, and so forth. Consciously and unconsciously we use nonverbal behaviors to communicate our feelings, liking, and preferences as well as to reinforce the meaning of our words.

Many people have great difficulties in communicating clearly and accurately to other individuals how they feel, despite the fact that awareness, acceptance, and expression of feelings are crucial for psychological health and for building and maintaining fulfilling relationships. Expressing warmth and liking is especially important for establishing and keeping friendships. The previous chapter focused on constructive ways of expressing feelings verbally. This chapter focuses on the skills necessary for effective nonverbal expression of feelings. The objectives of this chapter are to:

1. Remind you of the importance of the congruence between your verbal and nonverbal messages in communicating your feelings to another person clearly and accurately

2. Increase your awareness of how you communicate feelings to others

3. Provide skill practice in expressing feelings nonverbally

NONVERBAL COMMUNICATION

Actions speak louder than words. Because nonverbal messages tend to be less conscious we tend to believe them even more than the words people say. In communicating effectively with other individuals it may be more important to have a mastery of nonverbal communication than fluency with words. In a normal two-person conversation, the verbal components carry less than 35 percent of the social meaning of the situation, while more than 65 percent is carried by nonverbal messages (McCroskey, Larson, and Knapp 1971). That may seem surprising to you, but we communicate by our manner of dress, physique, posture, body tension, facial expression, degree of eye contact, hand and body movements, tone of voice, continuities in speech (such as rate, duration, nonfluencies, and pauses), spatial distance, and touch, as well as by words. In order to communicate effectively with other people, therefore, you must be as concerned with the nonverbal messages you are sending as with the verbal ones, if not more so. It is the nonverbal messages that most clearly and powerfully communicate liking and disliking, acceptance and rejection, and interest and boredom.

Eye contact is one nonverbal way to provide information (such as liking, attentiveness, competence, and credibility), regulate interaction (eye contact has an important role in initiating communication and in maintaining a conversation once it has begun), express intimacy (people look more at others whom they like than at those they dislike), exercise social control (eye contact increases when we attempt to be persuasive), and facilitate the accomplishment of tasks (eye contact helps to closely coordinate behavior). Facial expressions convey a variety of emotions, and these basic emotional expressions can be identified by people of very different cultures. Cultures may differ, however, in the *display rules* that govern the circumstances in which an emotion will be expressed. Interpersonal distance is a more abstract form of communication, but it, too, is an important means of conveying information. Four major zones (intimate, personal, social, and public) define the distances between people that accompany different types of interchange.

In comparison with verbal language, nonverbal behavior is very limited. Usually nonverbal messages are used to communicate feelings, likings, and preferences, and they customarily either reinforce or contradict messages that are communicated verbally. Feelings, in particular, are communicated more by nonverbal messages than by the words a person uses. Facial expressions and tone of voice are especially important in communicating feelings. Smiles, for example, communicate friendliness, cooperativeness, and acceptance of other individuals. There appears to be more eye contact between people who like each other than between people who do not like each other. Emotional meanings are communicated quite accurately through voice tone and inflection.

The problem is that it is often difficult to know for sure what another person really feels. People often say one thing but then do another. Someone can seem to like you but never say so. A person can say he or she likes you, but somehow you do not feel the statement is sincere. Feelings are often misunderstood and misinterpreted for two major reasons: (1) the ambiguity of nonverbal messages and (2) the frequent contradictions between verbal and nonverbal messages.

Since nonverbal messages are inevitably ambiguous, the receiver cannot be sure about what the sender is feeling. For one thing, the same feeling can be expressed nonverbally in several different ways. Anger, for example, can be expressed by jumping up and down or by a frozen stillness. Happiness can be expressed through laughter or tears. Any single nonverbal message, furthermore, can arise from a variety of feelings. A blush may show embarrassment, pleasure, nervousness, or even anger. Crying can be caused by sadness, happiness, excitement, grief, pain, or confusion. Also there are wide differences among social groups as to the meaning of many nonverbal messages. Standing close to the receiver may be a sign of warmth to a person from one cultural background and a sign of aggressiveness and hostility to a person from another cultural background. In understanding nonverbal messages, the receiver must interpret the sender's actions. As these actions increase in ambiguity, the chance for misinterpretation increases.

It is often difficult to make accurate judgments about the feelings of other people because of the different degrees of feelings or contradictory kinds of feelings being expressed simultaneously through verbal and nonverbal messages. We have all been in situations in which we have received or sent conflicting messages on verbal and nonverbal channels. The parent who screams, "I WANT IT QUIET AROUND THIS HOUSE," or the teacher who says, "I've always got plenty of time to talk to a student," are examples. Sometimes a person may say, "I like you," but communicate nonverbally, "Don't come close to me," by using a cold tone of voice, looking worried, and backing away. When receiving such conflicting messages through two different channels, we tend to believe the messages that we perceive to be harder to fake. This is often the nonverbal channel. You are, therefore, more apt to believe the nonverbal communication than the verbal one. Such contradictory communications are known as double binds and can make the receiver anxious and suspicious.

When communicating your feelings, it pays to take special care that your verbal and nonverbal messages are congruent. It is when your verbal and nonverbal messages are redundant and reinforce and complement each other that you will be most successful in effectively communicating what you feel. Especially when communicating liking and acceptance, avoid stooped shoulders and downcast eyes (signs of depression and disappointment) and keep your posture erect with your head held high (signs of self-acceptance and well-being). Keep good eye contact because it communicates that you are open to communication, involvement, and feedback. People tend to avoid eye contact when they want to hide their feelings, when they are tense, when they are interacting with someone they dislike, or when they are attempting to cut off social contact.

Nonverbal messages, then, are more powerful in communicating feelings than are verbal messages, but are also more ambiguous and difficult to interpret accurately. To communicate your feelings clearly and accurately to another person, you need to be skillful in both the verbal and nonverbal ways of expressing feelings. Above all, you need to make your verbal and nonverbal messages congruent with each other. The following exercises will help you become more aware of the ambiguity of nonverbal messages and of how you presently communicate feelings nonverbally, and they will help you become more skillful in the use of nonverbal cues to communicate feelings.

Exercise 6.1: Communication Without Words

The objective of this exercise is to increase your awareness of the ambiguity of expressing feelings in nonverbal or in behavioral ways. Given below are a series of situations. Each involves the expression of feelings through certain nonverbal behaviors. The procedure for the exercise is:

1. Divide into groups of three.

2. For each situation describe *two different* feelings (within the person named) that might have given rise to such a nonverbal expression of feelings.

3. Compare your answers with the answers of the other members of your trio. Discuss until you understand each other's answers.

4. In the group as a whole, share your feelings and reactions to the exercise. What did you learn? How would you react if someone in the group behaved similarly to the people in the situations described? Are there any times when the nonverbal expression of feelings is more effective than the verbal description of feelings?

The situations are:

1. Helen, who had been talking a lot in the group, suddenly became silent. Describe two feelings that might have caused Helen to do this.

2. Without expression, Dale suddenly changed the subject of the group's discussion. What are two different feelings that might have been responsible for Dale's changing the subject?

3. Whenever Keith made a comment in the group, he watched the leader's face. What are two different feelings that might have led Keith to watch the leader so intently?

4. While the group discussion was going on, Betty became more and more tense and restless. Finally, she got up abruptly and left the room without saying a word. Describe two different feelings that might have caused Betty to leave.

5. Roger was describing in a serious manner a fight he and a friend had had earlier. In the middle of his discussion, Dale began to laugh. Describe two different feelings that might have caused Dale to laugh.

Exercise 6.2: Interpreting Others' Nonverbal Cues

The objectives of this exercise are (1) to demonstrate the ambiguity of nonverbal cues in communicating feelings and (2) to illustrate how many different feeling reactions the same nonverbal cues can give. For this exercise you need from five to ten pictures cut out of magazines. Each picture should have at least one person in it who is expressing a feeling. The procedure for this exercise is:

1. Number the pictures. Pass each picture around the group.

2. Each person answers the following questions about each picture:

    a. How do the individuals in the picture feel?

    b. How does this picture make you feel?

3. The group then shares their answers for each picture.

    a. How similar were your interpretations of what the individuals in the pictures felt?

    b. How similar were the feelings you had in response to the pictures?

    c. If you have dissimilar answers, what makes the pictures so ambiguous?

   d.   Could different people interpret your own nonverbal cues in as many different ways as the group interpreted the nonverbal cues of the individuals in the pictures?

Exercise 6.3: How Do You Express Your Feelings?

The objective of this exercise is to increase your self-awareness of the ways in which you express your feelings. Given below are descriptions of feelings you may have experienced. For each of these you are to report two different ways that you express such feelings. The first answer should be something you would say that would express your feelings. The second answer should report how you might express such feelings by actions and without using words. The procedure for this exercise is:

1. Divide into groups of three.
2. Write out your answers to the various situations.
3. Compare your answers with the answers of the other members of your trio. Discuss until you understand each other's answers. Then discuss:
   a.   What did I learn about the way I usually express my feelings?
   b.   In what ways would it be helpful for me to change the ways I usually express my feelings?
   c.   In what ways would it be helpful for each of you to change the ways you usually express feelings?
4. In the group as a whole, share your feelings and reactions to the exercise. Then list as many principles for constructively expressing feelings as you can think of.

The descriptions are:

1. When you feel bored with what is going on in a discussion, how do you usually express your feelings?

   Using words: _____

   Without using words: _____

2. When you feel very annoyed with another person with whom you want to build a better relationship, how do you usually express your feelings?

   Using words: _____

   Without using words: _____

3. When another person says or does something to you that hurts your feelings deeply, how do you usually express your feelings?

   Using words: _____

   Without using words: _____

4. An acquaintance asks you to do something that you are afraid you cannot do well. You also want to hide the fact that you feel inadequate. How do you express your feelings?

    Using words: _____

    Without using words: _____

5. You feel affection and fondness for someone else but at the same time can't be sure the other person feels the same way about you. How do you usually express your feelings?

    Using words: _____

    Without using words: _____

6. Your close friend is leaving town for a long time, and you feel alone and lonely. How would you usually express your feelings?

    Using words: _____

    Without using words: _____

Exercise 6.4: Using Nonverbal Cues to Express Warmth and Coldness

The objective of this exercise is to increase your skills in the use of nonverbal cues to express warmth. In order to increase your awareness of the nonverbal cues that express warmth, you will be asked to role play the expression of coldness as well as the expression of warmth. Some of the nonverbal cues that can indicate either warmth or coldness are listed in the table below.

Nonverbal cue	Warmth	Coldness
Tone of voice	Soft	Hard
Facial expression	Smiling, interested	Pokerfaced, frowning, disinterested
Posture	Lean toward other; relaxed	Lean away from other; tense
Eye contact	Look into other's eyes	Avoid looking into other's eyes
Touching	Touch other softly	Avoid touching other
Gestures	Open, welcoming	Closed, guarding oneself, and keeping other away
Spatial distance	Close	Distant

The procedure for the exercise is:

1. Divide into pairs. Designate one person *A* and the other *B*.

2. Person A makes three statements about his childhood in a warm way. Then Person A makes three statements about his childhood in a cold way.

3. Person B gives Person A feedback of how successfully he role played the nonverbal expression of warmth and coldness.

4. Reverse roles and repeat steps 2 and 3.

5. Find a new partner. Repeat steps 2 and 3 with your new partner. This time discuss the characteristics of a person you want as a friend.

6. Find a new partner. Repeat steps 2 and 3 with your new partner. This time discuss what you could do to improve your relationship with your partner.

7. Discuss the exercise in the group as a whole.

   a. Did you find it easy to role play warmth and coldness? Why or why not?

   b. How well did each of you master the skills of expressing warmth and coldness nonverbally?

   c. Are there other ways to express warmth nonverbally?

   d. What were your reactions and feelings to the exercise?

8. Go around the group and give each other feedback concerning the typical nonverbal messages you send in the group. How would you describe each other's nonverbal behavior? What is most distinctive about each other's nonverbal behavior? If you were to suggest one way for each person to change his nonverbal behavior, what would it be?

Expressing warmth is a vital skill for building and maintaining fulfilling relationships. More than any other behavior, warmth communicates liking, concern, and acceptance of another person. You should practice the nonverbal expression of warmth until you are sure that you can communicate it effectively when you want to.

Exercise 6.5: Actions Speak Louder Than Words

The following exercise will give you a chance to practice nonverbal communication of feelings. You may not use words and sounds during this exercise, but must communicate only by nonverbal means, such as facial expressions, eye contact, gestures, posture, and touch. The procedure for the exercise is:

1. Form groups of six. Sit on the floor in a circle. Do not use a table. Deal out a deck of ordinary playing cards until everyone has the same number of cards and there are at least three cards left in the draw-deck. The draw-deck is placed face down in the center of the circle.

2. The winner of the game is the person who gets rid of all her cards first. You get rid of your cards by correctly identifying the feelings expressed by other group members and by accurately communicating feelings to the other group members.

3. Group members take turns expressing one feeling. To begin, the person on the

dealer's left selects a card from her own hand and lays it face down in front of her. She is now the expresser. The remaining group members are to identify the feeling she expresses. Then she expresses nonverbally the feeling on the card. The feeling each card represents is listed in item 9. The other people check their hands to see if they have a card that matches the feeling that was expressed. If so, they place the card(s) face down in front of them. If not, they pass.

4. When all the cards are down for the first round, they are all turned face up at the same time. If one or more of the receivers have matched the expresser's card, the expresser puts her card and all the matching cards face down on the bottom of the draw-deck.

5. Any group member who put down a wrong card must return it to his hand and draw an additional penalty card from the top of the draw-deck. You draw the same number of penalty cards from the draw-deck as the number of cards you put down in front of you.

6. If no other group member matched the expresser's card, then the expresser failed to communicate and she returns her card to her hand and draws a penalty card from the draw-deck. In this case the other people return their cards to their hands but *do not* draw penalty cards.

7. When you have two or three cards representing the same feeling, you must play all the cards if you play one of them. If you have several queens, for example, you must play all of them, if you play queens at all. So, as expresser or receiver, you may get rid of two or three cards. Or you may have to draw two or three penalty cards.

8. The expresser may use any nonverbal or unspoken behavior she wishes in order to communicate accurately the feeling she is portraying. No words may be spoken or sounds made. You may wish to use your hands, your head, your whole body, and you may involve other group members by touching them or engaging them in a nonverbal interchange.

9. Each card represents a different feeling.

2 = contentment	9 = anger
3 = shyness	10 = hope
4 = indifference	Jack = happiness
5 = fear	Queen = joy
6 = frustration	King = warmth
7 = loneliness	Ace = love
8 = sorrow	Joker = admiration

10. Discuss the following questions:

   a. Was it difficult or easy to express feelings nonverbally? Why or why not?

   b. Was it difficult or easy to interpret the nonverbal expressions? Why or why not?

   c. What nonverbal messages were most and least understandable?

   d. What did I learn about myself from this exercise?

Exercise 6.6: Recognizing Cues for Affection or Hostility

The following exercise is aimed at providing you with an opportunity to see if you can tell the difference between messages indicating affection and messages indicating hostility. Listed below are twenty messages. In the spaces provided, write an *A* if you think the message indicates affection and an *H* if you think the message indicates hostility. Then check your answers with the answers at the end of the chapter. Discuss with your group members any that you missed until you are sure you understand them.

_____ 1. Looks directly at the other person and gives undivided attention.

_____ 2. Greets the person in a cold, formal manner.

_____ 3. Engages in friendly humor.

_____ 4. Yawns or shows other signs of boredom.

_____ 5. Has a relaxed posture and does not appear tense or nervous.

_____ 6. Sits close to the other person.

_____ 7. Interrupts repeatedly.

_____ 8. Leans toward the other person as an expression of interest.

_____ 9. Sits relatively far away.

_____ 10. Responds directly and openly to the other person's request to know one's opinions, values, attitudes, and feelings.

_____ 11. Exhibits a cold, nonreceptive facial expression.

_____ 12. Uses the other person's vocabulary in explaining things.

_____ 13. Makes encouraging, reassuring remarks to the other person.

_____ 14. Lays traps for the other person (e.g., "A minute ago you said . . . and now you are contradicting yourself!").

_____ 15. Makes casual physical contact with the other person as an expression of liking (e.g., pat on the back, touch on the arm).

_____ 16. Says, "That stupid remark is about what I would expect from someone like you."

_____ 17. Shows consideration for the physical comfort of the other person by taking the person's coat, offering a more comfortable chair, adjusting the window, and so forth.

_____ 18. Sneers and appears amused when the other person is sharing personal feelings.

_____ 19. Hedges or rebuffs the other person when asked a "personal" question.

_____ 20. During the conversation looks repeatedly at the clock, out the window, away from the other person, or at papers on the desk.

IMPORTANCE OF MAKING YOUR VERBAL AND NONVERBAL MESSAGES CONGRUENT

There is no way to emphasize too much the importance of making congruent your verbal and nonverbal messages for communicating feelings. If you wish to express warmth, your words, facial expression, tone of voice, posture, and so on must all communicate warmth. Contradictory messages will only indicate to the other person that you are untrustworthy and will create anxiety about the relationship. Some psychologists have stated that receiving contradictory verbal and nonverbal messages for a long period of time from someone you love can result in mental illness. For a person to believe that your expression of feelings is real and genuine, your verbal and nonverbal messages must be congruent.

CHAPTER REVIEW

Test your understanding of the nonverbal expression of feelings by answering true or false to the following statements. The answers are at the end of the chapter.

True   False   1. It is possible to communicate verbally without giving nonverbal clues.

True   False   2. The verbal message is more believable than the nonverbal message.

True	False	**3.** In comparison with nonverbal actions, the verbal language is very limited.
True	False	**4.** Direct eye contact indicates dislike for the other person.
True	False	**5.** Feelings are misunderstood partly because the verbal and nonverbal messages are often incongruent.
True	False	**6.** Feelings are misunderstood partly because the nonverbal messages are often unclear.
True	False	**7.** Leaning away from another person is an expression of coldness.
True	False	**8.** Contradictions between verbal and nonverbal messages will tell the receiver that the sender is untrustworthy.
True	False	**9.** Contradictions between verbal and nonverbal messages will make the receiver suspicious.
True	False	**10.** Continued contradictory messages from a loved one can cause mental illness.

Indicate below the skills you have mastered and the ones you need more work on.

1. I have mastered the following:
   ____ Being aware of how I express my feelings nonverbally
   ____ Using nonverbal cues to express my feelings accurately
   ____ Being congruent in the way my verbal and nonverbal messages express feelings
   ____ Using nonverbal cues to express warmth.
2. I need more work on:
   ____ Being aware of how I express feelings nonverbally
   ____ Using nonverbal cues to express my feelings accurately
   ____ Being congruent in the way my verbal and nonverbal messages express feelings
   ____ Using nonverbal cues to express warmth.

You should now understand from this chapter the importance of having your nonverbal messages agree with your verbal messages. Also, you should have developed skill in interpreting and expressing different feelings nonverbally. This skill will be helpful in the next chapter, which deals with how to listen and respond to others in a helpful way.

ANSWERS

Recognizing Cues for Affection or Hostility: 1. A; 2. H; 3. A; 4. H; 5. A; 6. A; 7. H; 8. A; 9. H; 10. A; 11. H; 12. A; 13. A; 14. H; 15. A; 16. H; 17. A; 18. H; 19. H; 20. H.

Chapter Review: 1. false; 2. false; 3. false; 4. false; 5. true; 6. true; 7. true; 8. true; 9. true; 10. true.

7 *Helpful Listening and Responding*

RESPONDING TO ANOTHER PERSON'S PROBLEMS

When someone is talking to you about something deeply distressing or of a real concern to her, how should you listen and respond in order to be helpful? How do you answer in ways that will both help the person solve her problem or clarify her feelings and at the same time help build a closer relationship between that person and yourself?

Perhaps the most important thing to remember is that you cannot solve other people's problems for them. No matter how sure you are of what the right thing to do is or how much insight you think you have into their problems, the other people must come to their own decisions about what they should do and achieve their own insights into the situation and themselves. So how do you listen and respond to ensure that other people will make their own decisions and gain their own insights?

In listening and responding to other people's messages, there are two basic things that determine the effectiveness of your help:

1. Your intentions and attitudes as you listen and give your response

2. The actual phrasing of your response

The exercises that follow deal with both of these. Your intentions are the most important single factor in helping other people to solve their problems. The appropriate phrasing of your response involves considerable skill, but skill alone is not enough. It is only when the skills in phrasing responses reflect your underlying attitudes of acceptance, respect, interest, liking, and desire to help that your response will be truly helpful. Your response is helpful when it helps the other person explore a problem, clarify feelings, gain insight into a distressing situation, or make a difficult decision. In order to examine the intentions or attitudes with which you can respond to someone asking for help with a problem or a concern, we will go through the following exercise.

Exercise 7.1: Listening and Response Alternatives

The objectives of this exercise are to (1) identify your response style, (2) understand the different types of responses you can use in a situation in which the sender has a problem he wants help with, and (3) determine when each type of response may be most effective in helping other people with their problems and in building a closer relationship between the other people and yourself. Each of the response alternatives used in this exercise communicates underlying intentions and attitudes. The procedure is:

1. Using Answer Sheet A, and working by yourself, complete the questionnaire on Listening and Response Alternatives. Specific instructions are on the Answer Sheet.

2. Using Answer Sheet B, and working by yourself, identify the underlying intent of each response given in the questionnaire. Specific instructions are on the Answer Sheet.

3. Using the Scoring Key in the Appendix, score Answer Sheet A. Write the number of times you used each type of response in the appropriate spaces on the Answer Sheet.

4. Read the next section, which is on intentions underlying the responses. Then divide into groups of three and score Answer Sheet B, discussing each response until everyone understands it.

5. Combine two triads into a group of six. On Table 7.1 (p. 184), mark the frequency with which each member of the group used each type of response.

6. Use the questions on page 184 to discuss with your group the results summarized in Table 7.1

Answer Sheet A: Identifying Personal Responses

Read the twelve statements in the questionnaire and circle on this Answer Sheet the response that best represents what you would say to the speaker if you were trying to form a close relationship with him and to help him solve his problems.

1. a : b : c : d : e		7. a : b : c : d : e	
2. a : b : c : d : e		8. a : b : c : d : e	
3. a : b : c : d : e		9. a : b : c : d : e	
4. a : b : c : d : e		10. a : b : c : d : e	
5. a : b : c : d : e		11. a : b : c : d : e	
6. a : b : c : d : e		12. a : b : c : d : e	

Response   *Frequency*

E   _____

I   _____

S   _____

P   _____

U   _____

Answer Sheet B: Identifying the Intent of a Response

Study pages 178-184, on which the five basic intentions underlying the responses to the problems presented in the questionnaire are discussed. Then go back through the questionnaire and classify the responses to each problem according to the five categories. Read each of the twelve problem statements and identify the intent underlying each of the alternative responses by marking a *P* for probing, *I* for interpretative, *E* for evaluative, *S* for supportive, and *U* for understanding.

Item	1	2	3	4	5
1.					
2.					
3.					
4.					
5.					
6.					
7.					
8.					
9.					
10.					
11.					
12.					

Questionnaire on Listening and Response Alternatives

In this exercise, statements are made by several people about situations they face. Little or no information is presented about the nature of the person speaking. Following each statement is a series of five possible responses you might make in trying to help the person solve his or her problem. See Answer Sheet A for specific directions on how to complete this exercise.

1. **David.** "I'm determined to be a success, and I know I can do it if I just work hard enough. I may have to work 18 hours a day and stay chained to my typewriter, but if that's what it takes, I'll do it. My home life and my family may suffer, but it will be worth it in the end. I will be a success, and that's all that matters."

    a. You seem to be a person who wants badly to succeed at your job. That is understandable, but it may stem from your insecurity about your own competence and ability.

    b. I guess we all, at some time or other, go through a period where we want to achieve success. Lots of people worry about whether their family will suffer while they work so hard. I'm sure everything will turn out all right for you and your family.

    c. I think you are right. Hard work always pays off. Keep at it!

    d. You see yourself as a very ambitious person. Yet you're unsure about whether you want your family to suffer because of the long hours you believe you will have to work in order to be successful.

    e. Can you tell me a little more about why success is important to you? What will you do when you've achieved this success? Will you be happy? Will it give you all that you want out of life?

2. **Roger.** "I never seem to have enough time to do the things I enjoy. Just as I'm ready to go enjoy a nice game of golf or tennis, my brother reminds me of some writing I need to do, or my wife saddles me with household chores. It's getting harder and harder to have the fun out of life that I expect to have. It's depressing!"

    a. Wanting to have fun is OK, but don't you think you should do some work too? I certainly wouldn't play golf if I thought that later I would regret not having worked. Life does have responsibilities.

    b. It's upsetting that your work and household responsibilities are increasing to the extent that you don't have time for the fun and recreation you want.

    c. Maybe your leisure activities are just a way of getting out of the unpleasant jobs you should do.

    d. I'm curious. How much time do you spend on your favorite sports?

    e. You're in a busy time of your life right now. I bet you will have more leisure time as you get older.

3. **Frank.** "I never have any luck with cars. Every car I've ever gotten has been a lemon. Not only have I paid handsomely for the cars, but just when they are

out of warranty, something goes wrong. The car I have now needs a new engine. What's wrong with me? Why should I have all the bad luck?"

a. You're wondering if it is your fault somehow that every car you own breaks down and has to have costly repairs. All the money you have to pay for car repairs depresses and angers you.

b. Your anger about the poor quality of the cars you have owned is being turned against yourself and experienced as depression. Aren't the companies that made the cars to blame?

c. What kind of cars do you buy? How many cars have you owned?

d. Everyone has bad luck sometimes. I'm sure the next car you own will be more reliable. It's really not your fault the cars have turned out to be lemons. No one can tell how much repair a car will need when he first buys it.

e. You're always buying foreign cars. What you need is an American car that has a good warranty.

4. **Edythe.** "My older brothers pick on me constantly. They are always telling me what to do. I get pretty tired of their always harping at me to stand up straight or checking out my dates before I go out. What's worse, they tell things about me that are embarrassing. I've complained to my mother, and she tells them to stop, but they just keep on."

a. How often do you have serious talks with your brothers? Have you tried telling them how you feel?

b. You feel angry at your brothers because they pick on you, tell you what to do, are inconsiderate of your feelings, and want to pass judgment on your choice of dates, is that it? And you also feel helpless to change the situation, don't you?

c. I think you ought to be more understanding of your brothers. After all, they would not do it if they did not care about you.

d. Relax. Older brothers often act like that for a while. It's traditional. Once they see you have grown up, they will get off your back.

e. You resent being treated like a child. Part of establishing your independence as a person is feeling angry at people who don't treat you like an adult.

5. **Helen.** "When I was younger, I used to fight my parents because I wanted to get married. Now I'm married and I keep thinking of how good it was to be single and have no responsibilities to tie me down. I can't go anywhere without a bunch of kids clinging to me. It's rough, and there's nothing I can do about it."

a. I understand how you feel. I often feel that way too. But before long your children will grow up and then you will have all the freedom you want.

b. Let's explore how you arrange your time. How often do you wish to go somewhere without your children? How often do you hire babysitters?

c. You feel resentful and trapped because being married and having children don't allow you the freedom to go places and do things when you want to.

d. You say you fought your parents to get married. Now you feel resentful about the loss of freedom. Could it be that you are really angry at your parents for not stopping you from getting married in the first place?

e. Sounds to me as if you are stuck. You will just have to put up with the situation until your children are grown.

6. **Keith.** "I'm really depressed. I have a good job and I make an adequate salary, but I'm not happy. I guess working is not all it is cracked up to be. I have some money saved. I did not do too well in school before, but maybe I will quit work and go back to school. I don't know what I should do."

a. How long have you felt this way? Have the feelings just started recently, or have you always felt depressed about what you were doing?

b. In other words, you're depressed and puzzled because your job isn't fulfilling, but school wasn't either, and they are the only two alternatives you see yourself as having.

c. Depression is often anger turned against oneself. Perhaps you're angry at yourself for not feeling fulfilled by what you are doing.

d. If you didn't do so well in school before, you probably won't do any better now. You should be satisfied with having a good job; many people don't, you know.

e. Lots of people have trouble making up their minds. There are a lot of people who don't like their jobs and who really don't want to go back to school. You don't need to feel depressed.

7. **Dale.** "I wish I could find a way to finish college without going to classes. I register each quarter, intending to go, but I get sidetracked and end up dropping out. I've been enrolled for 6 years. My parents would kill me if they knew how many credits I need to graduate!"

a. It sounds as if you're just wasting time and money. You should probably just stop trying to go to school and get a good job instead.

b. You feel guilty because you keep letting your parents think you are trying to finish college when in fact you are doing other things. It bothers you not to meet their expectations.

c. Possibly if you tell me a little more about how you get sidetracked and what it is that you do while being sidetracked, we can get a clearer idea about what is involved.

d. Many people have trouble finishing college. It's not unusual. Maybe you should quit. Your parents will understand if you explain things to them.

e. Let's see if I understand you correctly. You're upset because you can't seem to finish college even though your parents really want you to, and you're worried about how they would react if you quit going to school. Right?

8. **David.** "All this work is driving me crazy! It seems as if I spend every waking moment working. I don't have any time to relax with my friends and family.

No matter how hard I work I never seem to get caught up. I have so many responsibilities. I don't know how I'm going to get everything done."

- **a.** Don't feel so bad. I'm sure that if you just keep at it, you'll get things done and have the leisure you need.
- **b.** You're obviously trying to do too much. What you need to do is cut down on your commitments so you'll have more free time.
- **c.** You feel frustrated and angry that your work doesn't get finished and you can't enjoy your family and friends more; you work hard, but your responsibilities always seem to increase faster than your ability to meet them.
- **d.** Can you tell me more about the specific nature of your responsibilities, the way you schedule your time, and how you acquire new responsibilities?
- **e.** How you spend your time probably reflects your true values. Perhaps you prefer your work over your family and friends. Could it be that you consider your work more important than enjoying life?

9. **Roger.** "I never seem to get anywhere on time. I don't know why. People bug me about it and sometimes they get pretty angry. I try to keep a schedule, but it never seems to work out. I have an important golf game coming up and I'm afraid I'm going to be late for it. I don't know what to do to change."

- **a.** In other words, you feel frustrated with yourself because you always seem to be late and somewhat worried about the way other people react to your lateness.
- **b.** I'm wondering if you have investigated ways of managing your schedule more effectively. How often are you late? Are there some things you are always late for and other things you are never late for?
- **c.** You are obviously not very organized, and of course people will be angry when you treat them with such inconsiderateness. Perhaps you should ask someone more punctual to pick you up when you have an important engagement.
- **d.** I really wouldn't worry. Being late is not so bad. I'm sure that no one is really angry about such a little thing as arriving late.
- **e.** Being late is sometimes caused by passive-aggressiveness, where you want to punish other people but also are afraid to take responsibility for your actions.

10. **Frank.** "I just never seem to have any money. I have a good-paying job, but it seems as soon as I get my pay check, it's gone. Then I have to scrimp and save the rest of the month. Now my car needs a new engine and I don't know where I'm going to get the money to pay for it."

- **a.** Tell me more about how you manage your money. Have you tried budgeting? What are your major expenses?
- **b.** You're feeling depressed on account of your chronic lack of money and your uncertainty over how you are going to pay for your needed car repairs.
- **c.** You may be wasting money on nonessentials. I think if you tried keeping a budget, you would be able to manage much better.

    d. I'm sure the money for your new car engine will turn up. Don't worry. You have always managed in the past.

    e. Depression such as you are experiencing often comes from a feeling of being helpless to solve your problems. Once you feel that you have some control over your financial problems, you'll feel better.

11. **Edythe.** "I just hate to bring my dates home to meet my family. I don't mind my boyfriends meeting my parents, but I wish there was some way to keep my older brothers out of the act. The way they give my dates the third degree scares them away. It's embarrassing."

    a. Embarrassment is often caused by older siblings, especially when they view you as a little girl. We have to plan to get them to see you as an adult and start treating you as one.

    b. It sounds as if they are pretty inconsiderate. Most people have siblings who embarrass them at some point, but your brothers sound as if they are really out of line.

    c. Just wait. I bet that soon you will meet someone who won't be scared off by your brothers.

    d. You feel angry about the way your brothers embarrass you by questioning your boyfriends, and you want to avoid such situations while at the same time allowing your parents to meet your dates.

    e. Just what do your brothers do to your dates? What specific questions do they ask?

12. **Frances.** "I don't know about my children. David works too hard, Roger plays too much, Frank is always broke, Edythe married someone none of us have met, Helen got married too early, Keith quit school to work and now wants to quit work to go to school, and Dale isn't close to graduating after 6 years of college. You do your best and look how they turn out! It's enough to make a person give up."

    a. You are worried about your children and yet feel helpless to change them. Each child seems to have some problem and you are unsure how well their lives will turn out.

    b. Can you explain further how you feel about your children?

    c. Don't worry. I'm sure they will turn out all right. All parents must worry about their children some time or another.

    d. Tell your children to straighten out. Either they listen to their mother or else they aren't worth talking to.

    e. You have certain expectations for each of your children, and they aren't living up to what you expect. These expectations are upsetting you.

INTENTIONS UNDERLYING THE RESPONSES

When other people want to discuss a problem or concern of theirs with you, there are at least five ways in which you can listen and respond:

1. Advising and evaluating
2. Analyzing and interpreting
3. Reassuring and supporting
4. Questioning and probing
5. Paraphrasing and understanding

Each of these alternative ways of responding communicates certain intentions. All of them, at one time or another, will be helpful. None of the responses can be labeled as good or bad, effective or ineffective. All have their place in helping other people solve their problems and gain insight into their difficulties. But some of the above responses are more helpful than others in building friendships and helping people explore further their feelings and thoughts. In exploring the intentions underlying the responses in the preceding questionnaire, the person with the problem will be called the sender and the person giving the response will be the receiver.

Advising and Evaluating (E)

Giving advice and making a judgment as to the relative goodness, appropriateness, effectiveness, and rightness of what the sender is thinking and doing are among the most common responses we make when trying to help others. These responses communicate an evaluative, corrective, suggestive, or moralizing attitude or intent. The receiver implies what the sender *ought* or *might* do to solve the problem. When advice is timely and relevant, it can be helpful to another person. Most often, however, when you give advice and evaluation you build barriers that keep you from being helpful and developing a deeper friendship.

For one thing, being evaluative and giving advice can be threatening to other people and make them defensive. When people become defensive they may closed-mindedly reject your advice, resist your influence, stop exploring the problem, and be indecisive. Why? Because giving advice and passing judgment often communicate that the receiver is assuming that her judgment is superior to that of the sender's. When a person has a problem, she does not want to be made to feel inferior. For another thing, being evaluative often seems to be a way of avoiding involvement with another person's concerns and conflicts. While it is quick, fast, and easy, it also allows the receiver to generalize about the sender's problems, and this communicates that the receiver does not care to take the time to understand the sender's problems fully. In addition, advice can encourage people not to take responsibility for their own problems. Even when praise is used to influence others, it can communicate that the sender must meet certain expectations before she is of value. Finally, advice and evaluation often tell more about the giver's values, needs, and perspectives than about the receiver's problems. Thus, if you wish to be helpful and further a relationship, you should usually avoid such phrases as "If I were you . . . ," "One good way is . . . ," "Why don't you . . . ?" "You should . . . ," "You ought to . . . ," "The thing to do is . . . ," and "Don't you think . . . ?"

It is important to avoid giving advice and evaluation in the early stages of helping other people understand and solve their problems and difficulties. There is a place for advising and evaluating, but there are other responses that are usually more helpful.

Analyzing and Interpreting (I)

When analyzing or interpreting the sender's problems and difficulties, the receiver's intentions are to teach, to tell the sender what his or her problem means, to inform the sender how the sender really feels about the situation, or to impart some psychological knowledge to the sender. In interpreting the sender's problems, the receiver implies what the sender might or ought to think. Analyzing or interpreting attempts to point out some deep hidden reason that makes the sender do the things he or she does. It attempts to give the person some additional insight through an explanation. Through such statements as, "Ah, ha! Now I know what your problem is," or, "The reason you are upset is . . . ," the receiver tries to teach the sender the meaning of the sender's behavior and feelings.

This suggestion will often make the sender defensive and will discourage her from revealing more thoughts and feelings for fear that these will also be interpreted or analyzed. Most of us react negatively when someone else implies that he knows more about us than we do.

When the receiver tries to analyze or interpret the sender's behavior, thoughts, and feelings, the receiver may communicate "I know more about you than you know yourself." People will usually respond better when you help them think about themselves and their feelings than if you try to figure out what causes them to do the things they do. It also frees you from being an "expert" on human behavior.

Reassuring and Supporting (S)

Supportive and reassuring responses indicate that the receiver wants to reassure, be sympathetic, or reduce the intensity of the sender's feelings. When the receiver rushes in with support and reassurance, this

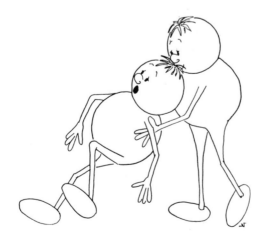

often denies the sender's feelings. Statements such as, "It's always darkest just before the dawn," and "Things will be better tomorrow," frequently end up communicating a lack of interest or understanding. Supportive statements are, however, frequently used by people trying to help a friend, student, or child. It's distressing to see a friend depressed, so all too often a person will communicate, "Don't be depressed," rather than listening carefully and helping clarify the causes and potential solutions for the depression. While there are times when other people need to be reassured as to their value and worth or supported in their reactions and feelings, reassurance and support are often ways of saying, "You should not feel as you do."

Questioning and Probing (P)

Probing by asking questions indicates that the receiver wants to get further information, guide the discussion along certain lines, or bring the sender to a certain realization or conclusion the receiver has in mind. In asking a question, the receiver implies that the sender ought or might profitably develop or discuss a point further. Questioning is, however, an important skill in being helpful to people who wish to discuss their problems and concerns with you. In using questions skillfully, it is necessary to understand the difference between an open and closed question and the pitfalls of the "why" question. An *open question* encourages other people to answer at greater length and in more detail. The *closed question* usually asks for only a simple yes or no answer. An example of an open question is, "How do you feel about your job?" while an example of a closed question is, "Do you like your job?" Because open questions encourage other people to share more personal feelings and thoughts, they are usually more helpful.

When you intend to deepen a relationship or help other people understand and solve their problems, it is usually recommended that you avoid why questions. To encourage people to give a rational explanation for their behavior may not be productive because most people do not fully know the reasons they do the things they do. Being asked why can make people defensive and encourages them to justify rather than explore their actions. Why questions are also often used to indicate disapproval or to give advice. For example, the question, "Why did you yell at the teacher?" may imply the statement, "I don't think you should have yelled at the teacher." Because criticism and advice tend to be threatening, people may feel less free to examine the reasons that led them to a particular action or decision. Instead of asking people to explain or justify their actions through answering why, it may be more helpful to ask what, where, when, how, and who questions. These

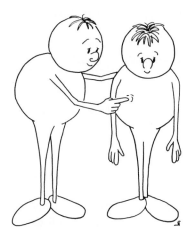

questions help other people to be more specific, precise, and revealing. For a more complete discussion of question asking, see Johnson (1979).

Asking questions skillfully is an essential part of giving help to other people who are discussing their problems and concerns with you. But questions, while they communicate that you are interested in helping, do not necessarily communicate that you understand. It may sometimes be more effective to change questions into reflective statements that encourage the person to keep talking. An example is changing the question, "Do you like swimming?" to a reflective statement, "You really like swimming." Reflective statements, which are discussed in the next section, focus on clarifying and summarizing without interrupting the flow of communication because they don't call for an answer.

Paraphrasing and Understanding (U)

An understanding and reflecting response indicates that your intent is to understand the sender's thoughts and feelings. In effect, this response asks the sender whether you, the receiver, have understood what the sender is saying and how she is feeling. This is the same as the paraphrasing response discussed in chapter 4. There are three situations in which you will want to use the understanding response. The first is when you are not sure you have understood the sender's thoughts and feelings. Paraphrasing can begin a clarifying and summarizing process that increases the accuracy of understanding. The second is when you wish to ensure that the sender hears what he has just said. This reflection of thoughts and feelings often gives the sender a clearer understanding of himself and of the implications of his present feelings

TABLE 7.1:   FREQUENCY WITH WHICH THE GROUP MEMBERS USED EACH TYPE
OF RESPONSE

Frequency	Evaluating	Interpreting	Supporting	Probing	Understanding	Total
0-2						
3-5						
6-8						
9-12						
Total	6	6	6	6	6	

and thinking. Finally, paraphrasing reassures the sender that you are trying to understand his thoughts and feelings.

In order to be truly understanding, you may have to go beyond the words of the sender to the feelings and underlying meanings that accompany the words. It is the true meaning of the statement and the sender's feelings that you paraphrase.

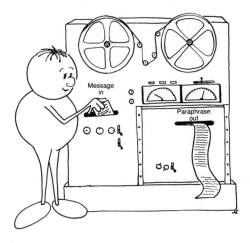

After you have finished the procedure for scoring both answer sheets, record the frequency with which each member of the group used each type of response. This can be done by taking one member of the group, asking her how many times she used the evaluating response, placing a tally mark in the appropriate box, then asking the member how many times she used the interpreting response, and so forth. When the recording is completed, you will have a tally mark for each group member under each type of response. Then, as a group, discuss the results summarized in the above table. The following questions may be helpful.

1. What are the most frequently used responses by the members of the group?

2. How frequently did each member use each of the responses?

3. How does a person trying to explain a problem to you react when you use each type of response?

4. When is each type of response most useful in helping other people with their problems and concerns and in building a relationship with them?

5. What responses tell the most about the receiver?

Exercise 7.2: Practicing the Five Responses

This exercise provides you with a chance to practice each of the five types of responses. The exercise consists of two parts, one in which you are given a problem statement and you write down what you would say (assuming you wanted to respond with each of the five types of intentions), and one in which you and another person make statements and practice with each other giving the different types of responses.

Part 1

Read the following paragraphs and write a response for each category. Do this by yourself.

"Sometimes I get so depressed I can hardly stand it. Here I am, twenty-five years old and still not married. It's not as if I haven't had any chances, but I've never really wanted to marry any of the guys I've dated. All my friends are married; I can't understand why I'm not. Is there something wrong with me?"

> Evaluative response
>
> Interpretative response
>
> Supportive response
>
> Probing response
>
> Understanding response

"I'm really concerned about a friend of mine named Jane. She never seems to take life seriously enough. She's dropped out of school, she gets a job, and then she quits after a week. She is using drugs and plans to move to a commune. I'm really worried that some day she'll ruin her life. I don't know what I should do."

> Evaluative response
>
> Interpretative response

Supportive response

Probing response

Understanding response

"I need your advice about my relationship with June. She wants us to get very serious. But I don't even know if I like her. We spend a lot of time together, I have fun when I'm around her, but she's all the time pushing me not to date other girls and to see her more often than I now do. I don't like to be pushed; but I don't want to hurt her by not dating her any more. What would you do?"

Evaluative response

Interpretative response

Supportive response

Probing response

Understanding response

Part 2

1. Divide into pairs. Discuss each other's answers and make suggestions as to how they might be improved.

2. Think of a problem you now are having either at your job or in school. It may be a major problem or it may be a minor one. Each person in the pair tells the other his problems. The receiver then gives an evaluative response, an interpretative response, a supportive response, a probing response, and then an understanding response.

3. Think of a problem you are having with your family. It may be either a minor or a major problem. Each person in the pair tells the other his problem. The receiver gives each of the five responses.

4. Think of a problem, either a major or a minor one, you are having with a friend. Each person in the pair tells the other his problem. The receiver gives each of the five responses.

5. In your pair, give each other the feedback concerning how well each of you can respond in the five ways discussed in this chapter. You may wish to continue practicing the different responses until you have mastered them to your satisfaction. This can be done by consciously applying them to your everyday conversations or by pairing up a member of your group and setting specific practice times for the two of you to increase your response skills.

COMPREHENSION TEST A

Test your understanding of responding to people's problems by answering true or false to the following statements. Answers are at the end of the chapter.

True	False	1. If you try hard enough, you can solve other people's problems for them.
True	False	2. The effectiveness of your help depends partly on your intentions and attitudes as you listen and give your response.
True	False	3. The phrasing of your response influences the effectiveness of your help.
True	False	4. Your intentions are of minor importance in helping people solve their problems.
True	False	5. A helpful response helps other people explore a problem, clarify feelings, gain insight, or make a difficult decision.
True	False	6. Giving advice is helpful to the sender's problems.
True	False	7. Telling the sender the underlying meaning of her feelings will bring a grateful response.
True	False	8. It's helpful to try and cheer up someone who's depressed.
True	False	9. Asking why questions will help the sender see the problem more clearly.
True	False	10. "You really hate your job" is a good example of a reflective statement.

HELPING PEOPLE SOLVE THEIR PROBLEMS

There are many times when a friend or acquaintance will wish to discuss a problem or concern with you. People do not often get very far in understanding their experiences and deciding how to solve their problems unless they talk things over with someone else. There is nothing more helpful than discussing a problem with a friend who is an effective listener. The first rule in helping other people solve their problems and understand distressing situations is to remember that all insights, understandings, decisions, and solutions occur within the other people, not within you. No matter how convinced you are that you know what the other people should do, your goal in helping must be to assist them in reaching their own decisions and forming their own insights.

The second rule in helping others solve their problems is to differentiate between an internal frame of reference (how the other person sees and feels about the situation) and an external frame of reference (how you see and feel about the other person's situation). You are able to give help to the extent that you understand and respond to the sender's frame of reference rather than imposing your frame of reference on the problem situation. It is not what makes you angry that is important, it is what makes the other person angry. It is not how you see things that matters, it is how the other person sees things. Your ability to be helpful to another person is related directly to your ability to view the situation from the other person's perspective.

Listening and responding in ways that help you understand the other person's perspective or frame of reference is always a tentative process. Many times the other person will not fully understand or be able to communicate effectively her perspective. While you are clarifying your own understanding of the other person's perspective, you will also be helping the other person understand herself better.

LISTENING AND RESPONDING ALTERNATIVES

The exercise on listening and responding alternatives is based on the work of Carl Rogers, a noted psychologist. Several years ago he conducted a series of studies on how individuals communicate with each other in face-to-face situations. He found that the categories of evaluative, interpretative, supportive, probing, and understanding statements encompass 80 percent of all the messages sent between individuals. The other 20 percent of the statements are incidental and of no real importance. From his observations of individuals in all sorts of different settings—businessmen, housewives, people at parties and conventions, and so on—he found that the responses were used by individuals in the following frequency: (1) evaluative was most used, (2) interpretative was next, (3) supportive was the third most common response, (4) probing the fourth, and (5) understanding the least. Finally, he found that if a person uses one category of response as much as 40 percent of the time, then other people see him as *always* responding that way. This is a process of oversimplification similar to stereotyping.

The categories of response are in themselves neither good nor bad. It is the overuse or underuse of any of the categories that may not be functional or the failure to recognize when each type of response is appropriate that interferes with helping the sender and building a better friendship. If, in answering the response alternatives questionnaire, you use only one or two of the responses, it may be that you overuse some types of responses while you underuse others. You can easily remedy that by becoming more aware of your responses and working to become proficient in using all five types of responses when they seem appropriate.

When is each response appropriate? From your own experience and from listening to the discussion of your group, you may have some good ideas. In terms of what is appropriate in the early stage of forming a friendship, two of the possible responses to be most sensitive to are the understanding and the evaluative responses. Basically, the understanding response revolves around the notion that when an individual expresses a message and that message is paraphrased in fresh words with no change of its essential meaning, the sender will expand upon or further explore the ideas, feelings, and attitudes contained in the message and achieve a recognition of previously denied meanings or feelings or move on to express a new message that is more meaningful to him. Even when the receiver has misunderstood and communicated a faulty understanding of the sender's ideas and feelings, the sender will respond in ways that will clarify the receiver's incorrect response, thus increasing the accuracy and clarity of communication between the two individuals.

It is the understanding response that is most likely to communicate to the sender that the listener is interested in the sender as a person and has an accurate understanding of the sender and of what he is saying, and it is this same response that most encourages the sender to go on and elaborate and further explore his problem. The understanding response may also be the most helpful for enabling the receiver to see the sender's problem from the sender's point of view. Many relationships or conversations are best begun by using the understanding response until a trust level is established; then the other categories of response can be more freely used. The procedures for engaging in the understanding response are rather simple (see chapter 4), and anyone who takes the time and effort can become quite skillful in their use.

As has been discussed in chapter 4, the major barrier to mutual understanding is the very natural tendency to judge, evaluate, approve, or disapprove of the messages of the sender. For this reason you should usually avoid giving evaluative responses in the early stages of a relationship or of a conversation about the sender's problems. The primary reaction to a value judgment is another value judgment (for example, "You say I'm wrong, but I think I'm right and you're wrong"), with each person looking at the issue only from his own point of view. This tendency to make evaluations is very much heightened in situations in which feelings and emotions are deeply involved, as when you are discussing a personal problem. Defensiveness and feelings of being threatened are avoided when the listener responds with understanding rather than with evaluative responses. Evaluative responses, however, may be helpful when you are specifically asked to make a value judgment or when you wish to disclose your own values and attitudes.

There will be times when another person tries to discuss an issue with you that you do not understand. *Probing responses* will help you get a clear definition of the problem before you respond. They may also be helpful if you do not think the sender is seeing the full implications of some of her statements. *Supportive responses* are useful when the person needs to feel accepted or when she needs enough support to try to engage in behavior aimed at solving her problem. Finally, *interpretive responses* are sometimes useful in confronting another person with the effect of her behavior on you; this situation will be further discussed in chapter 9. Interpretation, if carried out with skill, integrity, and empathy, can be a powerful stimulus to growth. Interpretation leads to insight, and insight is a key to better psychological living. Interpretation is one form of confrontation.

COMPREHENSION TEST B

Test your understanding of effective listening and responding by answering true or false to the following statements. Answers are at the end of the chapter.

True   False   1. Give advice freely, remembering that the insights and understandings happen within the receiver, not the sender.

True   False   2. There is a difference between how you see the situation and how the sender sees it.

True   False   3. Clarifying your understanding of the other person's perspective will help the other person to understand herself better.

True   False   4. Ninety percent of all messages between two people are evaluative, interpretative, supportive, probing, and understanding.

True   False   5. The frequency of the responses from most used to least used is in this order: evaluative, interpretative, supportive, probing, and understanding.

True   False   6. If a person uses one category of response as much as 40 percent of the time, he is seen as always responding that way.

True   False   7. Giving evaluative responses early is a barrier to mutual understanding.

True   False   **8.** The understanding response best helps the receiver see the sender's point of view and en-
courages further communication.

True   False   **9.** Probing responses help the receiver understand
what the problem is.

True   False   **10.** Interpretation is a form of confrontation.

PHRASING AN ACCURATE UNDERSTANDING RESPONSE

The second important aspect of listening with understanding is the phrasing you use to paraphrase the message of the sender. The phrasing of the response may vary in the following ways:

1. *Content.* Content refers to the actual words used. Interestingly enough, responses that are essentially repetitions of the sender's statements do not communicate the receiver's understanding to the sender. It seems that repeating a person's words actually gets in the way of communicating an understanding of the essential meaning of the statement. It is more effective if the receiver paraphrases the sender's message in the receiver's own words and expressions.

2. *Depth.* Depth refers to the degree to which the receiver matches the depth of the sender's message in his response. You should not respond lightly to a serious statement, and correspondingly, you should not respond seriously to a shallow statement. In general, responses that match the sender's depth of feeling or that lead the sender on to a slightly greater depth of feeling are most effective.

3. *Meaning.* In the receiver's efforts to paraphrase the sender's statements, he may find himself either adding meaning or omitting meaning. Some of the obvious ways in which meaning can be added are (1) completing a sentence or thought for the sender, (2) responding to ideas the sender has used for illustrative purposes only, and (3) interpreting the significance of a message. Perhaps the most obvious way meaning can be omitted is by responding only to the last thing the sender said.

4. *Language.* The receiver should keep the language he uses in his response simple in order to ensure accurate communication.

Exercise 7.3: Phrasing an Accurate Understanding Response

This exercise provides you with an opportunity to classify responses according to their wording. The procedure for the exercise is:

1. Each person should answer the questionnaire on the wording of an understanding response. The specific instructions are given on Answer Sheet A.

2. Study the categories of the understanding response given on pages 195-6. Then categorize the responses for each item in the questionnaire as to the type of understanding response it represents. The specific instructions are given on Answer Sheet B.

3. Using the Scoring Key in the Appendix, score Answer Sheet B. Indicate in the appropriate space on the Answer Sheet the number of times you used each type of wording.

4. Form groups of three and score Answer Sheet B, discussing each type of wording until everyone in the triad understands it.

5. Combine two triads into a group of six. On Table 7.2 (p. 196), mark the frequency with which each member of the group used each type of wording.

6. Use the questions on page 197 to discuss the results summarized in Table 7.2.

Answer Sheet A: Identifying Personal Responses

Read the nine statements in the questionnaire below and mark on this Answer Sheet the response that best represents what you would personally say to the speaker if you were trying to form a close personal relationship with him and help him solve his problems.

1. a : b : c : d	6.	a : b : c : d
2. a : b : c : d	7.	a : b : c : d
3. a : b : c : d	8.	a : b : c : d
4. a : b : c : d	9.	a : b : c : d
5. a : b : c : d		

Response	Frequency
A	_____
S	_____
P	_____
I	_____

Answer Sheet B: Identifying the Phrasing
of Understanding Responses

Study pages 195-6 on which the four different phrasings of understanding responses are discussed. Then read each of the nine statements below and identify the category of each understanding response by: I = identical content, P = paraphrasing content, S = shallow or partial meaning, and A = additional meaning.

Item	1	2	3	4
1.				
2.				
3.				
4.				
5.				
6.				
7.				
8.				
9.				

Questionnaire on Accurate Understanding

In this exercise there are nine consecutive statements made by a young man who has sought help from a friend because of some things that have gone wrong in his life. Each statement is followed by four possible responses. In considering each alternative response, read it as a tentative, questioning statement that asks, "Do I understand you correctly; is this what you mean?" See Answer Sheets A and B for specific instructions on what to do with these statements.

1. "Boy, am I ever discouraged! Everything is going wrong in my life. It seems that everything I do is doomed to failure. I might as well not even try."

   a. You feel discouraged and ready to give up because of failure.

   b. Your whole life is a mess and you feel suicidal.

   c. You are feeling discouraged because things aren't working out for you, is that right?

   d. You are feeling a little unhappy right now.

2. "For instance, yesterday at work I messed up my job, and the boss made me stay until I got it right. She was really mad at me. I felt awful."

   a. Your boss was in a bad mood.

   b. You messed up at work, and the boss made you stay late, and you felt awful.

   c. You were depressed because your boss was angry at you and saw you as not doing your job correctly.

   d. You're going to get fired because you can't do your job correctly.

3. "Because I had to stay late at work, I was late for my most important class. We had an exam and I know I flunked it. I didn't even have time to finish the test. And I have to pass this class to graduate!"

   a. You are flunking out of school because you messed up at work.

   b. You think you did badly on a test.

   c. Staying late at work made you late for an important exam, which you didn't finish.

   d. You are worried about whether you will graduate after having done badly on an important exam in a required class.

4. "Then I went over to my girl friend's house, and she was out on a date with someone else. That really tore me up! I started crying. I couldn't help it."

   a. You became even more depressed because when you needed someone to give you support and sympathy, your girl friend was gone on a date with another man.

   b. You have really given up, haven't you?

   c. You are feeling discouraged.

   d. Your girl friend was out on a date with someone else, and you cried about it.

5. "At this point I don't know whether to jump off a bridge or throw myself under a train. (Pause) What do you think?"

   a. You want me to tell you whether to jump off a bridge or get run over by a train, right?

   b. There doesn't seem to be any way out.

   c. You have decided to take revenge on the world by killing yourself, is that it?

   d. You want my advice.

6. "You know, I thought Carol really liked me. I can't believe she would be so dirty as to go out behind my back. Well, women are rotten, but I thought Carol was an exception."

   a. You don't have much confidence in women, but you thought Carol was different, and now you feel let down.

   b. You thought Carol was different from other women.

   c. Now you have proven that all women are rotten.

   d. You thought Carol really liked you until she went out behind your back.

7. "I really liked my job, too. The people are great to be around and the boss is usually easygoing. (Pause) I guess I'm the rotten apple in the barrel. It can't be fun to work with someone as incompetent as I am. I guess if I don't quit, I will get fired."

   a. You don't think you will ever be able to do any job well.

   b. You feel discouraged because you don't think you are doing very well at your job, even though you like it. You are afraid your co-workers don't like you even though you like them.

   c. You like your job and the people you work with, but you feel you are incompetent and will get fired.

   d. You're going to quit your job.

8. "My parents are really going to be happy when they find out I flunked out of school. They always told me I was aiming too high and couldn't do it. They have never had any confidence in me. (Pause) I guess that is why I don't have much confidence in myself."

   a. Your parents' and your own expectations are going to be met by your doing badly in school.

   b. Your parents will be happy about your flunking out of school because they don't have any confidence in you, which is why you don't have confidence in yourself.

   c. You think you are going to flunk out of school.

   d. Your parents really hate you, don't they?

9. "If I could just get over this slump, maybe I could make it. Things have been bad for me before, and somehow I managed to muddle through. If I can just hang on, maybe things will turn out all right."

   a. You are going through a slump, and you have been through slumps before, and maybe things will turn out all right.

   b. You want to get out of this slump.

   c. You are confident about the future.

   d. You feel some hope that if you just stay with it, things will work out for you, as they have in the past.

Types of Phrasing of an Understanding Response

After you have completed Answer Sheet A, study and discuss the following categories of the understanding response. Do not proceed until you are sure you understand each of the categories.

In the beginning of this section we discussed four aspects of an understanding response: content, depth, meaning, and language. The above questionnaire focuses upon two of these dimensions—content (either identical or paraphrased) and meaning (either partial or additional). In this questionnaire, all of the alternatives following the statements are so phrased as to appear to be attempts to communicate an understanding intent. For each statement, however, the alternatives differ in the following ways:

Identical content (I): a response in which the attempt at understanding is implemented in large part by simply repeating the same words used by the sender

Paraphrasing content (P): a response in which the attempt at understanding is implemented by rephrasing in fresh words the gist of the sender's expression without changing either the meaning or the feeling tone

Shallow or partial meaning (S): a response in which the attempt at understanding is implemented in a limited way by bringing in only a part of what the sender expressed or by undercutting or watering down the feeling tone expressed

Additional meaning (A): a response in which the attempt at understanding actually goes beyond the meaning of the sender and adds meaning not expressed by the sender.

After you have finished the procedure for scoring both answer sheets, mark the frequency with which each member of the group used each type of phrasing. In the group, discuss the results summarized in Table 7.2 and the consequences of using each type of phrasing. The following questions may be helpful:

TABLE 7.2:   FREQUENCY WITH WHICH THE GROUP MEMBERS USED EACH TYPE OF RESPONSE

Frequency of response	Type of responses			
	I	P	S	A
0–1	———	———	———	———
2–3	———	———	———	———
4–5	———	———	———	———
6–7	———	———	———	———
8–9	———	———	———	———

1. What type of phrasing was most commonly used by the members of the group?

2. What would be your feelings if a person used each type of phrasing in discussing your problems and concerns?

3. How may I develop my skills in paraphrasing to ensure the most effective phrasing of my response?

Exercise 7.4: Practicing the Phrasing of an Understanding Response

The next exercise provides you with practice in the phrasing of an understanding response. The exercise has two parts: one in which you are given a problem statement and you write down what you would say, and one in which you and another person make statements and practice with each other giving an appropriately phrased understanding response. The exercise is:

1. Read the following paragraphs and write an understanding response for each one. Do this by yourself. Be sure your response matches the paragraph in content, depth, language, and meaning.

   a. "I'm really upset! That stupid professor gave me a C on my research paper! I worked on it for 6 weeks, and it was twice as long as the paper Joe turned in, yet he got an A. That paper represented a lot of learning on my part. And he had the nerve to give me a C! What does he want anyway? Or is it that I'm just dumb?"

   b. "I need your help. There's a new girl who just moved in next door to you that I think I know. She may be a girl I dated several years ago; but I'm not sure since I haven't been able to get a close look at her. If she is the same girl I want to meet her; if she isn't the same girl, I don't want to meet her. Can you find out her name, telephone number, and where she grew up?"

2. Divide into pairs. Discuss each other's responses and make suggestions as to how they might be improved.

3. Think of a problem you are having with a friend or a member of your family. It may be a major problem or a minor problem. Each person in the pair should share his problem; the receiver gives an understanding response which is appropriate in content, depth, language, and meaning.

4. In the pairs, give each other feedback concerning the appropriateness of the content, depth, language, and meaning of the understanding responses. You may wish to continue practicing the phrasing of the understanding response until you have mastered it to your satisfaction. This can be done by consciously

applying it in your everyday conversations or by pairing up with a member of your group and setting specific practice times for the two of you to increase your skills.

Exercise 7.5: Expressing Acceptance Verbally

The purpose of this exercise is to give you an opportunity to practice communicating acceptance to another person. The skills involved in expressing acceptance are listening with understanding and expressing warmth. In this exercise you will conduct a discussion in which you practice listening with understanding and the expression of warmth. The procedure is:

1. Divide into trios. Two people will engage in a discussion; one person will observe. The role of the discussants is to express acceptance to each other. The role of the observer is to give the two discussants feedback concerning how successfully they communicated acceptance to each other. An observation sheet is provided below for the observer's use.

2. The two discussants spend 10 minutes discussing how their current close friendships were initiated and developed. Or they may discuss any topic that is of real interest to the two of them; do not spend more than 1 minute, however, on the selection of a topic to discuss. During the discussion the two participants

OBSERVATION SHEET: EXPRESSING ACCEPTANCE

Listening with understanding	*Person 1*	*Person 2*
Paraphrased other's feelings and ideas in own words	———	———
Did not indicate approval or disapproval	———	———
Depth of response was appropriate	———	———
Did not add or subtract meaning	———	———
Did not change the feeling tone	———	———
Negotiated for meaning	———	———
Language was understandable and appropriate	———	———
Did a perception check for other's feelings	———	———

Expressing warmth	*Person 1*	*Person 2*
Direct description of own feelings	———	———
Tone of voice	———	———
Facial expression	———	———
Posture	———	———
Eye contact	———	———
Touching	———	———
Gestures	———	———
Spatial distance	———	———
Congruence between verbal and nonverbal expressions of feelings	———	———

should be practicing both listening and understanding and expressing warmth. To listen with understanding is to paraphrase the other person's expressed feelings and ideas in your own words without any indication of approval or disapproval; this involves listening for meaning as well as listening to the other's words. To express warmth is to describe your feelings and to use the nonverbal cues of facial expression, tone of voice, posture, and so on in your discussion with your partner.

3. At the end of the 10-minute discussion, the observer and the two discussants give the two discussants feedback about how well they expressed acceptance to each other. Be specific.

4. Next, the trio switches roles so that one of the former discussants is now the observer, and the other two members conduct a discussion. Follow the instructions given in step 2. This time discuss what your greatest fears and hopes are about initiating friendships.

5. Conduct a feedback session according to the instructions given in step 3.

6. Switch roles once more and conduct a discussion on why you need friends. Follow the instructions given in steps 2 and 3.

Exercise 7.6: Level of Acceptance in Your Group

What is the level of acceptance in your group? You may wish to get everyone's opinion by completing the following questionnaire and summarizing the results. The purpose of this exercise is to provide a way in which the level of acceptance in your group may be assessed and discussed. The procedure is:

1. Each member of the group fills out the questionnaire below. Questionnaires should be unsigned so that no one's responses can be identified.

2. The results are tabulated in the Summary Table that follows the questionnaire.

3. Discuss the conclusions that can be drawn from the results.

4. What is contributing to the present high or low level of acceptance in the group?

5. How may the level of acceptance in the group be increased?

Questionnaire: Level of Acceptance

Think about the ways in which the members of your group normally behave toward you. In the parentheses in front of the items below, place the number corresponding to your perceptions of the group as a whole, using the following scale:

5 = They *always* behave this way.

4 = They *typically* behave this way.

3 = They *usually* behave this way.

2 = They *seldom* behave this way.

1 = They *rarely* behave this way.

0 = They *never* behave this way.

My fellow group members:

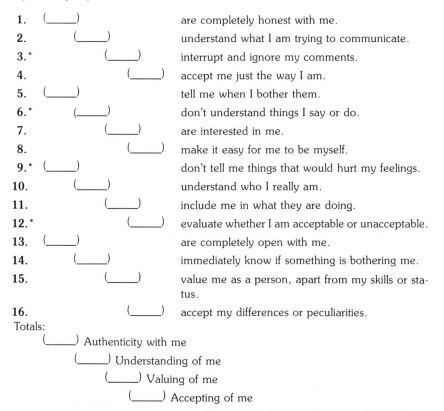

1. (_____)   are completely honest with me.
2.   (_____)   understand what I am trying to communicate.
3.*   (_____)   interrupt and ignore my comments.
4.   (_____)   accept me just the way I am.
5. (_____)   tell me when I bother them.
6.*   (_____)   don't understand things I say or do.
7.   (_____)   are interested in me.
8.   (_____)   make it easy for me to be myself.
9.* (_____)   don't tell me things that would hurt my feelings.
10.   (_____)   understand who I really am.
11.   (_____)   include me in what they are doing.
12.*   (_____)   evaluate whether I am acceptable or unacceptable.
13. (_____)   are completely open with me.
14.   (_____)   immediately know if something is bothering me.
15.   (_____)   value me as a person, apart from my skills or status.
16.   (_____)   accept my differences or peculiarities.

Totals:

(_____) Authenticity with me

(_____) Understanding of me

(_____) Valuing of me

(_____) Accepting of me

Add the total number of points in each column. Items with starred (*) numbers are reversed in the scoring—subtract from 5 the rating given to each before adding the totals for each column.

SUMMARY TABLE: LEVEL OF ACCEPTANCE

Score	Authenticity	Understanding	Valuing	Accepting
0–4				
5–8				
9–12				
13–16				
17–20				

CHAPTER REVIEW

Test your understanding of helpful listening and responding by answering true or false to the following statements. Answers are at the end of the chapter.

True	False	1.	The aim of a receiver is to help the other person come to her own understanding and solution to her problem.
True	False	2.	If your underlying attitude is not one of acceptance and liking, you won't be able to make a helpful response.
True	False	3.	The most helpful response to help people explore their feelings and thoughts is the probing response.
True	False	4.	"How do you feel about your job?" is an example of a closed question.
True	False	5.	"Do you like your teacher?" should be changed to "You like your teacher" to become a reflective statement.
True	False	6.	There is no difference between how you see and feel about a situation and how another person sees and feels about it.
True	False	7.	Just repeating what the sender says is effective paraphrasing.
True	False	8.	When you interpret the significance of a message, you are adding to the meaning of it.
True	False	9.	You will communicate more accurately if you use simple language in your responses.
True	False	10.	Responses that are slightly lighter in meaning than the sender's message are most effective.
True	False	11.	If you paraphrase and express warmth and liking, you will be able to convince other people that you accept them.
True	False	12.	If you are to accept another person, you must approve of the things he or she does.

Indicate below which skills you have mastered and which ones you need to work on further.

1. I have mastered the following:
   ____ Using the evaluative response
   ____ Using the interpretive response
   ____ Using the supportive response
   ____ Using the probing response
   ____ Using the understanding response
   ____ Matching the message in paraphrasing content
   ____ Matching the message in depth
   ____ Matching the message in meaning
   ____ Matching the message in language
   ____ Expressing acceptance verbally
2. I need more work on:
   ____ Using the evaluative response
   ____ Using the interpretive response
   ____ Using the supportive response
   ____ Using the probing response
   ____ Using the understanding response
   ____ Matching the message in paraphrasing content
   ____ Matching the message in depth
   ____ Matching the message in meaning
   ____ Matching the message in language
   ____ Expressing acceptance verbally

At this point, you should understand and be able to use appropriately evaluative, interpretative, supportive, probing, and understanding responses. You should understand how to make reflective statements and ask open questions. You should also be able to match a message in content, depth, meaning, and language. The next chapter will expand on an important factor in being able to respond helpfully to others: the acceptance of others—and of yourself.

ANSWERS

Comprehension Test A: 1. false; 2. true; 3. true; 4 false; 5. true; 6. false; 7. false; 8. false; 9. false; 10. true.

Comprehension Test B: 1. false; 2. true; 3. true; 4. false; 5. true; 6. true; 7. true; 8. true; 9. true; 10. true.

Chapter Review: 1. true; 2. true; 3. false; 4. false; 5. true; 6. false; 7. false; 8. true; 9. true; 10. false; 11. true; 12. false.

8 *Resolving Interpersonal Conflicts*

YOU CANNOT NOT NEGOTIATE

Not everything that is faced can be changed but
Nothing can be changed until it is faced.

James Baldwin

Betsy is frustrated. She is a member of a learning group that includes Meredith, who is the bossiest student in the class. Whenever Betsy tries to contribute to the group's work, Meredith interrupts her and takes over. No one else gets to contribute their ideas and conclusions. Betsy wants to be an equal participant in the group but believes that Meredith will not let her. What is she to do?

Storms are a natural and unavoidable aspect of the earth's weather system. Storms range in intensity from rainstorms to hurricanes. Some are accompanied by gentle rain, others by thunder and lightning. Similarly, interpersonal storms are a natural and unavoidable aspect of life that vary in intensity from mild to severe. Interpersonal storms have their origins in relationships among individuals. When individuals work together to achieve shared goals, participate in a division of labor, have complementary roles such as "student" and "teacher," and depend on each other's resources, storms are most likely to arise. Two people in a relationship are interdependent. What each does influences what the other does. But at the same time, each person has different perspectives, goals, and needs. *The combination of interdependence and differing perspectives makes it impossible for a relationship to be free from conflict.*

To understand conflicts of interests, you must first understand what wants, needs, goals, and interests are. There are many things each of us want. A *want* is a desire for something. Each person basically has a unique set of wants. A *need* is a necessity for survival. Needs are more universal. Every person needs to survive and reproduce (by using water, food, shelter, sex), belong (loving, sharing, cooperating), have power, have freedom, and have fun (Glasser, 1984). On the basis of our wants and needs we set goals. A *goal* is an ideal state of affairs that we value and are working to achieve. Our goals are related through social interdependence. When we have mutual goals we are in a cooperative relationship; when our goals are opposed, we are in a competitive relationship. Our *interests* are the potential benefits to be gained by achieving our goals.

Within relationships, the interests of the individuals at times are congruent and at times are in conflict. A *conflict of interests* exists when the actions of one person attempting to reach his or her goals prevent, block, or interfere with the actions of another person attempting to reach

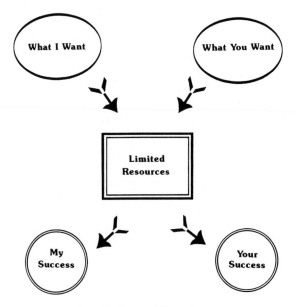

The Challenge of Negotiation

his or her goals (Deutsch, 1973). When two people both want the same library book, want to play the same position on an athletic team, want to be elected to the same student-body office, want to date the same person, or even want to use the pencil sharpener at the same time, they have a conflict of interests. In many classrooms teachers create a conflict of interests among students by having them compete for grades. *Both because they occur naturally and because they are deliberately created, conflicts of interests are common within relationships.*

Resolving a conflict of interests requires negotiation. Each person has needs and wants. To meet his/her needs and wants each person makes proposals to others. The other persons evaluate the proposal on the basis of how well it meets their needs and wants and either agree or make a counter-proposal. *Negotiation* is a process by which persons who have shared and opposed interests and want to come to an agreement try to work out a settlement (Johnson & F. Johnson, 1991; Johnson & R. Johnson, 1991). In order to resolve their different interests and continue to relate to each other in productive and fulfilling ways, negotiations must take place.

You spend a great deal of time negotiating, even when you do not think you are doing so. Every day you face the choice of negotiating agreements or engaging in hostilities. Negotiating occurs continually throughout your day, usually informally without you being fully aware

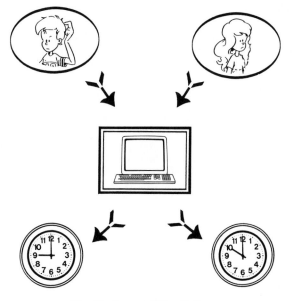

The Challenge of Negotiation

that it is going on. Conflicts continually occur, resolutions are negotiated, and individuals live with the consequences of the agreements they have made.

Exercise 8.1: Dividing Our Money

Some conflicts begin because there is only so much of something several people want, and no one can have as much as he or she would like. Salaries, promotions, office space, supplies, and even food are often the sources of such conflicts. When there is only so much money and several people have definite plans about how it should be used, not everyone has his or her plans adopted by the total group. This exercise focuses on such a conflict. It requires three people to divide some money two ways.

If you participate actively in this lesson, you will become more aware of how you manage such conflicts. You will also be able to give other participants feedback on how they act during such conflicts. The specific procedure is:

1. Divide into groups of three. Each person contributes twenty-five cents to the group; the seventy-five cents is placed in a pool.

2. The triad decides how to divide the money between two people. Only two people can receive money. The group has 15 minutes to make this decision. The group cannot use any sort of "chance" procedure such as drawing straws or flipping a coin to decide which two people get what amounts of money. Side agreements—for instance, to buy a soda for the person left out—are not allowed. It is all right for one person to end up with all the money. A clear decision must be reached as to how the money is to be divided between not more than two people.

3. The purpose of this exercise is to get as much money for yourself as you can. Try to convince the other two members of your triad that you should receive all the money. Tell them you are broke, poor, smarter than they are, or more deserving of the money. Tell them you will put it to better use or will give it to charity. If the other two people make an agreement to divide the money between themselves, offer one of them a better deal. For example, if they agree to split the money fifty-fifty, tell one person that you will let that person have fifty cents and will take only twenty-five cents if he or she agrees to split the money with you.

4. The majority rules. Whenever two people make a firm agreement to split the money a certain way, the decision is made. Be sure, however, to give the third person a chance to offer one of the two a better deal.

5. As soon as a decision is made, write your answers to these questions. Work by yourself.

   a. What were my feelings during the decision making?

b. How did I act during the decision making? What are the ways I handled the situation? Did I give up? Did I try to persuade others to my point of view? Did I try to take the money by force?

c. How would my conflict strategies be described during the decision making?

6. In your group of three, give each other feedback describing how you saw each other's actions during the decision making. Use the rules for constructive feedback. Make sure all members of your triad receive feedback.

7. Combine into a group of six and discuss the following questions.

a. What were the feelings present in each triad during the decision making?

b. How did members act in each triad during the decision making?

c. What conflict styles were present in each triad during the decision making?

d. What did we learn about conflict from the lesson?

Exercise 8.2: Nonverbal Conflict

Before you begin these exercises, please review the discussion of nonverbal exercises in chapter 3. The following nonverbal exercises dealing with various aspects of conflicts may be helpful in clarifying your feelings about conflict and your style of managing conflicts:

1. *Pushing and shoving:* Lock fingers with another person, with arms extended over your heads. Push against each other, trying to drive the other to the wall.

2. *Thumb wrestling:* Lock fingers with another person with your thumbs straight up. Tap your thumbs together three times and then try to pin the other's thumb so that the other cannot move it.

3. *Slapping hands:* Person A puts her hands out, palms down. Person B extends his hands, palms up, under Person A's hands. The object of the exercise is for Person B to try to slap the hands of Person A by quickly moving his hands from the bottom to the top. As soon as Person B makes a move, Person A tries to pull her hands out of the way before Person B can slap them.

4. *Pushing down to the floor and helping up:* In pairs, one person tries to push the other person down to the floor. No wrestling, but the person being pushed may resist if he or she wants to. After the person is pushed down to the floor, the pusher has to help the pushed person up. The person being helped up may still resist if he or she wants to.

5. *Unwrapping:* A member who is having internal conflicts is asked to make herself into a tight ball. Another person is chosen by her to "unwrap" her, or to open her up completely. The member may struggle against being unwrapped, or she may submit. Other members of the group may join in, some trying to keep the person wrapped and others trying to unwrap her. Or everyone in the group may pair up and take turns being unwrapped and unwrapping.

Exercise 8.3: My Conflict Strategies

Different people learn different ways of managing conflicts. The strategies you use to manage conflicts may be quite different from those used by your friends and acquaintances. This exercise gives you an opportunity to increase your awareness of what conflict strategies you use and how they compare with the strategies used by other people. The procedure is:

1. Form into groups of six. Make sure you know the other members of the group. Do not join a group of strangers.

2. Working by yourself, complete the questionnaire, "How I Act in Conflicts."

3. Working by yourself, read the next section, "Conflict Strategies: What Are You Like?" Then take out five slips of paper. Write the names of the other five members of your group on the slips of paper. On each slip of paper write one name.

4. On each slip of paper write the conflict strategy that most fits the actions of the person named.

5. After all group members are finished, pass out your slips of paper to the persons whose names are on them. You should end up with five slips of paper, each containing a description of your conflict style as seen by the other group members. Each member of your group should end up with five slips of paper describing his or her conflict strategy.

6. Score your questionnaire. Rank the five conflict strategies from the ones you use most to the ones you use least. This will give you an indication of how you see your own conflict strategy. The second most frequently used strategy represents your back-up strategy to be used if your first one fails.

7. Draw names to see who is first. Then proceed around the group in a clockwise direction. The first person describes the results of his or her questionnaire. This is the person's view of his or her own conflict strategies. Then the person reads each of the five slips of paper on which are written the views of the group members about his or her conflict strategy. Then the person asks the groups to give specific examples of how they have seen him or her act in conflicts. The group members should use the rules for constructive feedback. Repeat this procedure for every member of the group.

8. In your group, discuss the strengths and weaknesses of each of the conflict strategies.

How I Act in Conflicts

The proverbs listed below can be thought of as descriptions of some of the different strategies for resolving conflicts. Proverbs state traditional wisdom. These proverbs reflect traditional wisdom for resolving conflicts. Read each of the proverbs carefully. Using the scale given below indicate how typical each proverb is of your actions in a conflict.

5 = Very typical of the way I act in a conflict

4 = Frequently typical of the way I act in a conflict

3 = Sometimes typical of the way I act in a conflict

2 = Seldom typical of the way I act in a conflict

1 = Never typical of the way I act in a conflict

_____ 1. It is easier to refrain than to retreat from a quarrel.

_____ 2. If you cannot make a person think as you do, make him or her do as you think.

_____ 3. Soft words win hard hearts.

_____ 4. You scratch my back, I'll scratch yours.

_____ 5. Come now and let us reason together.

_____ 6. When two quarrel, the person who keeps silent first is the most praise-worthy.

_____ 7. Might overcomes right.

_____ 8. Smooth words make smooth ways.

_____ 9. Better half a loaf than no bread at all.

_____ 10. Truth lies in knowledge, not in majority opinion.

_____ 11. He who fights and runs away lives to fight another day.

_____ 12. He hath conquered well that hath made his enemies flee.

_____ 13. Kill your enemies with kindness.

_____ 14. A fair exchange brings no quarrel.

_____ 15. No person has the final answer but every person has a piece to contribute.

_____ 16. Stay away from people who disagree with you.

_____ 17. Fields are won by those who believe in writing.

_____ 18. Kind words are worth much and cost little.

_____ 19. Tit for tat is fair play.

_____ 20. Only the person who is willing to give up his or her monopoly on truth can ever profit from the truths that others hold.

_____ 21. Avoid quarrelsome people as they will only make your life miserable.

_____ 22. A person who will not flee will make others flee.

_____ 23. Soft words ensure harmony.

_____ 24. One gift for another makes good friends.

_____ 25. Bring your conflicts into the open and face them directly; only then will the best solution be discovered.

_____ 26. The best way of handling conflicts is to avoid them.

_____ 27. Put your foot down where you mean to stand.

_____ 28. Gentleness will triumph over anger.

____ **29.** Getting part of what you want is better than not getting anything at all.

____ **30.** Frankness, honesty, and trust will move mountains.

____ **31.** There is nothing so important you have to fight for it.

____ **32.** There are two kinds of people in the world, the winners and the losers.

____ **33.** When one hits you with a stone, hit him or her with a piece of cotton.

____ **34.** When both people give in halfway, a fair settlement is achieved.

____ **35.** By digging and digging, the truth is discovered.

Exercise 8.4: Confronting the Opposition

To resolve a conflict constructively, you and the other person have to discuss the conflict and negotiate a solution. For such a discussion to begin, one person must confront the other. Not all conflicts, however, can be successfully negotiated, and there may be times when it is advisable not to confront the opposition. The purpose of this exercise is to give you three specific examples of conflicts so that you can decide what you would do to make sure the conflicts are managed constructively. The procedure for the exercise is:

1. Working by yourself, read the first example of a conflict. Then rank the five alternatives from the best (1) to the worst (5) way to resolve the conflict. In deciding what is the best strategy to use, take into account the following:

    a. What are the person's goals?

    b. How important are the goals to the person?

    c. How important is the relationship to the person?

    d. What is the best way to:

        (1) improve the ability of the two people to relate to each other?

        (2) make their attitudes toward each other more positive?

        (3) reach an agreement that is satisfying to both people?

        (4) improve their ability to resolve future conflicts with each other?

    e. What is the most realistic thing to do?

2. Repeat this process for the second and third examples of conflicts.

3. Form a group of six members. In your group, rank the five alternative courses of action for the first example from the best (1) to the worst (5). Take into account the points listed in item 1.

4. Working as a group, list the interpersonal skills the person needs to discuss the conflict in a constructive way. You may wish to refer to the list of interpersonal skills on pages 361-365.

5. Repeat this procedure for the second and third examples.

6. Be prepared to report to the other groups the following:

    a. In what order did the group rank the five alternatives for each conflict example?

    b. What reasons does your group have for your ranking?

    c. What interpersonal skills are needed for a constructive discussion of the conflict?

Mr. Smith

You are a salesperson for a tire company. You work under a highly emotional sales manager, with whom you have a formal relationship. He calls you by your first name, but you call him "Mr. Smith." When he gets upset, he becomes angry and abusive. He browbeats you and your co-workers, and makes insulting remarks and judgments. These rages occur approximately once a week and last for about an hour. Most of the time, Mr. Smith is distant and inoffensive. He will tolerate no back-talk at any time. So far, you and your co-workers have suffered in silence during his outbursts. Jobs are scarce, and you have a spouse and a seven-month-old son to support. But you feel like a doormat and really do not like what Mr. Smith says when he is angry. The situation is making you irritable. Your anger at Mr. Smith is causing you to lose your temper more and more with your co-workers and family. Today he starts in again, and you have had it!

Rank the following five courses of action from 1 to 5. Put a 1 by the course of action that seems most likely to lead to beneficial results. Put a 2 by the next most constructive course of action and so forth. Be realistic!

_____ I try to avoid Mr. Smith. I am silent whenever we are together. I show a lack of interest whenever we speak. I want nothing to do with him for the time being. I try to cool down while I stay away from him. I try never to mention anything that might get him angry.

_____ I lay it on the line. I tell Mr. Smith I am fed up with his abuse. I tell him he is vicious and unfair. I tell him he had better start controlling his feelings and statements because I'm not going to take being insulted by him any more! Whether he likes it or not he has to shape up. I'm going to make him stop or else I'll quit.

_____ I bite my tongue. I keep my feelings to myself. I hope that he will find out how his actions are hurting our department without my telling him. My anger toward him frightens me. So I force it out of my mind. I try to be friendly, and I try to do nice things for him so he won't treat me this way. If I tried to tell him how I feel, he would only be angry and abuse me more.

_____ I try to bargain with him. I tell him that if he stops abusing me I will increase my sales effort. I seek a compromise that will stop his actions. I try to think of what I can do for him that will be worth it to him to change his actions. I tell him that other people get upset with his actions. I try to persuade him to agree to stop abusing me in return for something I can do for him.

_____ I call attention to the conflict between us. I describe how I see his actions. I describe my angry and upset feelings. I try to begin a discussion in which we can look for a way to reduce (1) his rages and (2) my resentment. I try to see things from his viewpoint. I seek a solution that allows him to blow off steam without being abusive to me. I try to figure out what I'm telling myself about his actions that is causing me to feel angry and upset. I ask him how he feels about my giving him feedback.

Ralph Overtrain

You work as a computer technician repairing computers. You make service calls to the customers of your company. Ralph Overtrain is one of your closest co-workers. He does the same type of work that you do. The two of you are often assigned to work together on large repair projects. You are married and have two children. Ralph is single and often has trouble with his girl friend. For the past several weeks, he has asked you to do part of his repair work because he feels too depressed and upset to concentrate on his work. You have agreed to such requests. Your wife is sick now, and you want to take some time off to visit her in the hospital. You ask Ralph if he would do part of your repair work so you can slip away and visit your wife. He refuses, saying that he is too busy and that it is your work, so you should do it. He says he sees no reason why he should do work you are getting paid for. You get more and more angry at Ralph. You see his actions as being completely selfish and ungrateful!

Rank the following five courses of action from 1 to 5. Put a 1 by the course of action that seems most likely to lead to beneficial results. Put a 2 by the next most constructive course of action, and so forth. Be realistic!

_____ I try to avoid Ralph. I am silent whenever we are together. I show a lack of interest whenever we speak. I want nothing to do with him for the time being. I try to cool down while I stay away from him. I try never to mention anything that might make him angry or remind me of his ungratefulness.

_____ I lay it on the line. I tell Ralph that I am fed up with his ungratefulness. I tell him he is selfish and a deadbeat. And I tell him he had better start paying back the favors I have done for him because I am not going to help him if he will not help me. Whether he likes it or not, he is going to do part of my work so I can visit my wife. I'm going to make him pay his debts to me.

_____ I bite my tongue. I keep my feelings to myself. I hope he will find out his behavior is wrong without my having to tell him. My anger toward him frightens me. So I force it out of my mind and try to be friendly. I try to do nice things for him so he will be willing to do a favor for me in the future when I need him to. If I tried to tell him how I feel, he would only be angry. Then he would be less likely to do me favors when I need him to in the future.

_____ I try to bargain with him. I tell him that if he does my work this time, I will do part of his work tomorrow. I seek a compromise that will allow me to visit my wife. I try to think of what I can do for him that will be worth it to him to take part of my work today. I tell him that other people don't see him as being reasonable and friendly. I try to persuade him to agree to take part of my work today in return for something I can do for him.

_____ I call attention to the conflict between us. I describe how I see his actions. I describe my anger and upset feelings. I try to begin a discussion in which we can look for a way to be more cooperative regarding each other's needs and to reduce my anger. I try to see things from his viewpoint. I seek a solution that allows him to feel he is only doing his work while at the same time allows me to visit my wife in the hospital. I try to figure out what I'm telling myself about his actions that is causing me to feel angry and upset. I ask him how he feels about my giving him feedback.

Donna Jones

In your upper-grade class this year, you have a student, Donna Jones, who seems to dislike you and everything about school. When you are interacting with her you can feel the resentment. She never seems to do anything overtly, but other students have reported incidences of Donna's making faces behind your back and making rude remarks about you and your assignments outside of class. On the morning of the math test, Donna has just dropped her papers on the floor for the third time and is disrupting the work of the other students. You have had enough, so you approach Donna and tell her to keep her papers on her desk, as she is interrupting the work of other students. As you turn to walk away, you notice grins on the faces of several students in front of you, and out of the corner of your eye you see Donna standing up and mimicking you behind your back.

Rank the five alternatives. Be realistic!

_____ I would ignore Donna and go back to my desk. I would arrange a way to seat her away from most of the other students and try to avoid any contact with her unless absolutely necessary. I would avoid any situation that could lead to conflict and hope that she changes as a result.

_____ I would turn around and "nail her" in the act. I'd tell her that I was fed up with her attitude and that it is time to shape up or ship out. If she's not able to work well in the classroom, she may find the principal's office more to her liking. Being firm and laying it on the line will change her behavior in a hurry.

_____ I would ignore Donna for the present, as I want to win her over to my side. Later I'd engage her in friendly conversation, find out what her hobbies are and about any pets she might have, establishing friendly feelings between us. She would then try harder on the tasks and not disrupt the class by ridiculing me anymore.

_____ I would take her up to my desk immediately and make a bargain with her that if she will stop disrupting the class and try to do the work, I'll let her be recess monitor for the week (something she has wanted to do for some time). I would continue to look for ways to trade off things she wanted to do for appropriate behavior in class.

_____ I would take her up to my desk and call attention to the conflict between us by describing how I saw her behavior and telling her that it makes me angry and upset. I'd explain what the problem is from my perspective and its effect on the other students and discuss possible solutions. I would ask for her perception of the conflict and what her feelings are, and I would keep discussing the situation until we had a solution that we both liked.

Exercise 8.5: Role Playing the Conflicts

Now that you have discussed the three examples of conflicts, it may be helpful to role play them. The purpose of this exercise is to role play the entire negotiation of a solution of the conflict between the two people. The procedure is:

1. Form groups of six. Take the first conflict, between the salesperson and Mr. Smith. One member should volunteer to play the part of each character. There are three conflict episodes, so each group member will play one role during the three role-playing episodes.

2. Spend up to 10 minutes role playing the conflict. Begin with the initiation of the strategy chosen by the group to be the most effective and continue through the entire negotiation of a solution to the conflict. The group members who are not playing a role observe in order to discuss the effectiveness of the person's actions in resolving the conflict.

3. In the group of six, discuss the role-playing episode:

    a. What were the strategies used to manage the conflict constructively?

    b. What interpersonal skills were used?

    c. What interpersonal skills were not used but might have been helpful?

    d. What changes in strategies would you make if you actually were in this situation?

4. Repeat this procedure for the second and third examples of conflicts.

5. What conclusions can your group make about managing conflicts on the basis of your role playing? Be ready to share your conclusions with the other groups.

Conflict Strategies

When you become engaged in a conflict, two major concerns you have to take into account are:

1. *Reaching an agreement that satisfies one's needs and meets one's goals.* This is why one negotiates. Each person has personal goals that he

or she wishes to achieve. You are in conflict because you have a goal or interests that conflict with another person's goal or interests. Your goal may be placed on a continuum between being of little importance to you to being highly important.

2. *Maintaining an appropriate relationship with the other person.* Some relationships are temporary while some are permanent. Some people you interact with infrequently while others you interact with several times a day. Within career and family settings you need to maintain caring and committed relationships so you can work together effectively to achieve mutual goals. With a store clerk you see only once, a pleasant but more impersonal interaction may be appropriate. Your relationship with the other person may be placed on a continuum between being of little importance to you to being highly important.

How important your personal goals are to you and how important the relationship is perceived to be affect how you act in a conflict. Given these two concerns within a relationship, there are five basic strategies that may be used to manage conflicts:

1. *The Turtle (Withdrawing).* If you act like a turtle, you give up both your goals and the relationship and, therefore, you avoid the other person and the issue. Avoiding a hostile stranger may be the best thing to do. Or you may wish to withdraw from a conflict until you and the other person have calmed down and are in control of your feelings.

2. *The Shark (Forcing).* If you act like a shark, you try to achieve your goals at all costs, demanding that the other person let you have your way, no matter how much it hurts the relationship. When the goal is very important but the relationship is not, such as when you are buying a used car, you may want to act like a shark and force. Never use forcing with someone you will have to relate to again soon.

3. *The Teddy Bear (Smoothing)*. If you act like a teddy bear, you give up your goals in order to maintain the relationship at the highest level possible. When the goal is of no importance to you but the relationship is of high importance, you may want to act like a teddy bear and smooth. When a colleague feels strongly about something, and you could care less, smoothing is a good idea. When you are smoothing, do so with good humor. Be pleasant about it. At times, to smooth you may need to apologize. Saying "I'm sorry" does not mean "I'm wrong." "I'm sorry" lets the other person know that you are sorry about the situation. When you think the other person's interests are much stronger or important than yours, smooth and give the other person their way.

4. *The Fox (Compromising)*. If you act like a fox, you give up part of your goals and sacrifice part of the relationship in order to reach an agreement. When both the goal and the relationship are moder-

ately important to you and it appears that both you and the other person cannot get what you want, you may want to negotiate like a fox. When there is a limited amount of money, and both you and a fellow employee want a large raise, for example, negotiating a compromise may be the best way to resolve the conflict. You can meet in the middle, each taking half, or flip a coin and let chance decide who will get their way.

5. *The Owl (Negotiating).* If you act like an owl, you initiate negotiations aimed at ensuring that you and the other person both fully meet your goals and maintain the relationship at the highest level possible. An agreement is sought that satisfies both you and the other person and resolves any tensions and negative feelings between the two of you. When both the goal and the relationship are highly important to you, you may want to act like an owl. Face the conflict. Negotiate to solve the problem. Think of solutions that will give both you and the other person what you want and will keep the relationship positive.

Each conflict strategy has its place. You need to be able to use any one of the five, depending on your goals and the relationship. In deciding which of the five strategies to use within any one conflict, there are six rules to consider (Johnson & Johnson, 1991):

1. *Do not withdraw from or ignore the conflict.* The procedure for withdrawing is to walk away and avoid the other person and your needs and goals related to the conflict. Refuse to identify and talk about the issue. Leave if the other person insists on doing so. In an ongoing relationship, withdrawal is inadvisable unless it is temporary in order to be able to negotiate more constructively at a later time.

High
Importance

R
E
L
A
T
I
O
N
S
H
I
P
S

Low
Importance

GOALS

High
Importance

2. *Do not engage in "win-lose" negotiations.* Voltaire once stated, "I know I am among civilized men because they are fighting so savagely." What he was describing was forcing. The procedure for forcing is to bring up the issue, take an extreme opening position, and refuse to compromise or reconsider until you absolutely have to. Forcing, however, is inappropriate within long-term relationships.

3. *Assess for smoothing.* Appropriate smoothing occurs when two people share mutual goals, each determines whose interests are stronger or more important, and one person gives up his or her interests to help the other. This is known as *one-step negotiating.*

4. *Compromise when time is short.* When time is short, and an ideal agreement cannot be discovered, compromise.

5. *Initiate problem-solving negotiations.* When both the issue and the relationship are important, you should negotiate. When the time is right, approach the other person and describe the conflict and your feelings. Invite him or her to do the same. Focus on the problem, not the person. Define the conflict in as small and specific a way as possible.

6. *Use your sense of humor.* Appropriate humor helps both you and the other person to manage the conflict constructively.

In following those rules there are a number of guidelines to keep in mind. First, *competent individuals use all five strategies, depending on the situation.* You need to practice all five strategies until they are thoroughly mastered. Although smoothing, negotiation, and compromise should dominate conflicts, there are times when forcing and withdrawal may prove useful. Second, *the most competent business executives, managers, and supervisors tend to use negotiations and smoothing as their dominant conflict strategies.* They tend to be highly relationship oriented, negotiating when the goals and needs involved in the conflict are important to them and smoothing when they are not. Incompetent business executives, managers, and supervisors tend to use forcing and withdrawal most frequently. *Within schools, teachers and administrators typically use forcing and withdrawal as their most frequent strategies.* When faced with misbehaving students teachers often first try to force the student to behave and then to expel the student from the classroom or school (which is a form of withdrawal). Thus, you will want to learn how to use all five strategies appropriately, especially negotiation and smoothing. Being able to choose how you wish to manage your conflicts empowers you considerably.

In some ways the five strategies present a simplified view of how most conflicts are managed. The complexities of the interaction between two individuals far exceed their initial approaches to the conflict. Conflicts can deteriorate. You need to be aware of your backup strategies as well as your dominant one. *Of most importance is the second most frequently used strategy, as that is the one you will tend to use when you are highly anxious and upset.* Within most conflicts there are initial strategies followed by backup strategies followed by other strategies that are based on what the other person is doing. You may wish to negotiate but, when faced with a colleague who is forcing, you may force back.

The use of certain strategies may increase the probability that other strategies will appear. Withdrawal, for example, often deteriorates into forcing. When individuals cannot withdraw any more, when they feel backed into a corner and have to deal with the conflict, they are likely to strike out and try to force the other person into letting them have their way. When a person attempts to smooth, and the other person responds with forcing and anger, withdrawal may follow. That, in turn, may be followed by forcing if the other person continues to be angry and competitive. Forcing creates counter-forcing. Even negotiations may deteriorate into forcing when (a) the timing is wrong and the other person does not respond constructively or (b) the person negotiating lacks the skills necessary to keep the management of the conflict constructive. When time is short, negotiating sometimes deteriorates into compromise. *The best time to confront is when the issue is small, concrete, and immediate.* This way issues are dealt with when they are most easily resolved.

Most of the time, you will want to act like either an owl and negotiate or like a teddy bear and smooth. In most conflicts, these are the two strategies that work best. When the goal is important to you, negotiate. When it is not, smooth. Because you almost always need to maintain

good relationships, you will rarely want to force or withdraw. Compromising is usually only helpful if negotiating has failed or when there is not enough time to resolve the conflict. Ideally, however, you will be able to use any of the five conflict strategies, depending on the situation. It is important that you can use each strategy skillfully.

One of the most difficult aspects of initiating problem-solving negotiations is managing emotions. Managing anger is especially problematic. If you try to hide it, very likely the problem will not be correctly identified and a wise agreement will not be reached. But if you express your anger destructively, the relationship may be severely damaged if not ruined. Anger is the focus of the next chapter.

COMPREHENSION TEST A

Test your understanding of the steps for resolving a conflict by taking the following quiz. Answers are at the end of the chapter.

1. Match the conflict strategy with the best situation for using it:

    ____ Goal and relationship very impor-   **a.** Withdraw
    tant

    ____ Goal and relationship moderately   **b.** Force
    important

    ____ Goal and relationship not impor-   **c.** Smooth
    tant

    ____ Goal important, relationship not   **d.** Compromise
    important

    ____ Goal not important, relationship   **e.** Confront
    important

True   False   2. It is a good idea to act the same way in every conflict.

True   False   3. The conflict strategy you adopt will depend on how important it is to you to maintain a good relationship with the other person and to achieve your personal goals.

True   False   4. The two most effective conflict strategies are confronting and compromising.

True   False   5. Defining the conflict carefully and constructively will make it easier to resolve.

True   False   6. Your ability to come up with satisfactory solutions depends on how well you understand how the other person's thoughts, feelings, and needs are different from yours.

True   False   7. The important thing about viewing the conflict from the other person's perspective is that you can see how to get her to agree to your point of view.

True   False   8. If the other person feels understood, he will not try to see your point of view.

True   False   9. By increasing the costs of continuing the conflict or by increasing the gains for resolving it, the motivation to resolve the conflict can be increased.

True   False   10. A conflict agreement should specify a joint position, future changed behaviors, and plans for dealing with behavior slips and for continuing the relationship.

Exercise 8.6: Which Strategy Would You Use?

1. Pick a real conflict that a member of your group is involved in. Write out five different ways of managing the conflict (forcing, withdrawal, smoothing, compromise, confrontation). Number the strategies from 1 to 5 and then number five spots in the room from 1 to 5.

2. Participants think of which strategy they would use. After considering the pros and cons of each option, they write down their choice and the reasons why it is the best option on the sheet of paper.

3. All participants signify their choice by going to the spot in the room that represents the option they have chosen. They pair up with another person who made the same choice, compare and combine their reasons, and make a list of three reasons why their choice is the best strategy. Everyone needs a copy of the reasons.

4. Form groups of up to five participants (one for each strategy). Each person presents the reasons for using the strategy he or she picked. The others listen carefully and then paraphrase the reasons. If the paraphrase is not accurate or complete, the individual presenting corrects the paraphraser. Follow the rules for good paraphrasing.

5. Participants decide if they wish to change their minds and choose a different strategy. They are asked to go to the spot they now think would be the best strategy to use. Then the number of persons in each spot is counted. The procedure may be repeated if there is time.

Paraphrasing Rules

Put yourself in the other persons's shoes. Restate the other person's ideas and feelings in your own words. State as correctly as possible the other's reasons for believing his or her option will make the best agreement. Start your remarks with *You want . . . ,* *You feel . . . ,* and *You think.* Show understanding and acceptance by nonverbal behaviors: tone of voice, facial expressions, gestures, eye contact, and posture.

Source: Johnson, D. W., and Johnson, R. T. (1991). *Teaching students to be peacemakers.* Edina, MN: Interaction Book Company.

Exercise 8.7: Using the Conflict Strategies

First, with a partner, write a story about two persons who have a conflict. *Second,* write out five different endings for the story, one for each of the strategies (Forcing, Withdrawal, Smoothing, Compromise, Confrontation). For each strategy, what would you do and what would you say? Record your answers in the table below.

USING CONFLICT STRATEGIES

	Actions and behaviors	Phrases
Withdrawal		
Forcing		
Smoothing		
Compromising		
Confronting		

You need to be competent in applying all five strategies. The most important, however, is confrontation. Working with a partner, write out what happens in each of the instances when two individuals use the different strategies listed below:

1.   Confronter against a withdrawer
2.   Smoother against a forcer
3.   Compromiser against a forcer
4.   Confronter against a smoother

Source: Johnson, D. W., and Johnson, R. T. (1991). *Teaching students to be peacemakers.* Edina, MN: Interaction Book Company.

NEGOTIATIONS TO SOLVE PROBLEMS

There are two ways to negotiate. You can negotiate to gain an advantage over another person or you can negotiate to solve a problem. If you have a short-term relationship with another person, lasting only a few minutes or a few hours, then you may decide to go for a win. But if you have a long-term relationship with a person that may last for several weeks or years or even the rest of your life, you will want to negotiate to solve problems. In *problem-solving negotiations* your goal is to discover a solution that will benefit everyone involved.

Imagine, for example, that you and another person are rowing a boat across the ocean and you cannot row the boat by yourself. You, therefore, seek food and water for the other person as well as for yourself. Otherwise, you will perish on the high seas. Most of your important relationships are cooperative—the better off, happier, and more successful the other person is, the better off, happier, and more successful you are.

When dealing with friends, classmates, colleagues, fellow employees, family members, neighbors, and bosses, you negotiate to solve the problem and, therefore, you have two concerns:

1.   *To negotiate in a way that gains benefits for all (as opposed to creating winners and losers).* Cooperators resolve conflicts as partners, side-by-side, not as adversaries. They are partners in a hard-headed, side-by-side search for a fair agreement advantageous to both sides. Otherwise you have to be careful when you pass dark alleys! One-sided settlements, imposed by whoever has the most power at the moment, are rarely stable or long lasting and typically damage the relationship.

2. *To negotiate in a way that improves the relationship and your ability to work together.* In long-term relationships, maintaining an effective working relationship is often more important than is meeting one's short-term needs and wants. In a marriage, for example, ensuring the survival of the marriage is almost always more important than meeting your immediate needs.

You negotiate differently within ongoing relationships than you do with strangers or acquaintances. Within ongoing relationships you are expected to show considerable concern about the other person's interests. You are, after all, striving to achieve the same goals, and the productivity and quality of life of both of you are affected by how the conflict is managed. Helping the other to achieve her goals is of some importance to you. How she can help you achieve your goals is of some importance to her.

Ongoing relationships are guided by a *norm of mutual responsiveness* (i.e., the rule that you should be committed to helping other people get what they want and fulfill their needs and they will do likewise). Within a work or personal relationship, there is an unspoken rule that each person is concerned about the other person's interests. A vigorous presentation of one's own interests, therefore, implies that these interests are genuinely important and that the other person should agree if it is at all possible. *One-step negotiations* occur: Each person (a) assesses the strength of his or her interests, (b) assesses the strength of the other person's interests, and (c) agrees that whoever has the greatest need is given his or her way. If both people follow the norm of mutual responsiveness, each will decide that the other person's goals are more important than his or her own goals about 50 percent of the time. If individuals are not equally responsive to each other's needs over time, the relationship breaks down.

Exercise 8.8: Which Books Do We Take?

Scientists have suddenly discovered that a large comet is going to strike the earth. All life, if not the earth itself, will be destroyed. Your group (four members) has been picked to move from Earth to a new planet. The conditions on the new planet will be harsh and difficult. You will be starting life over, trying to develop a farming and technological society at the same time. Because of the limited room in the spaceship, you can only bring three books. "Think carefully," the captain says. "You will never return to Earth. You will never be able to get more books from Earth."

1. Work by yourself. *First,* decide which book you personally want to bring. Choose the book you think will be most (a) important to save and (b) helpful to

starting a new civilization. *Second*, plan how to convince the other three members of your group that the book you have chosen should be chosen by the group.

2. Meet as a group. Only three books can go. You have to decide which three. You cannot take half of one and half of another. You cannot choose by chance (such as flipping a coin). Come to an agreement as to which three books your group will take and why. Each member should present the best case for the book he or she has chosen. The group must come to an agreement as to which three books they will take to the new planet. Each member must be able to explain the reasons why the three books were chosen.

3. As a group, *first* review *conflict of interests* and *negotiation* in this chapter. Explain how the above situation is a conflict of interests that requires negotiation to be resolved. *Second*, decide on four pieces of advice for negotiating resolutions to conflicts of interests. Write them down. Each member of the group needs a copy.

4. Each member of the group pairs up with a member of another group. Pair members (a) present the four pieces of advice decided on by their groups, (b) listen carefully to each other's presentation, and (c) take the best ideas from both groups and decide on four pieces of advice for negotiating resolutions of conflicts. Both members need a copy.

5. Return to your group of four. Members share their new lists. As a group, make a new list of four pieces of advice for negotiating resolutions to conflicts of interests, taking the best ideas from all members.

EFFECTIVE PROBLEM-SOLVING NEGOTIATING

A house divided against itself cannot stand.

Abraham Lincoln

On the eve of the Revolutionary War, English political philosopher Edmund Burke eloquently asked members of the House of Commons to head off the coming conflict by negotiating with the colonials: "All government—indeed, every human benefit and enjoyment, every virtue, and every prudent act—is founded on compromise and barter." His observation is still accurate. Negotiation is woven into the daily fabric of our lives. On the interpersonal level, we buy and sell houses and cars, jointly decide where to eat dinner, and bargain over salaries. On a larger scale, unions and management negotiate contracts, and nations arrange treaties and trade agreements. Failed negotiations may produce anything from minor inconveniences to nuclear holocaust.

Most people do not know how to negotiate effectively. Instead of negotiating, people may use such strategies to resolve their conflicts as physical violence, name calling and personal insults, or ostracizing someone until they give in. With different systems operating within a relationship, difficulties can result. Life gets much easier when all individuals are co-oriented and use the same negotiation procedure to resolve their conflicts. Since effective negotiating is typically not learned in families, from television, from movies, or from books, individuals must be directly and purposefully taught to negotiate.

Not only do individuals need to know how to negotiate effectively to improve the quality of their immediate lives, they need to know how to negotiate to be successful in their careers. Negotiating procedures and skills are keys to career success. A recent survey conducted for Accountemps (a large accounting, bookkeeping, and data processing temporary personnel service that is a division of Robert Half International Inc.) of vice presidents and personnel directors of 100 of the nation's 1,000 largest corporations found that the people who manage America's leading corporations spend over four working weeks a year dealing with the problems caused by employees who cannot resolve their conflicts with each other. In answer to the question, "What percent of management time is spent dealing with conflicts among employees," respondents revealed that executives spend an average of 9.2 percent of their time or, based on a 40-hour week, 4.6 weeks a year attempting to deal with employee conflicts and the difficulties and disruptions they cause. In 1976, the American Management Association sponsored a survey on conflict management (Thomas & Schmidt, 1976). The respondents included 116 chief executive officers, 76 vice-presidents, and 66 middle managers. They reported that about 24 percent of their time is spent dealing with conflict. The sources of conflicts they faced included misunderstandings, personality clashes, value and goal differences, substandard performance, disagreement over methods of work, lack of cooperation, competition, and noncompliance with rules and policies. School and hospital administrators, mayors, and city managers report that conflict resolution commands nearly 49 percent of their attention. In addition to taking up valuable management time, employee conflicts can seriously reduce any company's productivity and its ability to compete effectively in the marketplace. Knowing how to negotiate constructive resolutions to conflicts of interests is an essential skill that will significantly affect your career success.

Although negotiation takes place frequently every day, and knowing how to negotiate is a key to current and future quality of life and success, negotiating is not easy to do well. *There are five basic steps in negotiating a resolution to a conflict of interests:*

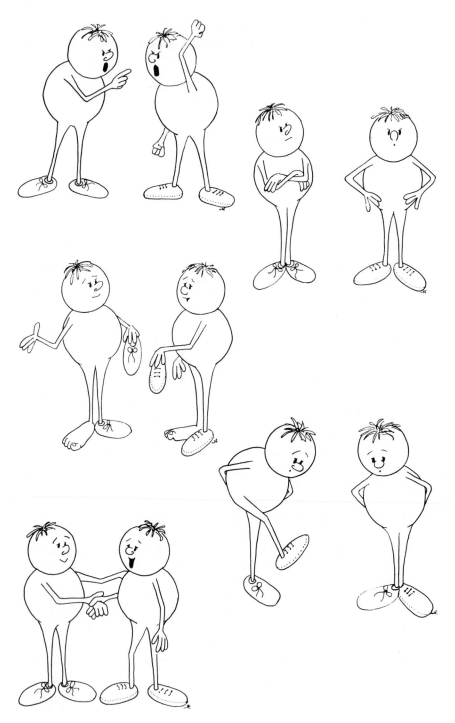

1. Jointly defining the conflict (what we want and how we feel)

2. Exchanging reasons and the rationale for our positions (our reasons why)

3. Reversing perspectives (my understanding of you, your understanding of me)

4. Inventing options for mutual benefit (three possible plans)

5. Reaching a wise agreement (let's shake)

Step One: Agreeing on a Definition of the Conflict

Sally Somnolent and Ms. Alert have a conflict. Sally sees it as very important that she get a good nap during class. Ms. Alert sees it as very important that Sally listen carefully in class to learn as much as possible. "The problem is that Ms. Alert is too authoritarian and uptight," Sally says. "The problem is that students nowadays are rude and lazy," Ms. Alert says. They do not agree on what the conflict is about. Agreeing on the definition of a conflict is like putting gas in an airplane. Without it, negotiations will never get off the ground.

Negotiations begin when you communicate to the other person that there is a conflict and you wish to resolve it. You say, "We have a conflict" and "I want to resolve it!" Then you share your perception of the conflict and invite the other person to do the same. *Conflicts cannot be resolved unless both parties bring out into the open what they want and how they feel.* Without a clear understanding of each other's interests, no constructive resolution is possible. *Each of us has a perfect right to our needs and goals and to expect that other people will treat us with respect and dignity.* Two of the major mistakes in defining a conflict are to be *aggressive* by trying to hurt the other person or to be *nonassertive* by saying nothing, giving up your interests, and keeping your feelings to yourself. You can *assert* your needs, goals, and feelings directly to another person in an honest and appropriate way that respects both yourself and the other person. Doing so enables you to act in your own best interests, to stand up for yourself without undue anxiety, to express honest feelings comfortably, and to exercise personal rights without denying the rights of others.

On the other hand, *everyone has a perfect right to refuse to meet your needs or facilitate your goal accomplishment if it is seen as destructive to his or her own interests to do so.* No one has to act against self-interest just to please someone else. After asserting your needs and goals, therefore, do not expect the other person to do exactly as you wish. *Do not confuse letting others know what you want with demanding that they act as you think they should.* Providing others with information about your interests is different from trying to force others to act in the ways you wish them to.

After expressing what you want and how you feel, and listening carefully to what the other person wants and how the other person feels, the conflict may be defined. How the conflict is defined will influence how easy the conflict is to resolve constructively.

It is not enough for a person to understand his or her position and feelings. They must be communicated and explained to the other person. The essential element of presenting your position is communicating it without "building hills as you go," "sabotaging your chances for agreement by alienating others," or "guaranteeing closed-minded rejection." Describe, don't accuse or label. Table 8.1 summarizes what is involved in negotiation.

A conflict is not defined until both you and the other person agree on a definition. Your definition of the conflict will affect how you act and feel in trying to resolve it. With a poor definition, you will feel miserable and act in ways that will make the conflict worse. With a constructive definition, you will feel confident and effective, and you will act in ways that resolve the conflict. It is important that you be able to define conflicts in a skillful way. Here are five rules that will help you do so:

Rule 1: Describe what you want (your interests). The Roman philosopher Seneca once stated, "If a man does not know to which port he is sailing, no wind is favorable." *The first step in defining a conflict is to describe what you want.* This involves:

1. Taking ownership of your interests by making *personal statements* that refer to "I," "me," "my," or "mine" and that describe your needs and goals.

2. Describing how the other person's actions are blocking what you want. In doing so, separate the behavior from the person by using a *behavior description.*

TABLE 8.1: RESPECT FOR SELF AND OTHERS

My respect for me	My respect for you
I have a perfect right to:	*You have a perfect right to:*
My needs and wants	Your wants and needs
Tell you what I want	Tell me what you want
Tell you how I feel	Tell me how you feel
Refuse to give you what you want	Refuse to give me what I want

We have a perfect right to negotiate with each other

3.   Separating the person from the problem. Attack the problem without blaming, labeling, accusing, or insulting the people.

4.   Focusing on the relationship by making relationship statements.

Rule 2: Describe how you feel. Thomas Watson, Jr., Chairman Emeritus of IBM Corporation, once commented that ''Many of us in business, especially if we are very sure of our ideas, have hot tempers.'' He then went on to describe his father, the founder of IBM, ''My father knew he had to keep the damage from his own temper to a minimum.'' Expressing and controlling your feelings is one of the most difficult aspects of resolving conflicts. It is also one of the most important. It is through experiencing and sharing feelings that close relationships are built and maintained. Feelings provide the cement holding relationships together as well as the means for deepening relationships and making them more effective and personal.

Within negotiations you must describe how you feel for at least two reasons. *First,* the only way other people can know how you are feeling and reacting is for you to tell them. There is a tendency in conflicts to hide feelings and reactions. You often do not want others to know how upset you really are. But if the conflict is to be resolved, you need to share your feelings and reactions. This helps other people understand how their actions are affecting you.

Second, unless feelings are openly recognized and expressed, the conflict will not be resolved. If individuals hide or suppress their anger, for example, they may make an agreement but they keep their resentment and hostility toward the other person. Their ability to work effectively with the other person is damaged as is their ability to resolve future conflicts constructively. And the conflict will tend to recur regardless of what the agreement is.

It is often difficult to express feelings, especially within conflict situations. Whenever there is a risk of being rejected or laughed at, expressing feelings becomes very difficult. The more personal the feelings, the greater the risk you may feel. It is also difficult to hide your feelings from other people. You may cry when you do not want to, get angry when it is best not to, or even laugh at a time that disturbs others. If you are angry and upset, typically the people you work with and the people around you will know. When you do not recognize, accept, and express your feelings a number of difficulties may arise. Relationships may deteriorate, conflicts may fester, bias may creep into your judgments, and the insecurities of your colleagues may increase.

Rule 3: Listen carefully to the other person's wants and feelings. Besides communicating clearly and descriptively your interests and feelings, you must listen carefully to the other person's interests and feelings. *To listen to another person you must (a) face the person, (b) stay quiet (until your turn), (c) think about what the person is saying, and (d) show you understand.* The keystone to good listening is paraphrasing. Often in a conflict it is helpful to follow the *paraphrasing rule*: Before you can reply to a statement, restate what the sender says, feels, and means correctly and to the sender's satisfaction. When you use paraphrasing, there is a rhythm to your statements. The rhythm is, You said . . . ; I say. . . . First you say what the sender said (You said). Then you reply (I say).

Rule 4: Jointly define the conflict as a mutual problem. Two drivers, coming from different directions, are roaring down a one-lane road. Soon they will crash head-on. If the two drivers define the situation as a competition to see who will "chicken out," they will crash and both will die. If the two drivers define the situation as a problem to be solved, they will tend to see a solution in which they alternate giving each other the right-of-way. Even simple and small conflicts become major and difficult to resolve when they are defined in a competitive, "win-lose" way. Even major and difficult conflicts become resolvable when they are defined as problems to be solved.

Rule 5: Jointly define the conflict as being small and specific. In defining a conflict, the smaller and more specific it is defined, the easier it is to resolve. Think small. The more global, general, and vague the definition of the conflict, the harder the conflict is to resolve. Defining a conflict as "She always lies" makes it more difficult to resolve than defining it as "Her statement was not true." When it comes to resolving conflicts, small is easy; large is hard!

These five rules provide a clear, useful way of defining a conflict. The more you follow these rules, the more skillful you will be in resolving conflicts. These five rules may be summarized as *I.U.D.* (*I*nform, *U*nderstand, and *D*efine).

Exercise 8.9: What I Want, What You Want

Conflicts begin when two people want the same thing. When one person says, "I want the ice cream bar" and another person says, "I want the ice cream bar," a conflict exists. It is OK to want something. Every person has needs. Every person every minute of the day wants something. To stand up for yourself, you have to let other people know what you want. *You have a perfect right to stand up for yourself.* So does the other person. You are both OK to stand up for what you want. The *first step* of negotiating is for each person to say what he or she wants. To practice the first and the last steps of negotiating, go through the procedure of:

1. I want . . . You want . . .
2. Meet me in the middle. OK. Shake.

Divide into groups of four. Form two rows of four participants each. The two rows face each other. Each person says to the person he or she is facing:

I want the cookie.	No, I want the cookie.
Let's meet in the middle.	
Each will get half.	
You cut.	
I'll choose.	OK. Shake.

Then move to the next person and say the same thing. Do not stop until you have practiced the sequence four times.

Where else can you use this procedure? Divide into pairs. Write down three places where you can use this procedure:

1. _____
2. _____
3. _____

Why is dividing the cookie in half a good idea?

Exercise 8.10: What I Want, What You Want. How I Feel, How You Feel.

It is not enough to say what you want. You also need to say how you feel. Sometimes you may feel angry. Sometiems you may feel frustrated. Sometimes you may feel afraid. In conflicts, everyone has feelings. Both sides need to say how they feel. You need to say how you feel. The other person needs to say how he or she feels. To stand up for yourself you need to let the other person know how you feel. To stand up for him- or herself, the other person needs to let you know how he or she feels. Both you and the other person have a perfect right to your feelings. The *second step* of negotiating is for each person to say how he or she feels. To practice the first, second, and last steps of negotiating, go through the procedure of:

1. I want . . . You want . . .
2. I feel . . . You feel . . .
3. Let's take turns. Flip a coin to see who goes first. OK. Shake.

Divide into groups of four. Form two rows of four participants each. The two rows face each other. Each person says to the person he or she is facing:

I want the book.	No, I want the book.
I feel frustrated.	I'm afraid you won't let me have the book.
Let's take turns.	
Flip a coin to see who goes first.	OK. Shake.

Then move to the next person and say the same thing. Do not stop until you have practiced the sequence four times.

Where else can you use this procedure? Divide into pairs. Write down three places where you can use this procedure:

1. _____

2. _____

3. _____

Why is flipping a coin a good idea?

Step Two: Exchanging Reasons for Positions

To be persuasive we must be believable; to be believable we must be credible; to be credible, we must be truthful.

Edward R. Murrow, Journalist

Once both you and the other person have expressed what you want and how you feel, listened carefully to each other, and jointly defined the conflict as a small and specific mutual problem, you must exchange the reasons for your positions. To do so, negotiators have to:

1. *Express cooperative intentions and enlarge the shadow of the future.* One of the most constructive things you can do in resolving a conflict is to highlight the long-term cooperative relationship. This is done in three ways. The *first* is to stress dealing with the conflict in a problem-solving way. Communicate that you and the other person will strive, side by side, to solve the problem rather than fight face-to-face to determine who wins. You want to say such things as, "This situation means that we will have to work together," "Let's

cooperate in reaching an agreement," "Let's try to reach an agreement that is good for both of us." The *second* is to state that you are committed to maximizing the joint outcomes. Successful negotiation requires finding out what the other person really wants and needs and showing him or her a way to get it while you get what you want. The *third* is to enlarge the shadow of the future by stating that you are committed to the continuation and success of the cooperative efforts you and the other person are involved in. In doing so, you must wish to point out (a) your long-term mutual goals and (b) the ways the two of you are interdependent and how that interdependence will continue for the foreseeable future.

The clear and unambiguous expression of cooperative intentions in negotiations results in higher quality agreements being reached in a shorter amount of time (i.e., better agreements faster). The other person becomes less defensive, more willing to change his or her position, less concerned about who is right and who is wrong, and more understanding of your views and ideas (Johnson, 1971, 1974; Johnson, McCarty, & Allen, 1976). The other person tends to see you as an understanding and trustworthy person in whom he or she can confide.

2. *Present your reasons, listen to the other person's reasons.* To say what you want and how you feel is not enough. You must also give your reasons for wanting what you want and feeling as you do. It is not enough to say, "I want to use the computer now, and I'm angry at you for not letting me have it." You must also say, "I have an important homework assignment due today and this is my only chance to get it done." Your reasons are aimed at (a) informing the other person and (b) persuading him or her to agree with you.

In listening carefully to the needs and wants of the other person, you must *stay flexible, changing your position and feelings when persuaded to do so.* Negotiating is a rational process. You are seeking a way to reach your goals and the other person is doing the same. How successful you are in reaching an agreement depends on how creatively you can think of alternatives that are good for both. This requires flexibility and a willingness to change your mind when you are persuaded that it is rational to do so.

Once both of you have explained your reasons, either of you may agree or disagree to help the other person to reach his or her goals. The decision to help the other person reach his or her goals or keep negotiating is based on two factors:

a. How important your goal is to you
b. How important the other person's goal is to him or her (based on the reasons he or she presents)

You must listen carefully to the reasons given and decide whether they are valid or not. If you decide that the other person's goals are far more important to him or her than yours are to you, then you may wish to agree at this point. Giving up your goals to help the other person reach his or her goals only works if he or she does the same for you 50 percent of the time. This is known as the *single step solution*.

If the other person's reasons are not valid, you need to point that out so he or she may see the inadequacies of his or her proposals. If neither the other person nor you are convinced to give up individual goals in order to fulfill the goals of the other person, then the two of you must reaffirm your cooperative relationship and explore each other's reasons at a deeper level.

3. *Focus on wants and needs, not positions.* The classic example of the need to separate interests from positions is that of a brother and sister, each of whom wanted the only orange available. The sister wanted the peel of the orange to make a cake; the brother wanted the inner part to make orange juice. Their positions, ("I want the orange!") were opposed, but their interests were not. Often, when conflicting parties reveal their underlying interests, it is possible to find a solution that suits them both.

   The heart of negotiation is meeting the goals of the other person while ensuring your goals are being met. The success of negotiation depends on finding out what the other person really wants, and showing him or her a way to get it while you get what you want. For a wise decision, therefore, reconcile wants, not positions. For every need or want, there usually exist several possible positions that could satisfy it. A common mistake is to assume that because the other person's position is opposed to yours, his or her goals must also be opposed. Behind opposed positions lie shared and compatible goals, as well as conflicting ones. To identify the other person's wants and needs ask "why," ask, "why not," and think about his or her choice, and realize that the other person has many different needs and wants.

4. *Clarify the differences between your and the other's interests before trying to integrate them into an agreement.* Conflicts cannot be resolved unless you understand what you are disagreeing about. If you do not know what you are disagreeing about, you cannot find a way to reach an agreement. You must understand the differences between your wants and needs and those of the other person. Only then will you be able to think of ways to satisfy both yourself and the other person so that the conflict can be resolved constructively. Your ability to come up with satisfactory solutions depends on your

understanding of how the other person's thoughts, feelings, and needs are different from yours. The more you differentiate between your interests and those of the other person, the better you will be able to integrate them into a mutually satisfying agreement. In discussing a conflict you try to find the answers to these questions: (a) What are the differences between my wants and needs and yours, (b) where are our needs and goals the same, (c) what actions of the other person do I find unacceptable, and (d) what actions of mine does the other person find unacceptable?

5. *Empower the other person.* During negotiations it is important that you do not let the other person feel powerless. Shared power and wise agreements go hand in hand. *There are two ways to empower the other person.* The *first* is by being open to negotiations and flexible about the option you like the best. If he or she can negotiate with you, then he or she has power and options. Willingness to negotiate is based on being open to the possibility that there may be a better option available than you now realize. Staying tentative and flexible means that you do not become overcommitted to any one position until an agreement is reached. *Second*, you provide power through choice among options. Generate a variety of possible solutions before deciding what to do. If Susan says to Mr. Johnson, "You have to agree to let me not do my homework," he will feel powerless. If Susan said, "Let's think of three possible agreements, and then choose the one that seems the best," both she and Mr. Johnson feel powerful.

The psychological costs of being helpless to resolve grievances include frustration, anxiety, and friction. When a person is powerless, he or she either becomes hostile and tries to tear down the system or becomes apathetic and throws in the towel. You do not want the other person to do either one. We all need to believe that we have been granted a fair hearing and that we should have the power and the right to gain justice when we have been wronged. If it becomes evident that we cannot gain justice, frustration, anger, depression, and anxiety may result.

Exercise 8.11: What I Want, What You Want. How I Feel, How You Feel. Why I Want It, Why You Want It.

It is not enough to say what you want. You must also say *why* you want it. You must have reasons for wanting something. And you must share your reasons with the other person. The other person needs to share his or her reasons with you. The *third step* of negotiating is to say why you want it (the cookie or the book). To practice the first, second, third, and last steps of negotiating, go through the procedure of:

1. I want . . . You want . . .
2. I feel . . . You feel . . .
3. I want it because . . . You want it because . . .
4. We could do it together.
   OK. Shake.

Divide into groups of four. Form two rows of four participants each. The two rows face each other.
Each person says to the person he or she is facing:

I want to play checkers.	No, I want to play checkers.
I feel frustrated.	I'm angry.
I'm frustrated because you are interfering with my playing checkers.	I'm angry because you won't let me play with the checkers.
We could play checkers together.	OK. Shake.

Then move to the next person and say the same thing. Do not stop until you have practiced the sequence four times.

Where else can you use this procedure? Divide into pairs. Write down three places where you can use this procedure.

1. _____
2. _____
3. _____

Why is playing checkers together a good idea?

Exercise 8.12: Differentiating Between Positions and Interests

For each of the following situations identify and write out each person's *position* and *interests* that caused them to take that position. Then find a partner and come to agreement on the answers. One member will be choosen randomly to give the pair's answers.

1. Sue wants the orange so she can use the peel to make an orange cake. Jim wants the orange so he can use the insides to make orange juice.

	Sue	Jim
Position	_____	_____
Interests	_____	_____

2. Jeremy wants the book so he can read it. Andrew wants the book so he can sit on it and see better.

	Jeremy	Andrew
Position	_____	_____
Interests	_____	_____

3. Davy wants the computer so he can write his science report. Tyler wants the computer to practice keyboarding.

	Davy	Tyler
Position	_____	_____
Interests	_____	_____

4. Jim wants the pencil so he can write with it. John wants the pencil to erase mistakes.

	Jim	John
Position	_____	_____
Interests	_____	_____

5. Betsy wants the ball so she can practice catching it. Sam wants the ball so she can practice throwing it.

	Betsy	Sam
Position	_____	_____
Interests	_____	_____

Whenever someones takes a position, ask them "why" in order to learn their interests.

Step Three: Understanding The Other's Perspective

> *The test of a first-rate intelligence is the ability to hold two opposed ideas in the mind at the same time, and still retain the ability to function.*
>
> *F. Scott Fitzgerald*

To reach a wise agreement, you must have a clear understanding of all sides of the issue, an accurate assessment of their validity and relative merits, and the ability to think creatively to come up with potential solutions that maximize joint outcomes and fulfill the interests of both you and the other person. All this requires that you are able to see the conflict from both your own and the other person's perspective. And you need to keep both in mind at the same time.

Juanita and Betsy work together as laboratory technicians in a large hospital. Juanita comes from a well-off upper-middle-class family. Betsy's parents had a hard struggle sending their daughter through college. Betsy and Juanita buy tickets for a state lottery in which they could win up to $5,000. When the drawing is held, they learn that they are both winners. Juanita says, "Hey, I won $5,000 in that lottery. Imagine that." Then she continues eating lunch and reading a magazine. Betsy starts jumping up and down shouting, "I won! I won! I won $5,000!" She throws her arms around her friend, crying and laughing in her excitement. Why did Juanita and Betsy react so differently to the news that they had each won $5,000 in a state lottery?

Each person has a unique *perspective* (a way of viewing the world and his or her relation to it) that is different from the perspectives of others. Your perspective is developed as a result of the ways in which you respond to your experiences as an infant, child, youth, and adult. Other people have developed their perspectives on the basis of their responses to their life experiences.

In order to negotiate successfully with another person, you must be able to take the other person's perspective and understand how the conflict appears to the other person. *Social perspective-taking* is the ability to understand how a situation appears to another person and how that person is reacting cognitively and emotionally to the situation. The opposite of perspective-taking is *egocentrism* or being unaware that other perspectives exist and that one's own view of the conflict is incomplete and limited.

Given that different people have different perspectives, that each person may have different perspectives at different times, and that misunderstandings often occur because we assume that everyone sees the world through our perspective, then an important issue for negotiations is to keep the other person's perspective in mind as well as your own, for a number of reasons [see Johnson & Johnson (1989) for a complete review of the research].

First, perspective-taking improves communication and reduces misunderstandings and distortions by influencing how messages are phrased and received. Negotiators often misunderstand and distort the positions of the others involved in the conflict due to poor communication. The better you understand the other person's perspective, the more able you are to phrase messages so the other person can easily understand them. If a person does not know what snow is, for example, you do not refer to "corn snow" or "fresh powder." In addition, understanding the other person's perspective helps you to understand accurately the messages you are receiving from that person. If the other person says, "That's just great," for example, the meaning reverses if you know the person is frustrated. You must be able to stand in the sender's shoes to understand accurately the meaning of the messages that person is sending you.

Second, perspective-taking is essential for a realistic assessment of common and opposed interests and an accurate assessment of their validity and relative merits. Often reaching an agreement requires the sacrifice of some of the opposed interests so that the common benefits, concerns, advantages, and needs may be built on. To propose workable alternative agreements you must understand how the other person sees the problem.

Third, the more able you are to take the other person's perspective, the broader the picture you get of the issue. Out of a mass of detailed information, people tend to pick out and focus on those facts that confirm their prior perceptions and to disregard or misinterpret those that call their perceptions into question. Each side in a negotiation tends to see only the merits of its case, and only the faults of the other side. It is not enough to understand logically how the other person views the problem. *If you want to influence the other person, you also need to understand empathetically the power of his/her point of view and to feel the emotional force with which he or she believes in it.*

Fourth, engaging in perspective taking tends to improve the relationship with the other person. You are more liked and respected when the other person realizes that you are seeing his or her perspective accurately and using it to create potential agreements that benefit both sides equally.

You ensure that you accurately see the situation from the other person's perspective by:

1. Asking for clarification or correction to make sure your understanding is accurate. This is called *perception checking*.
2. Stating your understanding of the other's wants and needs. This is often done by *paraphrasing*.

Exercise 8.13: My Understanding of You, Your Understanding of Me

Resolving conflicts takes more than understanding what you want and feel and why. You must also understand the other person. And you must make sure the other person knows you understand him or her. The *fourth step* of negotiating is to summarize what the other person wants and feels and why. To practice the first, second, third, fourth, and last steps of negotiating, go through the procedure of:

1. I want . . . You want . . .
2. I feel . . . You feel . . .
3. I want it because . . . You want it because . . .
4. My understanding of what you want, feel, and why is . . .
    Your understanding of what I want, feel, and why is . . .
5. You need it more than I do. You can have it.
    Thanks. Shake.

Put yourself in the other person's shoes. Restate the other person's ideas and feelings in your own words. State as correctly as possible what the other person wants, feels, and why. Start your remarks with, *You want . . .* , *You feel . . .* , and *You think . . .* Show understanding and acceptance by nonverbal behaviors: tone of voice, facial expressions, gestures, eye contact, and posture.

Divide into two rows of four people each. Face your partner. Go through steps 1–5 above to negotiate who gets to use the computer first. Emphasize your understanding of the other person. Then repeat with a new partner.

Where else can you use paraphrasing? Divide into pairs.
Write down three places where you can use this procedure.

1. _____

2. _____

3. _____

Why is letting the other person use the computer a good idea?

Exercise 8.14: Your Point of View

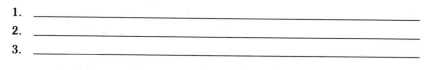

Everyone has his or her own point of view. Some people like Chinese food. Some people don't. If you like Chinese food you tend to assume that everyone does. If you like to be teased you assume that everyone likes to be teased.

In resolving conflicts it is important to understand the other person's point of view. An example of the need to understand others' points of view is given below. Read the story with your partner.

The Wise Men and the Elephant

Once upon a time, there were six wise men who lived in the same town. All six wise men were blind. One day, an elephant was brought to the town. The six men wanted to know what the elephant looked like. So they went to the elephant and started to touch it. The first one touched the elephant's big, flat ear. He felt it move slowly back and forth. "The elephant is like a fan," the first man cried. The second man felt the elephant's legs. "The elephant is like a tree," he cried. The third man was feeling the elephant's tail. "You are both wrong," he cried. "The elephant is like a rope." The fourth man was holding the elephant's trunk. "You are all wrong," he said. "The elephant is like a snake." The fifth man was touching one of the elephant's tusks. "The elephant is like a spear!" he yelled. "No, No!" the sixth man cried. "The elephant is like a high wall!" He was feeling the elephant's side. "Fan!" "Tree!" "Rope!" "Snake!" "Spear!" "Wall!" The six blind men shouted at each other for an hour. And they never agreed on what an elephant looked like.

Your Point of View Exercise

Working in your pair, answer the following questions. Then join another pair and share your answers.

1. Which blind man was right? _____
_____

2. What was their conflict based on? _____
_____

3. Were they really "wise"? How do you tell if someone is wise? _____
    _____

4. How could the wise men have discovered what an elephant really looks like?
    _____

5. What is the moral of the story? What does the story tell you about solving conflicts?
    _____
    _____

In your pair, rewrite the ending of the story to make it come out with a good solution to the conflict.

_____
_____
_____
_____
_____
_____

Step Four: Inventing Options For Mutual Gain

One completely overcomes only what one assimilates.

Andre Gide

The fourth step of negotiating is to identify several possible agreements. One will rarely do. People have a tendency to agree to the first reasonable solution that is proposed. But doing so shuts off consideration of even more advantageous agreements. Thus, make sure you generate at least three good alternative agreements before deciding on which one to adopt. To invent a number of potential agreements, you must avoid a number of obstacles and you must think creatively.

The four major obstacles that inhibit the inventing of a number of options are *judging prematurely* any new idea, *searching for the single answer* which leads to premature closure and fixation on the first proposal formulated as the single best answer, *assuming a fixed pie* (the less for you, the more for me), *shortsighted self-concern with your own immediate needs and goals*, and *defensively sticking with the status quo to avoid the fear of the unknown inherent in change.*

To invent creative options, you need to invent first and judge later, gather as much information as possible about the problem, see the problem from different perspectives and reformulate it in a way that lets new orientations to a solution emerge, broaden the options on the table rather than look for a single answer, search for mutual gains, invent ways of making decisions easily, propose possible agreements, and test each proposed agreement against reality. (What are its strengths and weaknesses? What does each person gain and lose? How does it maximize joint outcomes?)

Possible agreements include meeting in the middle, taking turns, sharing, letting the other person have it all, letting chance decide, package deals (in which several issues that are considered part of the agreement are settled), trade-offs (in which two different things of comparable value are exchanged), tie-ins (in which an issue considered extraneous by the other person is introduced, and you offer to accept a certain settlement provided this extraneous issue will also be settled to your satisfaction), and *carve-outs* (in which an issue is carved out of a larger context, leaving the related issues unsettled).

Agreement Menu

1. Meeting in the middle
2. Taking turns
3. Sharing
4. Letting the other person have it all
5. Letting chance decide
6. Package deal (several issues that are considered part of the agreement are settled)
7. Trade-off (two different things of comparable value are exchanged)
8. Tie-in (an issue considered extraneous by the other person is introduced and you offer to accept a certain settlement provided this extraneous issue will also be settled to your satisfaction)
9. Carve-out (an issue is carved out of a larger context leaving the related issues unsettled)

In inventing alternative agreements, it often helps to describe what you are doing and neglecting to do that creates and continues the conflict. Knowing how your actions help create and continue the conflict is essential for planning how to resolve it. And neglecting to do something constructive helps create and continue the conflict just as much as doing something destructive. You may want the other person to change. But the easiest thing to change is your own actions. If you wish to resolve a conflict, you must begin with deciding how to change your actions. It would be nice if everyone else changed so we would never have to. But you do not have control over the actions of others. They do. What you do have control over is your own actions. You can change your actions much more easily than you can change the other person's actions!

Exercise 8.15: Inventing Options for Mutual Gain

Resolving conflicts takes more than understanding yourself and the other person. You must also identify several possible solutions. In any conflict there are many ways to resolve it. The *fifth step* in resolving conflicts is to think of at least three plans to solve the problem. You can practice the first four steps of negotiating by going through the procedure of:

1. I want . . . You want . . .
2. I feel . . . You feel . . .
3. I want it because . . . You want it because . . .
4. My understanding of what you want, feel, and why is . . .
    Your understanding of what I want, feel, and why is . . .
5. Three plans to solve the problem are . . .
6. Let's pick Plan B.
    OK. Shake.

He Hurt Me, I'll Hurt You

Fred's friend yelled at him this morning on the playground. Fred feels sad and upset. When another friend, Ralph, says hello to him in line, Fred says, "Get out of here!"

Divide into two rows of four people each. Face your partner. Go through steps 1-6 above to negotiate a solution to the problem. Be sure to think of three plans before you choose one. Then repeat with a new partner.

Plan A: _____

_____

Plan B: _____

_____

Plan C: _____

_____

Exercise 8.16: Using Balance Sheets to Make Wise Decisions

Roger was a coin collector; his wife, Anne, loved to raise and show championship rabbits. Their income did not leave enough money for both to practice their hobbies, and splitting the cash they did have would not have left enough for either. The conflict over whether to spend their extra money on coins or rabbits was so severe that they were thinking about getting a divorce. Think of three optional agreements that would allow them to stay married. Then use the balance sheet to decide what to do. Use the following procedure.

1. Evaluate the first alternative agreement on the basis of the gains and losses for:
   a. Person 1.
   b. Person 2.
   c. Others in the class, school, family, and/or community.
2. Once all the gains and losses have been listed for the first alternative agreement, rate each in terms of its importance on a five-point scale from 1 (no importance) to 5 (extremely important).
3. Evaluate whether (a) each person will feel proud or ashamed if this alternative is agreed to and (b) it is important other people think that you have made the right decision.
4. Repeat these steps for each of the other alternative agreements.
5. After a balance sheet has been completed for each alternative agreement, rank the alternatives from "most desirable" to "least desirable."

CONFLICT DECISION BALANCE SHEET

	Gains	Rating	Losses	Rating	Approval
Person 1	_____	_____	_____	_____	_____
Person 2	_____	_____	_____	_____	_____
Others	_____	_____	_____	_____	_____

Repeat the process with the following two conflicts. Like the one above, they actually happened.

1.   Edythe and Buddy shared an office but had different work habits. Edythe liked to do her work in silence while Buddy liked to socialize in the office and have the radio on. Their conflict over noise became so severe that each went to their boss and demanded that the other be moved or even fired.

2.   Keith loved to spend his evenings talking to people all over the world on his ham radio set. From the time he got home from work until it was time to go to bed, he would sit with his ham radio conversing with far away people. His wife, Simone, felt cheated out of the few hours of each day they could spend together. Keith did not want to give up his radio time and Simone was not willing to forego the time they had together. The conflict became so severe that Simone was thinking about getting a divorce.

Pick a conflict you are presently involved in. Complete balance sheets for your conflict. Then negotiate with the other person some more.

Each of the three conflict examples given above actually happened. Here are the *solutions* that were negotiated with the help of a counselor.

1.   Roger and Ann decided to put all the first year's money into Ann's rabbits, and then after the rabbits were grown use the income from their litters and show prizes to pay for Roger's coins.

2.   Edythe and Buddy decided that on Mondays and Wednesdays Buddy would help keep silence in the office. On Tuesdays and Thursdays Edythe would work in a conference room that was free, leaving Buddy alone in the office to play the radio. On Fridays the two worked together on joint projects.

3.   Keith and Simone decided that four nights a week Keith would spend the evening talking with Simone. Afterwards he would stay up late and talk to his ham radio friends. On the following mornings Simone would drive Keith to work instead of having him go with a carpool, which allowed him to sleep later.

There are few problems that cannot be solved with the creative thinking of two problem-solving negotiators.

Step Five: Reaching A Wise Agreement

I never let the sun set on a disagreement with anybody who means a lot to me.

Thomas Watson, Sr., Founder, IBM

Given that we are all separate individuals with our own unique wants and needs, whenever we interact with others, we will have some interests that are congruent and other interests that are in conflict. It takes wisdom to manage the combination of shared and opposed interests and reach an agreement. *Wise agreements* are those that are fair to all participants, are based on principles, strengthen participants' abilities to work together cooperatively, and improve participants' ability to resolve future conflicts constructively. In other words, wise agreements are those that meet the following criteria:

1. *The agreement meets the legitimate needs of all participants and is viewed as fair by everyone involved.* To meet your and the other person's legitimate interests the agreement should clearly specify the responsibilities and rights of everyone involved in implementing the agreement. This includes:

   a. *The ways each person will act differently in the future.* These responsibilities should be stated in a *specific* (tells who does what when, where, and how), *realistic* (each can do what he or she is agreeing to do), and *shared* (everyone agrees to do something different) way.

   b. *How the agreement will be reviewed and renegotiated if it turns out to be unworkable.* This includes (a) the ways in which cooperation will be restored if one person slips and acts inappropriately and (b) the times participants will meet to discuss whether the agreement is working and what further steps can be taken to improve cooperation with each other.

2. *The agreement is based on principles that can be justified on some objective criteria* (Fisher & Ury, 1981). The objective criteria may be that everyone has an equal chance of benefiting (such as flipping a coin, having one cut and the other choose, or letting a third-party arbitrator decide), fairness (taking turns, sharing, equal use), scientific merit (based on theory, tested out, evidence indicates it will work), and community values.

3. *The agreement and the process of reaching the agreement strengthens participants' ability to work together cooperatively in the future* (the trust, respect, and liking among participants should be increased).

4. *The agreement and the process of reaching the agreement strengthen participants' ability to resolve future conflicts constructively.*

It is important that both you and the other person understand which actions trigger anger and resentment in the other. Criticism, put downs, sarcasm, belittling, and other actions often trigger a conflict. If the two of you understand what not to do as well as what to do, the conflict will be resolved much more easily.

Sometimes people find out later that they have made a bad agreement. You may have agreed to something you should not have, or you may have changed your mind, or you may have found out you cannot keep your side of the bargain. At that point, you reopen negotiations and try to find a workable resolution to the conflict.

Building a Bridge to Successful Resolution of a Conflict

Step Six: Try, Try Again

The final step for negotiating in a problem-solving way is: "Keep trying. Try, try again." No matter how far apart the two sides seem, no matter how opposed your interests seem to be, keep talking. With persistent discussion a viable and wise decision will eventually become clear.

NEGOTIATING IN GOOD FAITH

Everyone has a negotiating reputation. The promises of some people are to be believed. Other people rarely keep their commitments. You want to build a reputation of being someone who is honest, truthful, and trustworthy and, therefore, fulfills your promises. You want your word to be good.

There are strategies you can use when your word has not been good in the past. They are:

1. *Pay your debts.* Whatever you have agreed to do in the past and not yet done, do it. Once you have fulfilled past promises, your current promise will be more credible.

2. *Use collateral.* The collateral should be something of value, something the other person does not expect you to give up. While being significant enough to be meaningful, the collateral should not be something so outrageous that it is not believable. Promising to give someone $1,000 if you break your word is not believable.

3. *Have a cosigner who guarantees your word.* Find someone who trusts you that the other person trusts, and have them guarantee that you will keep your word.

REFUSAL SKILLS: THIS ISSUE IS NOT NEGOTIABLE

Not every issue is negotiable. Two important skills are:

1. Knowing when an issue is and is not negotiable
2. Being able to say "no" or "I refuse to negotiate this issue"

Negotiable issues include conflicts over (a) using something (computer, book, car, clothes), (b) agreeing on something (what to do, what to have for dinner, what movie to see), and (c) obtaining something (money, power, fame, clothes, friends). On most issues you benefit from negotiating and reaching an agreement.

There are times, however, when you will not want to negotiate. This may be because you do not like the other person, you see the issue as being nonnegotiable, you are uncomfortable with the issue, or you cannot do what the other person wants. You always have the option of saying "no" in negotiations. And you do *not* always need a clear reason. When you think someone is trying to manipulate you instead of solving a real problem, do not negotiate and do not make an agreement.

TABLE 8.2:   REASONS FOR SAYING "NO"

Clear	Unclear
Illegal	My intuition tells me "no"
Inappropriate	I am not sure
I will hurt other people	The right option is not there
I will not be able to keep my word	I have changed my mind

You will save considerable time and trouble by not persuading others to make agreements they do not wish to make and if you do not let others persuade you to agree to something you do not wish to do.

ACCURATE PERCEPTION OF YOUR OWN AND ANOTHER'S BEHAVIOR

In conflict situations, there are often perceptual distortions about your own and the other person's behavior, motivations, and position. Many of these distortions in perceptions are so common that they can be found in almost any conflict situation, whether it is between two people, two groups, or two countries. They include:

1. *Mirror image:* It is not uncommon for both you and the other person to feel that you are an innocent victim who represents truth and justice and who is being attacked maliciously by an evil enemy. In most conflicts, both people are firmly convinced that they are right and the other person wrong, and that they want a ''just'' solution but the other person does not.

2. *Mote-beam mechanism:* Often in conflict situations one clearly sees all the underhanded and vicious acts of the other person while being completely blind to identical acts engaged in by oneself. In most conflicts both people repress all awareness of the mean things they do to the other but become quite indignant about the mean things the other person does to them.

3. *Double standard:* Even if both people are aware of identical acts engaged in by themselves and the other person, there is a strong tendency to feel that what is legitimate for you to do is illegitimate for the other person to do.

4. *Polarized thinking:* It is common in conflict situations for both people to have an overestimated view of the conflict in which everything they do is good and everything the other person does is bad.

These misunderstandings escalate the conflict and make it more difficult to resolve it constructively. As long as you and the other person are each convinced that you are right and the other person is wrong, as long as you perceive every underhanded thing the other person does but ignore every underhanded thing you do, and as long as you apply a double standard to the behavior of yourself and the other person and think about the conflict in polarized, oversimplified ways, the conflict is bound to be destructive to your relationship.

In any conflict situation, you and the other person will usually have mixed feelings about each other. On the one hand you will feel hostile and wish that the other person would agree with your position; on the other hand, you will still feel affection for the other person and want to be agreeable to that person. When selective perception or distortions in perceptions operate, it is very easy to fall into a trap where you see only the hostile feelings of the other person and fail to see the positive feelings. This can very easily result in a self-fulfilling prophecy in which (1) you assume that the other's feelings are entirely hostile, (2) you take defensive action by either attacking the other person before he or she can attack you or cutting off contact with the other person, (3) your action intensifies the other person's hostility and decreases his or her positive feelings toward you, and (4) your original, but false, assumption is confirmed. Self-fulfilling prophesies are very common in conflict situations, and whenever you become involved in a conflict you should be careful not to fall into their traps.

Exercise 8.17: Old Lady/Young Girl

The objective of this exercise is to show how two people with different frames of reference can perceive the same event in two different ways. The procedure is:

1. Divide into two groups with an equal number of members in each group.

2. Each group receives a picture. The pictures are to be found in the Appendix at the end of this book. One group receives picture A and the other group receives picture B. Each group is asked to write out a description of the person in the picture, including such things as sex, clothing, hair style, and age.

3. Each member of the group is paired with a member of the second group. Each pair is given a copy of picture C. The two individuals are then asked to negotiate a common description of the person in the picture, including such things as sex, clothing, hairstyle, and age.

4. Conduct a discussion in the group as a whole concerning the results of the negotiations. Did you all see picture C in the same way? Once you perceived

the picture in one way, was it difficult to see it another way? In conflict situations, what influence do your background, previous experience, expectation, and frame of reference have upon how you see your behavior and the behavior of the other person?

5. Review the section on selective perception in chapter 4. How does the information in that section apply to this situation? How does it apply to most conflict situations?

Exercise 8.18: Role Reversal

The primary means of ensuring accurate perception of the conflict situation and of being able to communicate effectively with the other person is to gain as much insight as possible on how the other person perceives the conflict situation. This may be done through a procedure called role reversal. *Role reversal* may be defined as a procedure in which one or both of two people in a conflict present the viewpoint of the other. That is, given that A and B are in conflict, A presents B's point of view or B presents A's point of view, or both. The specific behaviors involved in role reversal are (1) the understanding response while (2) expressing warmth. A variety of research studies has demonstrated that the use of role reversal can eliminate misunderstandings and reduce distortions of the other person's point of view (Johnson, 1971).

Whenever you are in conflict with another person it is valuable to engage in role reversal in order to clarify each other's position and feelings. This exercise gives you an opportunity to practice role reversal. The procedure is:

1. Pick a current topic of interest on which there are differences of opinion in the group. Then divide the group in half, with each subgroup representing one side of the issue.

2. Each subgroup meets separately for 15 minutes to prepare to represent their side of the issue in negotiations with members of the other subgroup.

3. Each person in the subgroup is paired with a person from the other subgroup; each pair thus consists of persons representing opposite sides of the issue.

4. In the pair, designate the person A and B. Person A then is given up to 5 minutes to present her side of the issue. Person B then reverses his role by presenting Person A's position as if he were Person A.

5. Person B is then given up to 5 minutes to present his side of the issue. Person A role reverses.

6. The pair is then given 15 minutes to arrive at a joint agreement on the issue being discussed. During the 15 minutes they must obey the following rule: *Before either can reply to a statement made by the other, one person must accurately and warmly paraphrase the other's statement to the other's satisfaction.*

7. In the whole group discuss the impact of role reversal on your understanding and appreciation of the other side of the issue. Did role reversal help to reach

an agreement? Did it affect how you felt about each other during the negotiations? Did you feel it contributed to reaching a mutually satisfying agreement?

Exercise 8.19: Feelings in Conflicts

A basic aspect of any conflict is the feelings a person has while the conflict is taking place. Two common feelings are rejection and distrust. Many people are afraid of conflicts because they are afraid they will be rejected. And many people avoid conflicts because they do not trust the other person. The purposes of this exercise are to experience the feelings of rejection and distrust and to discuss how they influence your actions in conflicts. The procedure is:

Part 1: Rejection

1. Form into groups of four.
2. Pass out the instructions (p. 258) to each member of your group. The group has 10 minutes to select one person to be rejected and excluded from the group.
3. Combine two groups of four into a group of eight. Discuss the following questions:
   a. Did you feel rejected by the other members of your group of four?
   b. What is it like to feel rejected? What other feelings result from being rejected?
   c. How do you act when someone is rejecting you?
   d. When you are in a conflict, how can you act to minimize feelings of rejection on both your part and the part of the other person?

Part 2: Distrust

1. Form pairs.
2. Give each member of the pair an instruction sheet (p. 258). Your pair has 5 minutes to interact after you have both read the instructions.
3. Combine three pairs into a group of six and discuss these questions:
   a. Did you feel distrusted by the other member of your pair?
   b. Did you distrust the other member of your pair?
   c. How do you act when someone distrusts you?
   d. What is it like to feel distrusted? What other feelings result from being distrusted?
   e. When you are in a conflict, how can you minimize the feelings of distrust on both your part and on the part of the other person?
4. Be prepared to share with other groups your conclusions about how to minimize rejection and distrust.

Instruction Sheet for Exercise 8.19

Part 1

You are to try to get the person sitting on your right rejected from the group. Use any reason you can think of—he misses too many meetings, she's the only one in the group wearing a sweater, she's the shortest person—anything you can think of. Stick to this, and try to convince the other group members that this is the person who should be rejected. You can listen to the arguments of other people in the group, but don't give in. Be sure you talk about the person and not about rules for rejecting.

Part 2

Instructions A. Do not share these instructions with the other person in your pair. Your task for the next five minutes is to talk as positively and warmly as you can to the other person. Say only positive and friendly things, showing especially that you want to cooperate and work effectively with him or her in the future. Your conversation is to concentrate on him or her about your impression of that person, and the need for cooperation between the two of you. Don't talk about yourself. No matter what happens, you say only positive things. Keep the conversation moving along quickly. You are to speak first.

Instructions B. Do not share these instructions with the other person in your pair. The other person will speak first. Your task for the next five minutes is to talk with the other person in a way that shows distrust of him or her. Whatever the other person says, say something in return that communicates suspicion, distrust, disinterest, defiance, disbelief, or contradiction. Talk only about the things the other person talks about, and avoid starting conversation or bringing up new topics. Try not to help the other person out in any way. As an example, should your partner comment, "Say, I like the shirt you're wearing," you might respond, "What do you say that for? It's ugly. I don't like it at all. What are trying to accomplish by complimenting my shirt?"

SUMMARY

You negotiate to resolve conflicts of interests. *Conflicts of interests* exist when your actions interfere with or block another person from achieving his or her goal. *Interests* are the potential benefits to be gained by achieving goals. Goals are based on *wants* (a desire for something) and *needs* (a necessity for survival). On the basis of our wants and needs we set goals. A *goal* is an ideal state of affairs that we value and are working to achieve. When two or more people have mutual goals they are in a cooperative relationship; when the goals of two or more people are opposed they are in a competitive relationship. Resolving conflicts of interests requires negotiation. *Negotiation* is a process by which persons who have shared and opposed interests and want to come to an agreement try to work out a settlement. There are two types of negotiations. *Win-lose negotiations* occur when participants want to make an agreement more favorable to themselves than to the other persons. It is appropriate primarily when you will never have to work with the other person in the future. When buying a used car, for example, you engage in win-lose negotiations. The majority of the time, however, you negotiate within an ongoing relationship. That requires *problem-solving negotiations* where the goal is to reach an agreement that benefits everyone involved. Within ongoing relationships individuals are committed to the well-being of the other person as well as to their own well-being. In order to negotiate mutually beneficial agreements participants must state what they want and how they feel, state the reasons why they want what they do, reverse perspectives and summarize the other's position and interests, invent a series of possible agreements, and finally reach a wise decision.

Agreeing on a definition of the conflict requires that you state what you want and how you feel, listen carefully to the other person, and agree on a definition of the conflict that specifies it as a small and specific mutual problem to be solved. You inform, understand, and define (IUD). Exchanging reasons for your positions requires that you express cooperative intentions, exchange reasons, focus on interests not positions, explore how your interests are incompatible and compatible, and empower each other by giving choices. You gain understanding of the other person's perspective by paraphrasing and checking your perceptions of the other person's interests and reasons. You invent options for mutual gain by both inventing creative options and avoiding the obstacles to creative problem solving. You reach a wise agreement when the agreement meets the legitimate needs of all participants, when it is based on principles that can be justified on some objective criteria, when your ability to work cooperatively with the other person has been enhanced, and when your ability to resolve future conflicts constructively has been strengthened. Finally, you try, try again until a wise agreement is reached.

To negotiate in good faith you need to build a reputation as someone who is honest, truthful, and trustworthy. Not all issues, however, are negotiable. You must know the difference between a negotiable and a nonnegotiable issue. And you must be able to say "No, I will not negotiate on this issue" when it is appropriate to do so. One of the most problematic aspects of negotiating is to ensure that both people want to negotiate at the same time. Motivation to negotiate often must be coordinated.

Negotiations are inevitable. You negotiate every day and sooner or later you negotiate with everyone in your life. In deciding whether or not to negotiate and in ensuring that negotiations are effective and constructive, there are five basic strategies to choose from. Managing emotions, especially anger, is one of the most difficult aspects of negotiating. Managing your own anger and your responses to the anger of other individuals is covered in the next chapter.

Exercise 8.20: My Past Conflict Behavior

Think back over the interpersonal conflicts you have been involved in during the past few years. These conflicts may be with friends, parents, brothers and sisters, girlfriends or boyfriends, husbands or wives, teachers or students, or your boss or subordinates. On a separate sheet of paper list the five major conflicts you can remember from your past and the strategies you used and the feelings you had in resolving them.

Exercise 8.21: Disagreeing

We all have different opinions about many issues. Because we have different opinions, we often get into disagreements and arguments. How we act and feel during arguments is an important aspect of our conflict strategies. If you participate actively in this exercise, you will become aware of how you act and feel during disagreements. You will also be able to give feedback to other participants about their actions during the disagreements. The procedure is:

1. Form groups of six. Each member reads "The Fallout Shelter."

2. Working as a group, decide on the six people who are to go into the fallout shelter. You have 20 minutes to make the decision. During the discussion, argue strongly for your ideas and opinions. The future of the human species may depend on your group's decision. Make sure your group makes a good decision by arguing strongly for your opinions. Agree with the other group members only if they convince you that their ideas are better than yours.

3. Working individually, answer the following questions:
   a. What were my feelings when I disagreed with someone?
   b. What were my feelings when someone disagreed with me?
   c. How did I act when I wanted to convince someone to change his or her ideas?
   d. How did I act when someone was trying to convince me to change my ideas?
   e. How would my conflict strategies during the group discussion be described?

4. Draw straws to see who is going to be first. Then go around the group in a clockwise direction. Focusing on the member who is first, describe briefly how you saw his or her actions during the group discussion. Use the rules for constructive feedback given on pages 36–40. Make sure everyone in the group receives feedback before the exercise is over.

The Fallout Shelter

Your group is in charge of experimental stations in the far outposts of civilization. You work in an important government agency in Washington, D.C. Suddenly World War III breaks out. Nuclear bombs begin dropping. Places all across the world are being destroyed. People are getting into the available fallout shelters. Your group receives a desperate call from one of your experimental stations. They ask for your help. There are ten people at this station. But their fallout shelter only holds six. They cannot decide which six people should enter the fallout shelter. They have agreed that they will obey your group's decision as to which six people will go into the fallout shelter. Your group has only superficial information about the ten people. Your group has 20 minutes to make the decision. Your group realizes that the six people chosen may be the only six left to start the human species over again. Your group's decision, therefore, is very important. If your group does not make the decision within the 20 minutes allowed, all ten people will die. Here is what you know about the ten people:

> Bookkeeper, male, thirty-one years old
>
> His wife, six months pregnant
>
> Second-year medical student, male, militant black American
>
> Famous historian-author, forty-two years old, male
>
> Hollywood actress who is a singer and dancer
>
> Biochemist, female
>
> Rabbi, fifty-four years old, male
>
> Olympic athlete, all sports, male
>
> College student, female
>
> Policeman with gun (they cannot be separated)

Source: Johnson, D. W., and Johnson, R. T. (1992). *Creative controversy: Intellectual challenge in the classroom.* Edina, MN: Interaction Book Company.

CHAPTER REVIEW

Test your understanding of resolving interpersonal conflicts by taking the following quiz. Answers are at the end of the chapter.

True   False   **1.** If you have a really good relationship with someone, you'll not have conflicts.

True   False   **2.** You should avoid conflicts whenever possible.

True   False   **3.** Conflicts can give you energy and make your life more interesting.

True   False   **4.** Conflicts can help you understand yourself better and can deepen a relationship.

True   False   **5.** A conflict has been constructive if both people are satisfied with the results and the relationship is stronger.

True   False   **6.** The two major concerns you should take into account during a conflict are achieving your personal goals and keeping a good relationship with the other person.

True   False   **7.** You can build a climate of trust by making yourself vulnerable and by not exploiting the other person's vulnerability.

True   False   **8.** A cooperative interaction helps resolve conflicts by increasing interaction and thus taking your mind off the conflict.

Test your understanding of confrontation and negotiation by answering true or false to the following statements. Answers are at the end of the chapter.

True   False   **9.** Use confrontation when you want to solve a conflict, the relationship is strong, and the other person can respond constructively.

True   False   **10.** In confronting, you need to communicate your observation of the other person's behavior, your reaction, your interpretation, and your desire to understand the other person.

True   False   **11.** In confronting, it is important that you make your point and come out on top.

True   False   **12.** Two useful communication skills in confrontations are personal statements and the hit-and-run technique.

True   False   **13.** Confrontation should be used in almost all conflict situations.

True   False   **14.** Defining the conflict is a major part of confrontation and will help resolve the conflict.

True   False   **15.** Taking the other person's perspective will help you find mutually acceptable solutions to the conflict.

True   False   **16.** Many people avoid conflict for fear they will be rejected.

True   False   **17.** You should avoid any expression of anger in a confrontation.

True   False   **18.** ''I am upset about what you are doing and I'd like to talk to you about it'' is a good confronting statement.

19. Match the following conflict-management styles with their definitions:

___ The Teddy Bear

a. Solution must satisfy both parties.

___ The Fox

b. Smooth over conflict so relationship won't be harmed.

___ The Turtle

c. Seek a middle ground between the two extremes.

___ The Owl

d. Withdraw rather than face conflicts.

___ The Shark

e. Win conflict by overcoming the other person.

20. Match the following misperceptions with their definitions:

___ Mirror image

a. Everything I do is good; everything you do is bad.

___ Mote-beam mechanism

b. What is legitimate for me to do is illegitimate for you to do.

___ Double standard

c. I see the mean, underhanded things you do to me, but I don't see the mean, underhanded things I do to you.

___ Polarized thinking

d. I think I'm right and you're wrong; you think you're right and I'm wrong.

___ Self-fulfilling prophecy

e. I expected you to be hostile. I see only your hostile feelings and not your positive ones. I then take defensive action, which causes you to be more hostile.

What skills have you mastered, and what skills do you need more work on?

1. I have mastered the following:
   ____ An awareness of how I tend to manage conflicts
   ____ How to get an accurate perception of the conflict
   ____ How to communicate my expectations in a conflict
   ____ How to view the conflict from the other person's perspective
   ____ Knowing when to confront
   ____ Knowing what to say when confronting
   ____ Knowing what to avoid when confronting
   ____ Knowing how to build a mutually agreeable definition of the conflict
   ____ Knowing how to take the other person's perspective
   ____ Knowing how to negotiate a solution to the conflict
   ____ Knowing how to follow up on negotiated agreements

2. I need more work on:
   ____ An awareness of how I tend to manage conflicts
   ____ How to get an accurate perception of the conflict
   ____ How to communicate my expectations in a conflict
   ____ How to view the conflict from the other person's perspective
   ____ Knowing when to confront
   ____ Knowing what to say when confronting
   ____ Knowing what to avoid when confronting
   ____ Knowing how to build a mutually agreeable definition of the conflict.
   ____ Knowing how to take the other person's perspective
   ____ Knowing how to negotiate a solution to the conflict
   ____ Knowing how to follow up on negotiated agreements

In this chapter, you learned that conflicts, when handled constructively, are beneficial to a relationship. You identified your strategies for managing a conflict. You learned some of the perception problems that distort a relationship and how to make sure you have accurate communication in a conflict. You also learned how to ensure that you understand the other person's perspective in viewing the conflict. Finally, you learned how to negotiate with others as a way to solve interpersonal problems.

By now, you have learned when and how to use confrontation as a way of resolving conflicts. The next chapter will follow up by giving you ways of dealing with anger and stress, helping you to manage your feelings better.

ANSWERS

Comprehension Test B: 1. e, d, a, b, c; 2. false; 3. true; 4. false; 5. true; 6. true; 7. false; 8. false; 9. true; 10. true.

Chapter Review: 1. false; 2. false; 3. true; 4. true; 5. true; 6. true; 7. true; 8. false; 9. true; 10. true; 11. false; 12. false; 13. false; 14. true; 15. true; 16. true; 17. false; 18. true. 19. b, c, d, a, e; 20. d, c, b, a, e.

9 *Anger, Stress, and Managing Feelings*

If you are patient in one moment of anger, you will escape a hundred days of sorrow.

Chinese proverb

We are always under some stress as long as we are alive. Sometimes the stress is small—when we are asleep, for instance—and sometimes the stress is large, as when we are being attacked by muggers. But as long as we are alive, we are experiencing stress. Stress cannot be avoided, and our stress level is never at zero.

Besides the fact that stress is unavoidable, there are several aspects of stress that you should understand. One is that both too high and too low a stress level is damaging. If we experience too high a level of stress for too long, physiological problems such as headaches, ulcers, and muscle pains can develop. But boredom can make us just as sick as high distress. A certain amount of stress is necessary for meeting the challenges of our lives and for providing the energy required to maintain life, resist aggression, and adapt to constantly changing external influences.

Humans, as a species, are stress seeking. We seem to long for new experiences and new challenges. Traveling to the North Pole, climbing mountains, living in deserts, and exploring the bottom of the oceans are all activities for which we are biologically and socially ill-adapted, but we do them anyway. Humans seek out certain types of stress and enjoy it.

Another important aspect of stress is that the human body reacts to stress in a stereotyped, physiological way. Stress results in an emergency discharge of adrenalin and corresponding changes in the hypothalamus, pituitary, and thymus. Briefly, the autonomic nervous system and the endocrine system combine to speed up cardiovascular functions and slow down gastrointestinal functions. This equips us to take physical action to restore the situation and our internal physiological state to normal. It really does not matter whether we are reacting with great joy or great fear, our physiological response is the same. To understand stress fully, homeostasis must first be understood. *Homeostasis* is the ability to stay the same. The internal environment of our bodies (our temperature, pulse rate, blood pressure, and so forth) must stay fairly constant, despite changes in the external environment, or else we will become sick and even die. Stress alerts our bodies that action is needed to adapt to the external environment by changing our internal environment. The body then strives to restore homeostasis. *Stress,* therefore, can be defined as a nonspecific, general response of the body, signaling a need to perform adaptive functions so that normalcy or homeostasis can be restored.

There are many stressful events in our lives, from the death of a loved one to getting a speeding ticket. Stress affects both sexes and all ages. People in late adolescence or their twenties may be accumulating the effects of stress, effects that may not be apparent until their forties or fifties. Stress disorders are based on the slow developmental accumulation of psychological and physical stress responses throughout an individual's life. How you manage stress has great influence on your ability to reach out to other people, build a relationship, and maintain it over a long period of time. The quality of your relationships, on the other hand, determines how much stress you experience.

Exercise 9.1: Can Friends Help You Stay Well?

What is the level of stress and support in your life? You may wish to get an idea by completing the following questionnaires (California Department of Mental Health, 1981). The procedure is to complete the questionnaires, score them, and plot the results on the chart.

First complete the stress level and support network strength sections that follow.

Stress Level

Circle each stress event which you have experienced within the last 12 months. Then add the scores for each item you circled.

Personal

- (6) Serious injury or illness
- (6) Alcohol, drug, or emotional problem
- (4) Marriage
- (4) Death of close friend
- (2) Trouble with friends or neighbors
- (2) Begin or end school or training program

Work & Finances

- (6) Lost job, retired
- (4) Sold or bought home
- (2) Changed jobs, promotion
- (2) Trouble with boss

Family

- (10) Death of spouse or immediate family member
- (8) Divorce
- (6) Reconciliation or separation
- (4) Serious illness or injury of family member
- (4) Pregnancy or birth
- (4) Family arguments or trouble with in-laws
- (4) Child enters or leaves home
- (2) Relative moves into household
- (2) Moved to new residence

Stress Total:

Support Network Strength

Circle *one* response for *each* item. Then add the scores next to each item you circled.

1. At work, how many persons do you talk to about a job hassle?

    none (or not employed) (0)   one or two (3)   two or three (4)   four or more (5)

2. How many neighbors do you trade favors with (loan tools or household items, share rides, babysitting, etc.)?

    none (0)   one (1)   two or three (2)   four or more (3)

3. Do you have a spouse or partner?

    no (0)   several different partners (2)   one steady partner (6)

    married or living with someone (10)

4. How often do friends and close family members visit you at home?

    rarely (0)   about once a month (1)   several times a month (4)

    once a week or more (8)

5. How many friends or family members do you talk to about personal matters?

    none (0)   one or two (6)   three to five (8)   six or more (10)

6. How often do you participate in a social, community, or sports group?

    rarely (0)   about once a month (1)   several times a month (2)

    once a week or more   (4)

    Support Total:

Below, draw a line across each barometer where your scores for stress level and network strength fall.

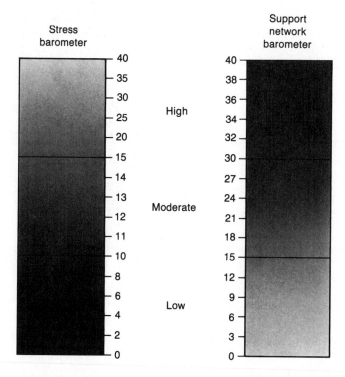

Stress barometer	Support network barometer

If your STRESS LEVEL score is:

Less than 10:
You have a *low stress level* and your life has been stable in most areas.

10-15:
You have a *moderate stress level* and there has been a lot of change in your life.

If your SUPPORT NETWORK score is:

Less than 15:
Your support network has *low strength* and probably does not provide much support. You need to consider making more social contacts.

15-29:
Your support network has *moderate strength* and likely provides enough support except during periods of high stress.

If your STRESS LEVEL score is:

16 or more:
You have a *high stress level* and there have been major adjustments in your life.

If your SUPPORT NETWORK score is:

30 or more:
Your support network has *high strength* and it will likely maintain your well-being even during periods of high stress.

The chart below illustrates the relationship between stress and the support we get from others. Using your ranking (*high, moderate, low*) from the previous exercise, put an "x" where your stress level and support network strength scores intersect. When your stress level is *lower* than your network strength, your score will be in the darker area of the chart. When your stress level is *higher* than your support strength, your score will fall in the lighter area. Darker colors indicate a greater likelihood of remaining well. Lighter colors indicate a higher risk of becoming ill.

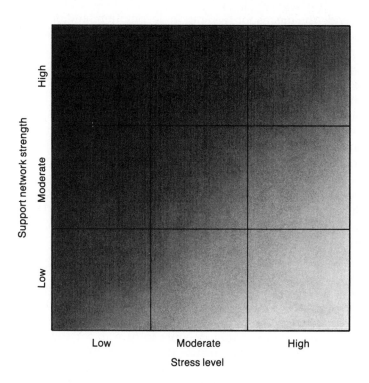

Exercise 9.1 was reprinted with permission of the California Department of Mental Health from *Friends can be good medicine.* Sacramento: State of California, Technical Report, 1981.

MANAGING STRESS THROUGH SOCIAL-SUPPORT SYSTEMS

One of the most effective ways of managing stress is through utilizing social-support systems involving other people who care about you and/or are sympathetic to your plight. Discussing stressful situations with friends and clarifying one's feelings through describing them to a sympathetic person are some of the most helpful strategies for managing stress. One of the first actions you should take when you find yourself experiencing stress, therefore, is to seek out friends and sympathetic acquaintances with whom to discuss the situation and your feelings.

There is a biological precedent for such a procedure. In the course of evolution, colonies of individual cells combined to form a single cooperative community in which competition was amply overcompensated by mutual assistance (because each member of the group could depend on the other for help). Different cells specialized, each undertaking different functions, some to look after food intake and digestion, others to provide the means for respiration, locomotion, and defense, still others to coordinate the activities of the entire colony. The evolution of diverse species was largely dependent on the development of processes that permitted many cells to live in harmony, with a minimum of stress between them, serving their own best interests by ensuring the survival of the entire complex structure. Stress within the body is managed through this complex division of labor in which different specialized cells work collaboratively to deal with threats to the productiveness of the entire colony. The indispensability of disciplined, orderly, mutually cooperative support is illustrated by its opposite—the development of cancer, whose most characteristic feature is that it cares only for itself. Cancer feeds on the other parts of the biological system to which it belongs until it kills the entire system, thus committing biological suicide, since a cancer cell cannot live except within the body in which it started its egocentric development.

Loneliness, isolation, and lack of social support during periods of stress do create physiological damage and aggravate the effects of stress. Isolating ourselves during stressful times is the equivalent of committing social suicide, since destroying or failing to maintain our relationships when we need them the most is self-destructive. When we are experiencing stress, we need other people to turn to for support. Yet many people have too few relationships they can count on as sources of support. In our complex, technological, bureaucratic world, a broad base of interpersonal support is important. In addition to whatever family we may have, we need friends and acquaintances who respect us, challenge us, provide resources for us, and who will be our mentors, evaluators, experts, and energizers. When we are experiencing stress, it is important to feel that we are not alone and to realize that by discussing situations with other people, we can alleviate stress and provide ourselves with relief from pain.

THE NATURE AND VALUE OF ANGER

Emotions are always involved in conflicts, and one of the most common is anger. When other people obstruct your goal accomplishment, frustrate your attempts to accomplish something, interfere with your plans, make you feel belittled and rejected, or indicate that you are of no value or importance, anger results. When you get angry at other people the results can be either destructive or constructive. The results are destructive when you express anger in a way that creates dislike, hatred, frustration, and a desire for revenge on the part of the other person, or when anger is repressed and held in, creating irritability, depression, insomnia, and physiological problems, such as headaches and ulcers. The results are constructive when you feel more energy, motivation, challenge, and excitement, and the other person feels friendship, gratitude, goodwill, and concern. In this chapter we shall examine anger in some depth and discuss how it can be managed so that constructive rather than destructive results occur.

Anger both causes and accompanies distress. Anger can result in tight muscles, teeth grinding, piercing stares, headaches, heart attacks, loud voices, projectiles, and smashed furniture. When we are angry our blood boils, we are fit to be tied, we have reached the end of our rope, and what happened is the last straw. Anger is an emotion that occurs regularly in the life of every person, more often and with greater intensity at some times than at others. Failure to manage anger constructively can lead to alienation of loved ones, disrupted work performance, and even cardiovascular disorder. However, proper recognition, understanding, acceptance, and channeling of anger can make life more comfortable, productive, and exciting. In order for anger to be managed constructively, its components must be identified, and its major functions must be understood. The useful and constructive aspects of anger must be promoted while the destructive and useless aspects of anger are quelled. Rules for constructive anger management must be followed.

The main components involved in most human anger are as follows:

1. Anger is usually a defense against something.

2. Anger occurs when we are not getting something we want or would like. We get angry when we are frustrated, thwarted, or attacked.

3. Anger has in it a sense of righteousness and a belief that one's personal rights have been violated. When we are angry, we usually believe that we are rightfully angry because the other person has acted unjustly or irrationally.

4. There is a narrowing of perceptual focus and priorities when we are angry. All our attention is focused on the person and behavior we are angry with.

5. There is a demand aspect of anger. It makes us demand that we get our way.

6. There is considerable physiological arousal that demands expression in physical action. We not only are ready to "fight or flee," there is a demand that we actually do so.

When we plan how to manage our anger constructively, we need to keep in mind that anger is a righteous but defensive reaction to frustration and aggression based on a unidimensional perceptual focus, a physical demand to take action, and a belief that we must get our way.

There are at least eight major functions of anger. Each is described briefly below.

1. *Anger provides energy and increases the vigor with which we act.* Anger helps us to move toward action and to utilize the energy provided by the physiological stress reaction for productive activity. Anger mobilizes us for action and thereby provides considerable physical energy to apply toward achieving our goals.

2. *Anger disrupts ongoing behavior by agitation, impulsiveness, and interference with attention and information processing.* Anger disrupts behavior, causing people to focus continually on the injustice that has been done to them or on the attack they are defending against rather than on tasks at hand or on receiving new information. It often causes us to act impulsively in ways aimed at correcting the perceived injustice or defending against the perceived aggressive actions of the other person.

3. *Anger facilitates the expression of negative feelings and negative feedback, which might not be expressed if we were not angry.* The constructive aspect of such communication is that it provides information we

need for accurate identification of problems and high-quality decision making. Anger is a sign something is going on that needs to be changed. It is only through facing such problems that they can be solved. Being angry and confronting another person in a way that leads to problem solving increases the trust within the relationship and increases confidence that the relationship is strong enough to handle future strains. Healthy relationships depend on the ability of both partners to give accurate but negative feedback to each other, and anger helps us to do so. But the potential negative aspect of such forthrightness is that the strength of the negative feelings or feedback may be inappropriate to the provocation, may be overstated, or may be stated in such an offensive and threatening way that the conflict is escalated and the other person becomes fearful and angry.

4. *Anger is a defense against vulnerability.* It changes internal anxiety to external conflict. Anger can overcome anxiety and fear and encourage us to take actions we would never take otherwise. A small child may strike out in anger against a much bigger peer. A subordinate may confront a boss she is afraid of. A very shy person who is angry may introduce herself to strangers. Such actions can be highly constructive or destructive, depending on the circumstances.

5. *Anger initiates or strengthens antagonism as an internal, learned stimulus for aggression.* Feeling angry can be a signal that aggressive actions are called for. Many times we become aggressive through habit when faced with a provocation and strike out verbally or physically at the other people in the situation.

6. *Anger can be a signal that an event is a provocation or that something frustrating or unpleasant is taking place.* Discovering that we are angry can help clarify or discriminate what is taking place within a situation.

7. *Anger helps us maintain a sense of virtue and righteousness in the face of opposition.* Anger helps us maintain a belief that we are right, justified, and superior.

8. *Anger can intimidate other people and is therefore a source of interpersonal power and influence.* When we want to overpower another person, get our way, or dominate a situation, being angry can often help us to do so.

Being angry at another person can be an unpleasant experience. We can make the other person resentful and hostile when we express anger.

We can become anxious after we have expressed anger as we anticipate rejection, counter-anger, and escalation of the conflict. Yet anger can have many positive effects on our problem solving if we learn to manage it constructively.

RULES FOR MANAGING ANGER CONSTRUCTIVELY

In managing your anger constructively, there is a set of rules to follow. *The first rule in managing anger is to recognize and acknowledge the fact that you are angry.* Anger is a natural, healthy, normal human feeling. Everyone feels it. You need not fear or reject your anger. For one thing, repressed, denied anger does not vanish, but often erupts suddenly in verbal and physical assaults on people and property as well as overreactions to minor provocations. In addition, repression and denial of your anger can create headaches, ulcers, muscle pains, and other physiological ailments. Remember that anger and aggression are not the same thing. You can express anger without being aggressive.

The second rule is to decide whether or not you wish to express your anger. This involves at least two steps: clarifying the intent of the other person and deciding how to respond. You first ask for clarification before deciding how to respond when someone has done something that you feel is aggressive or provocative in nature. Do not assume that aggression was intended without checking it out. It may be a misunderstanding, and you have nothing to be angry about. If it was not a misunderstanding you proceed to the second step of deciding how to respond. There are a number of considerations in making such a decision. The first is remembering that heightened anger makes you agitated and impulsive, and that impulsive, antagonistic acts can escalate conflict and get you into trouble. The second is remembering that your information-processing capacity will also decrease as your anger increases, making your analysis of what actions are needed somewhat suspect. Third, beware of the righteousness of your anger. In most situations it is not a matter of punishing people you think have acted in an unjust way. It is a matter of ensuring that a constructive outcome results from the situation. Do not attempt to prove you were right or that you are morally superior. Think of how to solve the problem. The fourth consideration is facing your anger and making the decision while the provocation is small. Don't disregard small irritations and little frustrations. Small feelings, if they are kept inside and allowed to build up, become big feelings. You may explode in an overreaction someday if you store up all your little frustrations and annoyances. Do not keep them inside. Finally, it is often helpful to delay taking action and talk the situation over with a colleague before deciding how to respond. Remember that it is usually better to keep your life clear, dealing with issues and provocations when they arise and when you feel angry, not after days or weeks of being upset. It is a good idea not to take flight by avoiding the person or situation, thus waiting and letting resentment and hostility build up. But there are times when avoidance may be the most effective action to take. When the expression of anger will be ineffective or destructive, you need to be able to switch to a more productive and suitable pattern of behavior.

The third rule is to express your anger directly and descriptively when it is appropriate to do so. Once you have expressed your anger constructively, let it go. The specific procedures and skills for expressing anger are discussed later in this chapter. Remember to take responsibility for your anger (the other person did not make you become angry; your anger resulted from your interpretation of the causes of the other person's behavior). Second, when you express anger towards a student or colleague, it is part of a confrontation and you must be willing to become more involved with the other person and the situation as your anger becomes clarified. Third, express your anger to the appropriate person and make it to the point. Do not generalize, but be specific about the provocation. Fourth, use the skills of accurate communication and constructive feedback (Johnson 1991). Nonverbal messages are more powerful in expressing feelings than are words, but they are also more difficult to understand. To communicate your anger clearly, you need to be skilled in both verbal and nonverbal communication, and you need to be able to make your words and nonverbal messages congruent with each other. Make the statement of your anger descriptive, accurate, and to the point, and express it to the appropriate person. Keep in touch with yourself and say it all. State the anger directly without being sarcastic. Use honest, expressive language and avoid name calling, accusations, put-downs, and physical attacks. Finally, make the expression of anger cathartic. Catharsis refers to the feeling of release of pent-up emotion that people experience either by talking about their troubles or by crying, laughing, shouting, or otherwise engaging in very active emotional release. Anger needs to be expressed in a way that terminates it and gets it over and done with. Anger is not a feeling to hold on to. If you have expressed it correctly, you should no longer feel angry afterwards.

The fourth rule of managing your anger constructively is to express it indirectly or react in an alternative way when direct expression is not appropri-

ate. If it is not appropriate to express your anger directly, free yourself from the anger before discussing the conflict with the other person. Feelings do need to be expressed. The stronger the feeling, the stronger the need for expression. In privacy you can swear at your boss, hit a punching bag, or swim hard while imagining what you would like to say to a certain acquaintance. There may be many times when you cannot express your anger directly to the person provoking you. Yet it is important to express your anger in a way that ends it. You do not want to stay angry forever. The sooner you get rid of the feelings, the happier your life will be. Expressing and terminating anger indirectly usually involves the following:

1. *Physical exercise:* There is a general maxim that when one is angry and wants to feel better tomorrow, then one should exercise today. Vigorous exercise like jogging, swimming, tennis, or volleyball provides physical release of energy that is important in releasing anger.

2. *Private physical expression:* Strongly express the feeling in private by shouting, swearing, crying, moaning, throwing pottery, pillow fights, and even hitting a pillow against a wall while yelling. This will provide a physical release of energy and anger.

3. *Psychological detachment:* Resolve the situation in your mind or resign yourself to it. Tell yourself things that can help. Give up thoughts of revenge and getting back at other people. You want to resolve the problem. You can put up with an unfair administrator. An obnoxious colleague is not really that bad. Let the negative feelings go; do not hang onto them. They will only make your life unpleasant. Another alternative is to change the way you view the provocation, thereby changing your feeling of anger. Through modifying your interpretations of what the other person's behavior means, you can control your feelings, responding with amusement or indifference rather than with anger. This skill is discussed at length later in this chapter.

4. *Relaxation:* Learn to relax when you wish so that you can relax yourself when your anger has been triggered. As you learn to relax more easily, your ability to regulate your anger will improve.

By learning alternative ways of reacting to provocations and indirect ways of expressing anger, you will be able to choose the most effective response. Such freedom gives you an advantage in situations in which other people are trying to provoke you, because the best way to take charge of such a situation is not to get angry when most people would expect or even want you to do so.

The fifth rule is to stay task oriented. You can control and contain your anger and usually be far more effective in managing the situation by staying task oriented. This means staying focused on what must be done in the situation to get the outcome you want. Especially when the other person is angry, do not get distracted by his or her anger; rather, stay focused on the task. Taking insults personally distracts you from your task and involves you in unnecessary conflict. Do not let yourself get sidetracked or baited into a quarrel. Recognize what the other person is doing, but do not be provoked by it; rather, stay task oriented and focused on the issue. There is evidence that anger directed toward a person will be far more destructive than will anger directed toward an issue. Viewing an incident as a personal affront is likely to result in disruptive and defensive anger, while viewing an incident as a problem to be solved is likely to result in discriminative, expressive, and energizing anger.

The sixth rule is to analyze, understand, and reflect upon your anger. Get to know yourself so that you recognize (a) the events and behaviors that trigger your anger and (b) the internal signs of arousal that signal you are becoming angry. You can control your anger. You can find your own buttons so that you know when someone else is pushing them. It is important for you to understand the regularities of your anger patterns—when, in what circumstances, and with whom you become angry—and then plan how to avoid frustrating, anger-provoking situations. And you can explicitly decide what you want and plan in detail how to manage situations to obtain it without getting angry. As you become more and more sharply tuned to the signs of tension and upset inside you, you will achieve greater ability to short-circuit the anger process. You can train yourself to use the initial flash of anger as a signal that anger is on the way and that you may therefore need to switch to a more productive and suitable behavior pattern. Signs of internal arousal can be alerting signals that you are becoming upset and that effective action is called for if a positive outcome is to result. Thus, you can learn to stop anger before it develops.

Anger often results from your believing that things are not going the way you want them to go or that you are powerless in a situation in which you want to be able to influence other people. Remember, you gain power and influence when you keep calm and refuse to get angry. Since anger is sometimes due to doubting yourself or letting yourself feel threatened by someone else, it is important to remember that you are a worthwhile person and that you have many strengths and competencies. This can keep you from feeling angry. And you should always beware of the righteousness of your anger. It can be blind.

The seventh rule is to congratulate yourself when you have succeeded in managing your anger constructively. Feel good about your success. Don't focus on your mistakes and failings or on the nastiness of other people. Focus on your ability to manage your anger constructively.

The eighth rule is to express emotions other than anger. Besides expressing negative feelings, it is important to express positive feelings while discussing a conflict. There are positive feelings, such as liking, appreciation, and respect, that strengthen your relationship with the other person. Both positive and negative feelings have to be communicated with skill in a conflict.

EXPRESSING ANGER CONSTRUCTIVELY

> *I was angry with my friend:*
> *I told my wrath, my wrath did end.*
> *I was angry with my foe:*
> *I told it not, my wrath did grow.*
>
> William Blake

Expressing anger constructively can be one of the most difficult aspects of resolving conflicts. There is a risk in expressing feelings such as anger. When you express anger, you have to worry about alienating the other person. Expressing anger could lead to losing the relationship or even losing your job. And you have to worry whether the other person will also get angry at you. Being exposed to the anger of others is painful.

To express anger constructively you must first be aware that you are angry, accept anger as natural and normal, and decide to express it. When feelings are repressed, denied, or ignored, they will come out later in one way or another. Keeping anger buried is usually harmful, causing a number of problems. First, it adds to your frustrations. This is not sensible. Getting angry over a frustration does not usually remove the frustration and always adds to your discomfort. Second, anger prevents you from solving problems. Being hateful simply fills your thoughts with delicious ways of getting even with others, not with how to get others to behave differently toward you. The net result is that things get worse and worse as you become angrier and angrier. Third, concealed anger is often displaced onto other persons. Not expressing anger at a student or colleague can lead to displacing anger at your friends, family, or some stranger. Hidden anger does not vanish, but often suddenly erupts in physical violence and assaults on both people and property. Fourth, anger can make you physically sick. Headaches, high blood pressure, and physical pains are not helpful when you are trying to resolve a conflict. Fifth, repeated failure to express anger in words sometimes produces the appearance of apathy. If you repeatedly fail to express anger in words, you may give the impression that you don't care. In the long run, keeping anger to yourself will only hurt you and your relationships.

There are several advantages to expressing anger directly in a conflict. Anger conveys to other people what your commitments are and which commitments must be respected or changed. Expressing anger can clear the air so that positive feelings can once again be felt and expressed. Problems that are being ignored are brought to the surface and highlighted through the expression of anger. Anger can override fear and feelings of vulnerability and lead you to act more competently in troublesome situations.

DIRECTLY EXPRESSING ANGER

To express your anger constructively, describe the other person's behavior, describe your feelings, and make your nonverbal messages congruent with your words. The purpose of asserting your anger is to create a shared understanding of the relationship so it may be improved or so you may be more effective in achieving your goals. You want the other person to know how you perceive and feel about his or her actions, and you wish to end up knowing how the other person perceives and feels about your actions. You want to discuss the situation until you and the other person have a common perspective or frame of reference in viewing the relationship and your interactions with each other.

Behavior Descriptions

In describing the other person's provocative actions, you need to be skillful in observing what actually occurred and in letting the other person know what behavior you are responding to by describing it clearly and specifically. To do this, you must describe visible evidence, behavior that is open to anyone's observation. Restrict yourself to talking about the actions of the other person. Using personal statements is also a good idea so that it is clear that you are taking ownership of your observations. An example of a good behavior description is, "Jim, by my count, you have just interrupted me for the third time." (Not, "Jim, you are really being rude," which is negative labeling, or, "Jim, you always want to be the center of attention," which imputes an unworthy motive.)

Descriptions of Your Own Feelings

You describe your feelings by using personal statements (referring to *I*, *me*, or *my*) and specifying the feeling by name or by action verb, simile or some other figure of speech. Your description will be more helpful and effective if it is specific rather than general ("You bumped my arm" rather than "You never watch where you are going"), tentative rather than absolute ("You seem unconcerned about completing our project" rather than "You don't care about the project and you never will"), and informing rather than demanding ("I haven't finished yet" rather than "Stop interrupting me"). This latter point needs reemphasizing because of its importance; the description of your anger should be noncoercive and should not be a demand that the other person must change. Avoid judgments of the other person ("You are egocentric"), name calling or trait labeling ("You're a phony"), accusations and imputing undesirable motives to the other person ("You always have to be the center of attention"), commands, demands, and orders ("Stop talking and listen!"), and sarcasm ("You're really considerate, aren't you?" when the opposite is meant). By describing your feelings about the other person's actions, your feelings are seen as temporary and capable of change rather than as permanent. It is better to say, "At this point, I am very annoyed with you" than "I dislike you and I always will."

Making Nonverbal Messages Congruent

In describing your feelings you need to make your nonverbal messages similar to your verbal ones. When you express anger verbally, your facial expression should be serious, your tone of voice cold, your eye contact direct, and your posture rather stiff. Contradictory verbal and nonverbal messages will only indicate to the other person that you are untrustworthy and will make the other person anxious.

Listening Skills

While discussing your anger with another person it is important to use good listening skills. Use *perception checks* to make sure that you are not making false assumptions about the other person's feelings and intentions (''My impression is that you are not interested in trying to understand my ideas. Am I wrong?'' ''Did my last statement bother you?''). And when negotiating the meaning of the other person's actions and in clarifying both your feelings and the feelings of the other person, use paraphrasing to make sure you accurately understand the other person and that the other person feels understood and listened to.

Assess Impact on Other

Take into account the impact your anger will have on the other person. While you will usually feel better after expressing anger constructively and directly to another person, the other person may feel alienated and resentful. After expressing anger directly, it is important to make sure that the other person has a chance to respond and clarify his or her feelings before the interaction is ended.

Summary

To express anger constructively, first describe the other person's provocative behavior and then describe your anger verbally while making your nonverbal messages congruent with your words. An example would be, ''Jim, by my count you have just interrupted me for the third time in the past half hour, and I am both frustrated and angry as a result'' (while maintaining a serious facial expression, a cold tone of voice, direct eye contact, and a rather stiff posture). You should then be ready to negotiate on the meaning of Jim's actions and on whether or not anger is the appropriate feeling to have.

In expressing anger your attitude should not be, ''Who's right and who's wrong?'' but rather, ''What can each of us learn from this discussion that will make our relationship more productive and satisfying?'' As a result of the discussion, each of you will act with fuller awareness of the effect of your actions on the other person as well as with more understanding of the other person's intentions. One, both, or neither of you may act differently in the future because of this increased awareness. Any change in future behavior needs to be self-chosen rather than compelled by a desire to please or a need to submit to the other person.

Finally, make sure the timing of the expression of your anger is appropriate. Generally, express your anger when there is time enough to discuss the situation and the provocation. The closer in time your reaction is expressed to the provocation, the more constructive the discussion will be.

ASSERTIVENESS AND AGGRESSIVENESS

All people have a perfect right to express their thoughts, feelings, opinions, and preferences and to expect that other people will treat them with respect and dignity. In interpersonal situations involving stress and anger, you may behave nonassertively, aggressively, or assertively. When you behave *nonassertively,* you say nothing in response to a provocation, keeping your feelings to yourself, hiding your feelings from others, and perhaps even hiding your feelings from yourself. Nonassertive behavior is often dishonest and involves letting other people violate your personal right to be treated with respect and dignity.

Aggressive behavior is an attempt to hurt someone or destroy something. It infringes on the rights of others and involves expressing your feelings indirectly through insults, sarcasm, labels, put-downs, and hostile statements and actions. Aggressive behavior involves expressing thoughts, feelings, and opinions in a way that violates others' rights to be treated with respect and dignity.

Assertive behavior involves describing your feelings, thoughts, opinions, and preferences directly to another person in an honest and appropriate way that respects both yourself and the other person. It enables you to act in your own best interests, to stand up for yourself without undue anxiety, to express honest feelings comfortably, and to exercise personal rights without denying the rights of others. Assertive behavior is direct, honest, self-enhancing self-expression that is not hurtful to others and is appropriate for the receiver and the situation.

In general, it is a good idea to raise your restraints and inhibitions against aggressive and nonassertive behavior and to lower any inhibitions, restraints, or anxieties you have about being assertive.

IRRATIONAL BELIEFS UNDERLYING ANGER AND A BLAME ORIENTATION

Long-term anger is based on two irrational beliefs. The first is that you must have your way and that it is awful not to get everything you want.

This is known as *catastrophizing*. The second is that people are bad and should be severely dealt with if they have behaved wrongly. If you see the cause of your frustration as being wicked people who deserve to be punished for their evil acts, you are stuck in a blame orientation. A blame orientation distracts you from finding a solution to your frustration.

Exercise 9.1: Understanding My Anger

Being aware of our feelings is an important and somewhat difficult task. Many of us were taught to hide our feelings. We learned to pretend we did not have them. This is especially true of feelings we consider negative, such as anger. We often keep our anger inside and act as if it were not there. We deny to ourselves that we are angry. In order to be aware of our anger and express it appropriately, we must understand what makes us angry.

The purpose of this exercise is to increase your awareness of what makes you angry. The procedure is:

1. Working by yourself, complete the statements given below on a separate sheet of paper. Be sure to write out your answers fully.

2. Form into groups of four. Take the first statement and discuss the answers of each member. Then go on to the second statement.

3. After you have finished discussing all sixteen statements, write down:

   a. The five major things that make your group members angry

   b. The five major ways in which your group members express their anger

   c. The five major conclusions your group has come to about what happens when anger is expressed.

4. Share your conclusions with the other groups, while they share their conclusions with you.

5. In your group of four, discuss how your group's conclusions compared with the conclusions of the other groups. Do you all feel anger for the same reasons? Do you all express your anger in the same way? Do you all feel the same way when someone is angry at you? Do you all agree on what consequences will result from expressing anger?

My Anger

Complete the following statements. Be specific. Try to think of times when you were angry or someone was angry at you. You may wish to substitute "co-workers" or "fellow students" for "friends" and "parents," or "boss" for "teacher."

1. I feel angry when my friends . . .
2. When I'm angry at my friends, I usually . . .
3. After expressing my anger, I feel . . .
4. The way I express anger usually makes my friends . . .
5. When my friends express anger toward me, I feel . . .
6. When I feel that way, I usually . . .
7. After reacting to my friends' anger, I feel . . .
8. My reactions to my friends' anger usually results in their . . .
9. I feel angry when my teacher . . .
10. When I'm angry at my teacher I usually . . .
11. The way I act when I'm angry at my teacher makes me feel . . .
12. The way I act when I'm angry at my teacher usually results in my teacher's . . .
13. When my teacher expresses anger at me, I feel . . .
14. When I feel that way I usually . . .
15. After reacting to my teacher's anger, I feel . . .
16. My reactions to my teacher's anger usually result in my teacher's . . .

Exercise 9.2: Defusing the Bomb Exercise

The purpose of this exercise is to discuss how you manage provocations. The procedure for the exercise is:

1. Divide into groups of three.
2. Read the following incident, and as a group answer these questions:
   a. How would you feel?
   b. What would you do?
   c. How would you maximize positive outcomes and minimize negative outcomes?
   d. What would you say to yourself to manage your feelings constructively?

Incident

You are a teacher at a suburban junior high school. You are sitting in your office when a parent, Ms. Jones, walks in without an appointment. Ms. Jones, in a very loud and angry voice, begins to demand that you reprimand one of your students, stating that the student is vicious and picks on Ms. Jones's son (who is a student in your class). Ms. Jones refuses to listen to your explanations, criticizes your ideas, and even brags about how well she understands teaching and child development. For the most part,

she is uninterested in anything you have to say. Finally, as you present your view once again, Ms. Jones calls you a stupid jerk.

Exercise 9.3: Managing Provocations

Novaco (1975) described a sequence of stages in managing a provocation constructively. Those stages are:

1. When possible, be prepared for a provocation.
2. Experience the provocation.
3. Cope with arousal and agitation.
4. Reflect on the experience and engage in self-reward for coping successfully.

For each stage, there are a number of statements people make to themselves to help them manage the provocation successfully. The assumption is that through controlling what you say to yourself before, during, and following a provocation you can change your conflict behavior and instruct yourself in more constructive behavioral patterns. The purpose of this exercise is to give you some practice in differentiating among the self-statements for each stage and applying them to a conflict situation you have recently been involved in. The procedure is:

1. Form into triads and classify the self-statements below according to the four stages of managing a provocation constructively.

2. Have each member of the triad then identify a conflict situation that usually creates anger and distress in him.

3. Working as a triad, take each conflict situation and work out a series of self-statements that can be used during each stage of managing the provocation constructively. Each member of the triad should leave the triad with a set of self-statements that will help her manage the conflict situation more constructively next time it appears.

Managing Provocations by Talking to Yourself

Given below are a number of statements that you could say to yourself to help yourself manage a conflict situation constructively. Working as a triad, classify each statement given below as belonging in one of Novaco's four stages of managing a provocation constructively. (For Key, see Appendix, pp. 369-70.)

Stage   →   *Self-Statement*

1. _____ I can work out a plan for handling this.
2. _____ As long as I keep cool, I'm in control here.
3. _____ Getting upset won't help.
4. _____ It worked!
5. _____ If I find myself getting upset, I will know what to do.
6. _____ You don't need to prove yourself.
7. _____ It's not worth it to get so angry.
8. _____ I could have gotten more upset than it was worth.
9. _____ I actually got through that without getting angry. Way to go!
10. _____ My anger is a signal that it's time to start talking to myself.
11. _____ If I start to get mad, I will just be banging my head against the wall. So I might as well just relax.
12. _____ This could be a bad situation, but I believe in myself.
13. _____ I'm doing better at handling myself in these situations all the time.
14. _____ My muscles are starting to feel tight. Time to relax and slow things down.
15. _____ Don't assume the worst or jump to conclusions. Look for positives.
16. _____ Before I go in, I need to take a few deep breaths, relax myself, make sure I feel comfortable and at ease.
17. _____ I didn't take anything personally. I sure feel better that way!
18. _____ I'm not going to let them get to me.

19. _____ He would probably like me to get really angry. Well, I'm going to disappoint him.

20. _____ I'll be able to manage this situation. I know how to regulate my anger.

21. _____ Calm down. I can't expect people to act the way I want them to.

22. _____ I've been getting upset for too long when it wasn't necessary. I have really improved in not getting angry!

23. _____ There won't be any need to get angry or upset.

24. _____ Don't get upset; just keep thinking about what I want to do to make sure I get what I want out of this situation.

25. _____ Keep focused on the task. Don't let them distract you into a quarrel.

26. _____ What is it I have to do to stay calm and be effective?

27. _____ There is no need to doubt myself. What he says doesn't matter.

28. _____ I am excellent at not reacting with anger when people provoke me.

MANAGING YOUR FEELINGS

I have known a great many troubles,
but most of them never happened.

Mark Twain

There are times when your relationships may result in great happiness, satisfaction, growth, and joy. There are other times when your relationships may result in depression, sadness, anger, worry, frustration, or guilt. You will be depressed occasionally about a relationship or angry at the way in which other people are treating you. If the feelings are dealt with constructively, they will not last very long. But if you have destructive patterns of interpreting what is happening in your life, you can be depressed and upset all the time. You can turn small events into tragedies. You could, for example, react as if a colleague's not liking you were as serious as finding out you have incurable cancer. There are people who are talented at taking an occasional small event and creating major feelings of depression or anger that stay with them for several days or weeks. Don't be one of them.

How you feel is important for your enjoyment of life and for your ability to relate effectively to other people. If you are depressed, angry, worried, and anxious about your relationships, then you need to take some sort of action. You need to get rid of negative feelings and to promote positive feelings, such as happiness, contentment, pride, and satisfaction.

To change negative or destructive feelings, you have two choices. You can try to change things outside of yourself; you can change jobs, friends, location, and careers. Your second choice is to change things within yourself; you can change your interpretations of what is happening in your life. Changing your interpretations will change your feelings. In choosing whether to try to change something outside of yourself or inside yourself, it is important to remember that the easiest thing to change in your life is yourself.

Let's take an example. Sam believes his boss is always picking on him. He thinks that his boss gives him the dirtiest jobs to do. Sam thinks that his colleagues are not made to work as hard as he is. The principal always seems to be criticizing Sam but not his colleagues. All this makes Sam angry, depressed, worried, and frustrated. Sam also feels that the situation is hopeless. "What can I do?" asks Sam. "My boss has all the power. He can fire me, but I can't do anything to him."

Sam has two choices. He can try to change his boss. Or he can try to change his feelings. Psychologists would tell Sam it is easier to change his feelings than to change his boss. What do you think?

TIPS ON SURVIVAL: HOW TO LIVE A LONG LIFE

Want to live a long time? Research studies have been done on survival in concentration camps, in prisoner-of-war camps, on cancer and heart-disease victims, and on old age. Five factors seem to be the most important for survival:

1. *Having deeply held goals and commitments.* These goals and commitments need to involve relationships with other people. People who lived the longest in concentration and prisoner-of-war camps, for example, were people who turned their concern outward and worked to help other people survive.

2. *Sharing your distress with other people.* Quiet, polite, passive, accepting, and well-behaved persons die. A person who openly shares her suffering with other people and is aggressive in getting her needs met will tend to live longer.

3. *High morale is important.* Depression kills. In concentration camps, in POW camps, and among cancer patients, people who become depressed die.

4. *Physical activity is an important survival factor.* Keeping yourself physically active will help you survive.

5. *Friendships and love relationships are vital.* Lonely people die. Isolated people die. People with good friends and loving relationships survive. Many psychologists believe that loneliness is the biggest personal-adjustment problem in the United States.

Want to live a long and happy life? Then build goals and commitments that are important to you and that involve other people's welfare. Share your moments of distress and discomfort with other people. Learn how to talk with other people about how you feel. Avoid depression and keep your morale high. Keep physically active. And constantly build and renew friendships and love relationships. We will all die someday. Let us hope that we don't die from lack of commitments, passivity, depression, inactivity, or loneliness.

DISPOSABLE FEELINGS: LIKE IT OR DUMP IT

The five aspects of expressing feelings to be discussed are:

1. Gathering information through your five senses.
2. Interpreting the information.
3. Experiencing the feelings appropriate to your interpretations.
4. Deciding how you intend to express your feelings.
5. Expressing your feelings.

It is your interpretations that cause your feelings, not the events in your life. Feelings are not caused by events and people around you; they are caused by the ways in which you interpret your experiences. Your boss or teacher cannot upset you; only the interpretations you make about their behavior can upset you. Your friends cannot upset you; only the interpretations you make about your friends' behavior can upset you. This means that you can control your feelings. You can decide which feelings you would like to keep and expand. You can decide which feelings you would like to dump and get rid of. Your feelings are disposable!

Depending on your interpretations, you can feel satisfaction, pride, enjoyment, fun, contentment, and challenge about your relationships. Or you can feel depressed, anxious, worried, angry, sad, hopeless, and helpless about your relationships. When your interpretations result in feelings that contribute to a painful and troubled life, you are managing your feelings destructively. When you have feelings of depression and anxiety, your work suffers, the people around you suffer, and you are just no fun to be around. Maintaining relationships means that you are able to manage your interpretations so that you are not overly depressed, anxious, angry, or upset.

Your interpretations are heavily influenced by the assumptions you make about what is good or bad, what you do or do not need, and what causes what in the world. Sometimes people have assumptions that cause them to be depressed or upset most of the time. You can assume, for example, that your boss has to like you more than any other employee. Since there is always somebody your boss will like better than you, such an assumption will keep you unhappy. You will be depressed because your boss does not like you best! Assumptions such as this one are irrational. An *irrational assumption* is a belief that makes you depressed or upset most of the time. The belief (such as, the boss has to like me best or else my life is ruined) is accepted as true without any proof. If you believe your boss has to love you or else life is unbearable, you have an irrational assumption. If you believe that you have to be perfect or else you are absolutely worthless, you have an irrational assumption. If you believe that everyone in the world has to think you are absolutely marvelous or else you will be miserable, you have an irrational assumption. If you think you are unemployable because you can't immediately find a job, you have an irrational assumption. Irrational assumptions can only make you feel miserable because they lead to depressing interpretations. All you have to do to ruin your life is to make a few irrational assumptions and refuse to change them no matter how much pain they cause!

It takes energy to have destructive feelings. It takes energy to hold onto irrational assumptions. It takes energy to make interpretations that lead to miserable feelings. It takes energy to try to ignore, deny, and hide these miserable feelings. The fewer irrational assumptions you have, the more energy you will have for enjoying yourself and your relationships. The more quickly you get rid of your irrational assumptions and the destructive feelings they cause, the more energy you will have for enjoying yourself and your relationships.

To maintain constructive relationships you need to:

1. Be aware of your assumptions.
2. Know how they affect your interpretation of the information gathered by your senses.
3. Be able to tell how rational or irrational your assumptions are.
4. Dump your irrational assumptions.
5. Replace your irrational assumptions with rational ones.

You can change your irrational assumptions. The easiest way is to (1) become highly aware of when you are making an irrational assumption; (2) think of a rational assumption that is much more constructive; and (3) argue with yourself until you have replaced your irrational assumption with a rational one.

Irrational assumptions are learned. Usually they are learned in early childhood. They were taught to you by people in your past. Irrational assumptions are bad habits just like smoking or alcoholism. What was learned as a child can be unlearned as an adult. If you keep arguing against your irrational assumptions, you will soon develop rational ones. Do not let yourself feel bad just because you have bad thinking habits.

Exercise 9.4: Assumptions, Assumptions, What Are My Assumptions?

What are common irrational assumptions? How do you know if your assumptions are rational or irrational? One way is to compare them with the following list of rational and irrational assumptions taken from the writings of Albert Ellis (1962). Do you make any of these assumptions? Do you have any of the irrational assumptions listed below? Do you make any of the rational assumptions listed below? Can you tell the difference between the rational and the irrational ones?

Read each of the statements listed below. Write *yes* for any assumption that describes how you think. Write *no* for any assumption that does not describe how you think. Then reread each statement. Write *R* for the rational assumptions. Write *I* for the irrational assumptions. Keep your answers. You will use them in a later lesson.

Common Assumptions

_____ 1. I must be loved, liked, and approved of by everyone all the time or I will be absolutely miserable and will feel totally worthless.

_____ 2. It would be nice if I were liked by everyone, but I can survive very well without the approval of most people. It is only the liking and approval of close friends and people with actual power over me (such as my boss) that I have to be concerned with.

_____ 3. I have to be absolutely 100 percent perfect and competent in all respects if I am to consider myself worthwhile.

_____ 4. My personal value does not rest on how perfect or competent I am. Although I'm trying to be as competent as I can, I am a valuable person regardless of how well I do things.

_____ 5. People who are bad, including myself, must be blamed and punished to prevent them from being wicked in the future.

_____ 6. What is important is not making the same mistakes in the future. I do not have to blame and punish myself or other people for what has happened in the past.

_____ 7. It is a total catastrophe and so terrible that I can't stand it if things are not the way I would like them to be.

_____ 8. There is no reason the world should be the way I want it to be. What is important is dealing with what is. I do not have to bemoan the fact that things are not fair or just the way I think they should be.

_____ 9. If something terrible could happen, I will keep thinking about it *as if* it is actually going to take place.

_____ 10. I will try my best to avoid future unpleasantness. Then I will not worry about it. I refuse to go around keeping myself afraid by saying, "What if this happened?" "What if that happened?"

_____ 11. It is easier to avoid difficulties and responsibilities than to face them.

_____ 12. Facing difficulties and meeting responsibilities is easier in the long run than avoiding them.

_____ 13. I need someone stronger than myself to rely on.

_____ 14. I am strong enough to rely on myself.

_____ 15. Since I was this way when I was a child, I will be this way all my life.

_____ 16. I can change myself at any time in my life, whenever I decide it is helpful for me to do so.

_____ 17. I must become upset and depressed about other people's problems.

_____ 18. Having empathy with other people's problems and trying to help them does not mean getting upset and depressed about their problems. Over-concern does not lead to problem solving. How can I be of help if I am as depressed as others are?

_____ 19. It is terrible and unbearable to have to do things I don't want and don't like to do.

_____ 20. What I can't change I won't let upset me.

Exercise 9.5: Interpretations

The assumptions we make greatly influence our interpretations of the meaning of events in our life. These interpretations determine our feelings. The same event can be depressing or amusing, depending on the assumptions and interpretations we make. The purpose of this exercise is to focus a group discussion on the ways in which assumptions affect our interpretations and how we feel.

1. Form groups of four. Take the ten episodes below and discuss the following questions:

    a. What irrational assumptions is the person making?

    b. How do these assumptions cause the person to feel the way she does?

    c. What rational assumptions does the person need in order to change her feelings into more positive feelings?

2. In your group, discuss assumptions each of you have that influence your feelings of depression, anger, frustration, distress, and worry. When you are experiencing each of these feelings, what assumptions are causing you to feel that way? How can you change these assumptions to make your life happier?

Episodes

1. Sally likes to have her co-workers place their work neatly in a pile on her desk so that she can add her work to the pile, staple it all together, and give it to their supervisor. Her co-workers, however, throw their work into the supervisor's basket in a very disorderly and messy fashion. Sally then becomes very worried and upset. "I can't stand it," Sally says to herself. "It's terrible what they are doing. And it isn't fair to me or our supervisor!"

2. Jill has been given responsibility for planning next year's budget for her department. This amount of responsibility scares her. For several weeks she has done nothing on the budget. "I'll do it next week," she keeps thinking.

3. John went to the office one morning and passed a person he had never met in the hallway. He said, "Hello," and the person just looked at him and then walked on without saying a word. John became depressed. "I'm really not a very attractive person," he thought to himself. "No one seems to like me."

4. Dan is an intensive-care paramedic technician and is constantly depressed and worried about whether he can do his job competently. For every decision that has to be made, he asks his supervisor what he should do. One day he came into work and found that his supervisor had quit. "What will I do now?" he thought. "I can't handle this job without her."

5. Jane went to her desk and found a note from her supervisor that she had made an error in the report she worked on the day before. The note told her to correct the error and continue working on the report. Jane became depressed. "Why am I so dumb and stupid?" she thought to herself. "I can't seem to do anything right. That supervisor must think I'm terrible at my job."

6. Heidi has a knack for insulting people. She insults her co-workers, her boss, customers, and even passersby who ask for directions. Her boss has repeatedly told Heidi that if she doesn't change she will be fired. This depresses Heidi and makes her very angry at her boss. "How can I change?" Heidi says. "I've been this way ever since I could talk. It's too late for me to change now."

7. Tim was checking the repairs another technician had made on a television set. He found a mistake and became very angry. "I have to punish him," he thought. "He made a mistake and he has to suffer the consequences for it."

8. Bonnie doesn't like to fill out forms. She gets furious every day because her job as legal secretary requires her to fill out form after form after form. "Every time

I see a form my stomach ties itself into knots," she says. "I hate forms! I know they have to be done in order for the work to be filed with the courts, but I still hate them!"

9. Bob is very anxious about keeping his job. "What if the company goes out of business?" he thinks. "What if my boss gets angry at me?" "What if the secretary I yelled at is the boss's daughter?" All day he worries about whether he will have a job tomorrow.

10. Jack is a very friendly person who listens quite well. All of his co-workers tell their problems to Jack. He listens sympathetically. Then he goes home deeply depressed. "Life is so terrible for the people I work with," he thinks. "They have such severe problems and such sad lives."

Exercise 9.6: Changing Your Feelings

Now that you have discussed how people can make their assumptions more constructive, you may want to apply your own advice to yourself. The purpose of this exercise is to give you a chance to discuss your own negative feelings and see what assumptions are causing them. The procedure is:

1. Form groups of four. Draw straws to see who goes first in your group. Then go around the group in a clockwise direction. Each member completes the following statements:

    a. What depresses me about school or work is . . .

    b. When I get depressed about school or work I . . .

    c. The assumptions I am making that cause me to be depressed are . . .

    d. Constructive assumptions I can adopt to change my depression to more positive feelings are . . .

    Listen carefully to what each group member says. If he is not sure of his assumptions, help him clarify them. Give support for making his assumptions more constructive.

2. Now go around the group again and discuss how each member completes these statements:

    a. The things I worry about are . . .

    b. What I do when I get worried is . . .

    c. The assumptions I am making that cause me to be worried are . . .

    d. Constructive assumptions I can adopt to change my worry to more positive feelings are . . .

3. Now try anger:

    a. The things I get angry about are . . .

    b. What I do when I get angry is . . .

    c. The assumptions I am making that cause me to be angry are . . .

    d. Constructive assumptions I can adopt to change my anger to more positive feelings are . . .

4. Let's see how you feel about your career!

    a. The negative feelings I have when I think about my career are . . .

    b. The things I do when I have those feelings are . . .

    c. The assumptions I am making that cause the feelings are . . .

    d. Constructive attitudes I can adopt to change these feelings to more positive ones are . . .

5. Discuss in your group what the members learned about themselves and the ways in which they manage their feelings.

Exercise 9.7: How Do I Manage My Feelings?

There are five questions below. Each question has two parts. Check *a* if your way of managing feelings is best described by the *a* part of the question. Check *b* if your way of managing feelings is best described by the *b* part of the question. Think about each question carefully. Be honest. No one will see your answers. The results are simply for your own self-awareness.

1. _____ a. I am fully aware of what I am sensing in a given situation.

    _____ b. I ignore what I am sensing by thinking about the past or the future.

2. _____ a. I understand the interpretations I usually make about other people's actions. I investigate my feeling by asking what interpretation is causing it. I work to be aware of interpretations I am making.

    _____ b. I deny that I make any interpretations about what I sense. I ignore my interpretations. I insist that I do not interpret someone's behavior as being mean. The person *is* mean.

3. _____ a. I accept my feeling as being part of me. I turn my full awareness on it. I try to feel it fully. I take a good look at it so I can identify it and tell how strong it is. I keep asking myself, "What am I feeling now?"

    _____ b. I reject my feeling. I ignore it by telling myself I'm not angry, upset, sad, or even happy. I deny my feeling by telling myself and others. "But I'm not feeling anything at all." I avoid people and situations that might make me more aware of my feelings. I pretend I'm not really feeling the way I am.

4. _____ a. I decide how I want to express my feeling. I think of what I want to result from the expression of my feeling. I think of what is an appropriate way to express the feeling in the current situation. In my mind, I review the sending skills.

_____ **b.** Since I've never admitted to having a feeling, I don't need to decide how to express it! I don't think through what might happen after I express my feelings. I never think about what is appropriate in a situation. When my feelings burst I am too emotional to remember good sending skills.

5. _____ **a.** I express my feelings appropriately and clearly. Usually, this means describing my feeling directly. It also means using nonverbal messages to back up my words. My words and my nonverbal messages communicate the same feeling.

_____ **b.** I express my feelings inappropriately and in confusing ways. Usually, this means I express them indirectly through commands, accusations, put-downs, and evaluations. I may express feelings physically in destructive ways. My nonverbal messages express my feelings. I shout at people, push or hit them, avoid people, refuse to look at them, or don't speak to them. I may hug them, put my arm around them, give them gifts, or try to do favors for them. My words and my nonverbal messages often contradict each other. I sometimes smile and act friendly toward people I'm angry at. Or I may avoid people I care a great deal for.

MANAGING ANGER CONSTRUCTIVELY: A CHECKLIST

1. Anger occurs when we are not getting something we want or would like (when we feel frustrated, thwarted, attacked, belittled, devalued).

2. Anger can:
   a. Add to your frustrations. This is not sensible. Getting angry over a frustration does not usually remove the frustration and always adds to your discomfort.
   b. Prevent you from solving problems. Being hateful simply fills your thoughts with delicious ways of getting even with others, not with how to get others to behave differently toward you. The net result is that things get worse and worse as you become angrier and angrier.
   c. Make you physically sick.

3. Beware of its:
   a. Narrowing of perceptual focus and priorities
   b. Righteousness, blame orientation, and desire to punish
   c. Demand that you get your way
   d. Physiological arousal

4. Rules:
   a. Recognize and acknowledge your anger.
   b. Decide whether you wish to express it. Know how to detach and let it go if you decide not to.
   c. When it is appropriate to do so, express anger directly and descriptively. Once you have expressed your anger constructively, let it go.
   d. Express it indirectly or react in an alternative way when direct expression is not appropriate.
      1. Physical exercise
      2. Private physical expression
      3. Psychological detachment
      4. Relaxation
   e. When the other person is angry, stay focused on the task/issue. Do not get distracted by his or her anger.
   f. Analyze, understand, and reflect upon your anger.
5. Anger is based on two irrational beliefs:
   a. You must have your way. It is awful not to get everything you want.
   b. People are bad and should be severely dealt with if they have behaved wrongly. They are wicked for frustrating you and deserve to be punished.
6. Express your anger constructively:
   a. Describe the other person's behavior.
   b. Describe your anger.
   c. Make your verbal and nonverbal messages congruent.
   d. Check your perceptions of the other person's behavior and the assumptions you are making about the meaning of the behavior.
   e. Paraphrase the other person's replies.

CHAPTER REVIEW

Test your understanding of anger, stress, and managing your feelings by answering true or false to the following statements. Answers are at the end of the chapter.

True	False	1. A certain amount of stress is beneficial.
True	False	2. It is important to deal with anger in some way.
True	False	3. The first step to managing angry feelings is to identify the feelings as they begin.
True	False	4. You can change anger by looking at events differently or talking yourself out of it as you feel anger arise.
True	False	5. You can deal with anger constructively by repressing your feelings.
True	False	6. Hitting someone in the mouth is not a constructive way to deal with anger.
True	False	7. The best way to deal with anger is to talk over the situation with the person who made you angry.
True	False	8. If you can't talk over the problem, you can get rid of your angry feelings by vigorous exercise or private yelling or crying.
True	False	9. A good way to deal with stress is to discuss your feelings with a friend.
True	False	10. Isolating yourself during times of stress is self-destructive.

Indicate below which skills you have mastered and which skills you still need more work on.

1. I have mastered the following:
   ____ An understanding of stress and how to deal with it
   ____ An awareness of what makes me angry
   ____ An understanding of how I behave when angry
   ____ An understanding of my irrational beliefs and how to minimize them
   ____ An understanding of how to express anger constructively
   ____ An understanding of how to change my interpretations of situations

2. I need more work on:
   ____ An understanding of stress and how to deal with it
   ____ An awareness of what makes me angry
   ____ An understanding of how I behave when angry

____ An understanding of my irrational beliefs and how to minimize them

____ An understanding of how to express anger constructively

____ An understanding of how to change my interpretations of situations

You have read about how to deal with stress, anger, and managing your feelings. You should have a greater awareness of what makes you angry, how to minimize anger, and how to express anger constructively. As you practice the suggestions in this chapter, you will find that you have more constructive control over your feelings and relationships. As you continue to practice the skills you have learned in this book, you will learn how to "reach out" to others in a way that will result in more rewarding relationships for them and for you.

ANSWERS

Chapter Review: 1. true; 2. true; 3. true; 4. true; 5. false; 6. true; 7. true; 8. true; 9. true; 10. true.

10 Building Relationships With Diverse Others

INTRODUCTION

We live in one world. The problems that face each person, each community, each country cannot be solved without global cooperation and joint action. Economically, for example, there has been a globalization of business reflected in the increase in multinational companies, coproduction agreements, and offshore operations. As globalization becomes the norm, more and more companies must translate their local and national perspectives into a world view. Companies that are staffed by individuals skilled in building relationships with diverse peers have an advantage in the global market.

Interacting effectively with peers from different cultures, ethnic groups, social classes, and historical backgrounds does not come naturally. For 200,000 years humans lived in small hunting and gathering groups, interacting only infrequently with other nearby small groups. Today we are required to communicate effectively with people cross-culturally, through the generation gap, among races, between genders, and across those subtle but pervasive barriers of class. No wonder this feels uncomfortable—we have never been required to do it before!

Diversity among your acquaintances, classmates, coworkers, neighbors, and friends is increasingly inevitable. North America, Europe, and many other parts of the world are becoming more and more diverse in terms of culture, ethnicity, religion, age, physical qualities, and gender. You will be expected to interact effectively with people with a wide variety of characteristics and from a wide variety of backgrounds. In order to build relationships with diverse peers, you must:

1. Accept yourself.
2. Lower the barriers to building relationships with diverse peers.
3. Recognize that diversity exists and is a valuable resource.
4. Build friendships with diverse peers.
5. Highlight important mutual goals that require cooperative action and develop a common ground on which everyone is cooriented.
6. Clarify misunderstandings.

ACCEPTING YOURSELF

> *"If I am not for myself, who will be for me? But if I am only for myself, what am I?"*
>
> The Talmud

Two basic human needs are to:

1. Join with others in a cooperative effort to achieve something great.
2. Be a unique and separate individual who is valued and respected in one's own right.

In order to meet this second need, you must accept yourself as you are and build a distinct image of yourself as a certain kind of person who has an identity differentiated and discernible from that of others. The greater your self-acceptance, the more stable and integrated your personal identity. Building a coherent, stable, and integrated identity that summarizes who you are as a separate, autonomous, and unique individual is the first step in building constructive relationships with diverse peers.

The Person You Think You Are

What kind of person are you? How would you describe yourself to someone who does not know you? Would your description be disjointed and

contradictory, or would it be organized and consistent? Would it change from day to day, or would it stay the same over a period of years? Do you like yourself, or do you feel a basic sense of shame and contempt when you think of yourself? We all need a strong and integrated sense of personal identity that serves as an anchor in life.

Early philosophers advised us to "know thyself" and poets have told us, "To thy own self be true." We have taken their advice. Hundreds of books have been written dealing with how to get to know yourself and the *Oxford English Dictionary* lists more than 100 words that focus on the self, from *self-abasement* to *self-wisdom*. When you form a conception of who you are as a person you have an identity.

Your *identity* is a consistent set of attitudes that defines "who you are." It is a subjective self-image that is a type of cognitive structure called a self-schema. A *self-schema* is a generalization about the self, derived from past experience, that organizes and guides your understanding of the information you learn about yourself from interacting with others. You have multiple schemas, multiple identities, and multiple selves. They include your view of your physical characteristics (height, weight, sex, hair and eye color, general appearance), your social roles (student or teacher, child or parent, employee or employer), the activities you engage in (playing the piano, dancing, reading), your abilities (skills, achievements), your attitudes and interests (liking rock and roll, favoring equal rights for females), and your general personality traits (extrovert or introvert, impulsive or reflective, sensible or scatterbrained). Your *gender identity* is your fundamental sense of your maleness or femaleness. Your *ethnic identity* is your sense of belonging to one particular ethnic group. Your identity consists not only of various self-schemas that you currently possess but of selves that you would like to be or that you imagine you might be. These "potential selves" include ideals that you would like to attain and standards that you feel you should meet (the "ought" self). They can originate from your own thoughts or from the messages of others.

Each of your self-schemas is viewed as being positive or negative. You generally look at yourself in an evaluative way, approving or disapproving of your behavior and characteristics. Your self-schemas are arranged in a hierarchy. The more important an identity is, or the higher it stands in the hierarchy, the more likely it is to influence your choices and your behavior.

To cope with stress you need more than one self. The diversity and complexity of the identity reduces the stress you experience. Self-complexity provides a buffer against stressful events. If you have only one or two major self-schemas, any negative event is going to have an impact on most aspects of your identity. The woman who sees herself primarily as a wife, for example, is likely to be devastated if her husband says he wants an immediate divorce. In contrast, the individual who has a more complex representation of self may be more protected from negative events that primarily involve only one or two of several roles. The woman who sees herself not only as wife, but also as a mother, lawyer, friend, and tennis player, will have other roles to fall back on when impending divorce threatens her role of spouse. People with more complex identities are less prone to depression and illness; they also experience less severe mood swings following success or failure in one particular area of performance.

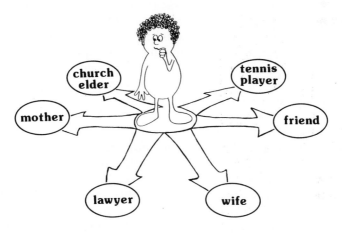

Why Have an Identity

There are a number of reasons why having a clear identity is important. First, our identity provides stability to our lives. The world can change, other people can change, your career and family life can change, but there is something about yourself that remains the same. During infancy, childhood, adolescence, and early adulthood, a person has several identities. The physical changes involved in growth, the increasing number of experiences with other people, increasing responsibilities, and general cognitive and social development, all cause changes and adaptations in self-definition. But the final result has to be a coherent and unified personal identity.

Second, our identity directs what information, out of all the information available, we select to attend to. In order to make sense out of all the available information, we selectively process that which past experience indicates is important for us. Having a self-schema speeds the processing of information relevant to our view of ourselves. Information congruent with our view of ourselves is processed easily, but information that contradicts our view of ourselves is resisted and may be screened out entirely. If we see ourselves as intelligent, for example, we tend to see our high grades as being caused by our abilities and efforts. If we receive two As and two Cs we will tend to see the As and ignore the Cs.

Third, our identity provides consistency to our lives. Generally, we work to minimize any contradictions in our view of ourselves. Our identity organizes and revises the incoming information so that it is consistent with our view of ourselves. The incoming information is revised to fit our identity by having information relevant to it added or by altering inconsistent information. A low grade is perceived to be the result of bad luck and incompetent teachers. If we get low grades, then creative expression, not grades, are seen to be an indication of intelligence. We twist what we perceive so that it fits into our existing schemas.

Fourth, we remember what fits into our self-schemas and forget what does not. We remember our successes and forget our failures. Our identity facilitates the memory of information relevant to our view of ourselves. It even reconstructs memory so the events we remember fit our view of ourselves.

Finally, we seek out information and experiences that validate our schemas. When we see ourselves as intelligent we seek out evidence "proving" that we are intellectually superior people.

The way in which our existing identity affects the processing of new incoming information may result in a number of biases about ourselves. There is often an *illusion of control* of events that occur purely by chance. If you win the New York Lottery, for example, you tend to ascribe your success to your intelligence in picking the right number rather than seeing it resulting from dumb luck. There is a *false consensus effect* in which you believe that most other people would act the way you do. If you take home pencils and paper from the office, you tend to believe that everyone does so. There is an *above average effect bias* in which the vast majority of people view themselves as being above average on any category or trait that is socially desirable. You tend to see yourself as more positive than you really are. There is, however, a small minority of people who tend constantly to evaluate themselves in an unrealistically negative way. There is a *beneffectance effect* in which you claim credit for success and deny responsibility for failure. When students do well on examinations, for example, they state the tests are valid but when they obtain poor grades, they question the validity of the tests. Finally, there is a *cognitive conservatism* effect in which, once your view of yourself has developed, there is a conservative tendency to maintain and reinforce it and to resist changing it.

Building Your Identity

To loosely paraphrase Goethe, "Character is produced in the stream of life, not in solitude." Your identity is produced in interaction with other people. All of the influences on self-awareness discussed in the previous chapter related to building an identity. In addition, by adopting a number of social roles and building a broad range of experiences, you define who you are. By adopting the roles of student, tutor, friend, neighbor, boss, subordinate, engineer, carpenter, sailor, skier, minister, or cook, for example, you acquire a number of social roles that define you both to yourself and to other people. The more varied and extensive your experiences and the more you experience a wide variety of social roles, the more clearly defined your identity becomes.

Your identity builds from identifying with real, historical, and fictional people. You imitate and internalize aspects of individuals who have emotional significance for you. You identify with your parents, older siblings, teachers and friends. You also identify with historical characters such as Benjamin Franklin or Jane Addams.

The formation and increasing integration of your identity continue throughout life. It is a process that is constantly occurring. In adolescence, however, there is a marked crisis in which individuals struggle with integrating and updating their identities. The danger of adolescence is failing to resolve this crisis by "getting it all together." Luckily, you are never too old to define more clearly who you are.

Building Pride in Your Ethnic Identity

Each person must develop an awareness and appreciation of their own cultural, ethnic, religious, and historical background. Part of your identity is based on your identification with and appreciation of the culture and homeland of your ancestors. Usually, the more respect you have for your cultural heritage the more respect you have for yourself.

Deciding Whether You Are Acceptable or Unacceptable

> *Show me the sensible person who likes himself or herself? I know myself too well to like what I see. I know but too well that I'm not what I'd like to be.*
>
> *Golda Meir*

How do you decide whether you have value? You at least have choices. First, you can make conclusions about yourself on the basis of how you think other people see you. If other people like you, you tend to like yourself. This is called *reflected self-acceptance*. Second, you can believe that you are intrinsically and unconditionally acceptable. This is called *basic self-acceptance*. Third, you can base your conclusions about your self-worth on how well you meet external standards and expectations. This is known as *conditional self-acceptance*. It is characterized by "if-then" logic. "If I meet the external standards and expectations placed on me by other people, then I am of value. If I don't, then I am worthless." Fourth, you can estimate how positively your attributes compare with those of your peers. This is called *self-evaluation*. Fifth, you can judge how your real self compares with your ideal self, that is, compare what you think you are and what you think you should be. This is known as *real-ideal comparison*. Most people use one or more of these procedures for making judgments about their self-worth. It is important that you learn not only to accept yourself but also learn a constructive method of judging your self-worth from the information that is available to you about yourself. Usually, an unconditional, basic self-acceptance is viewed as the most constructive way to determine your self-acceptance.

Some of the Benefits of Self-Acceptance

There is a common saying that goes, "I can't be right for someone else if I'm not right for me!" *Self-acceptance* is a high regard for yourself or, conversely, a lack of cynicism about yourself. There are a number of benefits to accepting yourself as you are, and a relationship exists among self-acceptance, self-disclosure, and being accepted by others. The more self-accepting you are, the greater your self-disclosure tends to be. The greater your self-disclosure, the more others accept you. And the more others accept you, the more you accept yourself. A high level of self-acceptance, furthermore, is reflected in psychological health. Psychologically healthy people see themselves as being liked, capable, worthy, and acceptable to other people. All of these perceptions are based on self-acceptance. Considerable evidence abounds that self-acceptance and acceptance of others are related. If you think well of yourself you tend to think well of others. You also tend to assume that others will like you, an expectation that often becomes a self-fulfilling prophecy.

DIFFICULTIES WITH DIVERSITY

Once you are accepting of yourself, you are in a position to be accepting of others. There are, however, a number of barriers to accepting diverse peers. They include prejudice, the tendency to blame the victim, and cultural conflict.

Prejudice

To know one's self is wisdom, but to know one's neighbor is genius.

Minna Antrim

Building relationships with diverse peers is not easy. The first barrier is prejudice. Prejudice, stereotyping, and discrimination begin with categorizing. In order to understand other people and yourself, categories must be used. *Categorizing* is a basic human cognitive process of conceptualizing objects and people as members of groups. We categorize people on the basis of *inherited traits* (culture, sex, ethnic membership, physical features) or *acquired traits* (education, occupation, lifestyle, customs). Categorizing and generalizing are often helpful in processing information and making decisions. At times, however, they malfunction and result in stereotyping and prejudice.

To be prejudiced means to prejudge. *Prejudice* can be defined as an unjustifed negative attitude toward a person based solely on that individual's membership in a group other than one's own. Prejudices are judgments made about others that establish a superiority/inferiority belief system. If one person dislikes another simply because that other person is a member of a different ethnic group, sex, or religion, that is prejudice.

One common form of prejudice is ethnocentrism. *Ethnocentrism* is the tendency to regard our own ethnic group, culture, or nation as better or more ''correct'' than others. The word is derived from *ethnic,* meaning a group united by similar customs, characteristics, race, or other common factors, and *center.* When ethnocentrism is present, the standards and values of our culture are used as a yardstick to measure the worth of other ethnic groups. Ethnocentrism is often perpetuated by *cultural conditioning.* As children we are raised to fit into a particular culture. We are conditioned to respond to various situations as we see others in our culture react.

Prejudices are often associated with stereotypes. A *stereotype* is a set of beliefs about the characteristics of the people in a group that is applied to almost all members of that group. Typically, stereotypes are widely held beliefs within a group and focus on what other cultural and ethnic groups, or socioeconomic classes are ''really like.'' Woman have been stereotyped as being more emotional than men. Men have been stereotyped as being more competitive than women. Tall, dark, and handsome men have been stereotyped as being mysterious. Stereotypes distort and exaggerate in ways that support an underlying prejudice or fundamental bias against members of other groups. Stereotypes are resistant to change because people believe information that confirms their stereotypes more readily than evidence that challenges them. Stereotypes almost always have a detrimental effect on those targeted, interfering with the victim's ability to be productive and live a high quality life.

Stereotypes reflect an *illusionary correlation* between two unrelated factors, such as being poor and lazy. Negative traits are easy to acquire and hard to lose. When you meet one poor person who is lazy you may tend to see all poor people as lazy. From then on, any poor person who is not hard at work the moment you notice him or her may be perceived to be lazy. Our prejudiced stereotype of poor people being lazy is protected in three ways. Our prejudice makes us notice the negative traits we ascribe to the groups we are prejudiced against. We tend to have a *false consensus bias* by believing that most other people share our stereotypes (see poor people as being lazy). We tend to see our own behavior and judgments as quite common and appropriate, and to view alternative responses as uncommon and often inappropriate. Finally, we often develop a rationale and explanation to justify our stereotypes and prejudices.

When prejudice is put into action, it is discrimination. *Discrimination* is an action taken to harm a group or any of its members. It is a negative, often aggressive action aimed at the target of prejudice. Discrimination is aimed at denying members of the targeted groups treatment and opportunities equal to those afforded to the dominant group. When discrimination is based on race or sex, it is referred to as racism or sexism.

Diversity among people can either be a valued resource generating energy, vitality, and creativity, or it can be a source of prejudice, stereotyping, and discrimination. To reduce your prejudices and use of stereotypes, these steps may be helpful:

1. Admit that you have prejudices (everyone does, you are no exception) and commit yourself to reducing them.
2. Identify the stereotypes that reflect your prejudices and modify them.
3. Identify the actions that reflect your prejudices and modify them.
4. Seek feedback from diverse friends and colleagues about how well you are communicating respect for and valuing of diversity.

Blaming the Victim

It is commonly believed that the world is a just place where people generally get what they deserve. If we win the lottery, it must be because we are nice people who deserve some good luck. If we are robbed, it must be because we are careless and want to be punished for past misdeeds. Any person who is mugged in a dark alley while carrying a great deal of cash may be seen as "asking to be robbed." Most people tend to believe that they deserve what happens to them. Most people also believe that others also get what they deserve in the world. It is all too easy to forget that victims do not have the benefit of hindsight to guide their actions.

When someone is a victim of prejudice, stereotyping, and discrimination, all too often they are seen as "doing *something* wrong." *Blaming the victim* occurs when we attribute the cause of discrimination or misfortune to the personal characteristics and actions of the victim. The situation is examined for potential causes that will enable us to maintain our belief in a just world. If the victim can be blamed for causing the discrimination, then we can believe that the future is predictable and controllable because we will get what we deserve.

Blaming the victim occurs as we try to attribute a cause to events. We constantly interpret the meaning of our behavior and events that occur in our lives. Many times we want to figure out *why* we acted in a particular way or why a certain outcome occurred. If we get angry when someone infers we are stupid, but we could care less when someone calls us "clumsy," we want to know why we are so sensitive about our intelligence. When we are standing on a street corner after a rainstorm and a car splashes us with water, we want to know whether it was caused by our carelessness, the driver's meanness, or just bad luck. This process of explaining or inferring the causes of events has been termed *causal attribution*. An attribution is an inference drawn about the causes of a behavior or event. Any behavior or event can have a variety of possible causes. We observe the behavior or event and then infer the cause. When our boss criticizes our work, for example, we can attribute his or her behavior to a grouchy mood, being under too much pressure, disliking us, or the sloppiness of our work. Early in childhood we begin observing our own behavior and draw conclusions about ourselves. We seem to have a fundamental need to understand both our own behavior and the behavior of others.

In trying to understand why a behavior or event occurred, we generally choose to attribute causes either to:

1. Internal, personal factors (such as effort and ability)
2. External, situational factors (such as luck or the behavior/personality of other people)

For example, if you do well on a test, you can attribute it to your hard work and great intelligence (an internal attribution) or to the fact that the test was incredibly easy (an external attribution). When a friend drops out of school, you can attribute it to a lack of motivation (an internal attribution) or lack of money (an external attribution).

People make causal attributions to explain their successes and failures. Frequently such attributions are *self-serving*, designed to permit us to take credit for positive outcomes and to avoid blame for negative ones. We have a systematic tendency to claim our successes are due to our ability and efforts while our failures are due to bad luck, evil people, or a lack of effort. We also have a systematic tendency to claim responsibility for the success of group efforts ("It was all my idea in the first place and I did most of the work") and avoid responsibility for group failures ("If the other members had tried harder, this would not have happened.").

The opposite happens when someone is suffering from depression (as a pervasive condition, not as an isolated reaction to an unfortunate turn of events). Failures are inferred to be caused by personal factors ("It's all my fault!" "Everything I touch turns out rotten!") and successes are inferred to be caused by luck or other people. The more a person attributes the failures to causes that are stable and enduring ("It's my general personality"), global (likely to affect many outcomes), and internal (something about him- or herself), the more likely the person is to become more depressed. People who think this way are likely to say "I'm an unlovable person" when a relationship goes awry instead of saying, ''Maybe he/she just had a bad day.'' In this age of soaring expectations, life is inevitably full of personal failures. We get bad grades, we do not get the job we want, our salary is lower than what we think it should be, a person we want to form a relationship with does not like us. The way we attribute blame for our failures can drive us into depression.

Attributing the causes of others' failure and misfortune to their actions rather than to prejudice and discrimination can be a barrier to building constructive relationships with diverse peers. Bad things do happen to good people. Racism does exist. Innocent bystanders do get shot. It is usually a good idea to suspend any tendency to blame the victim when interacting with diverse peers.

Culture Clash

Another common barrier to building relationships with diverse peers is cultural clashes. A *culture clash* is a conflict over basic values that occurs among individuals from different cultures. The most common form is members of minority groups questioning the values of the majority. Common reactions by majority group members when their values are being questioned are feeling:

1. *Threatened:* Their responses include avoidance, denial, and defensiveness.
2. *Confused:* Their responses include seeking more information in an attempt to redefine the problem.
3. *Enhanced:* Their responses include heightened anticipation, awareness, and positive actions that lead to solving the problem.

Many cultural clashes develop from threatening, to confusing, to enhancing. Once they are enhancing, they are no longer a barrier.

As prejudice, stereotyping, and discrimination are reduced, the tendency to blame the victim is avoided, and cultural clashes become enhancing, the stage is set for recognizing and valuing diversity.

RECOGNIZING AND VALUING DIVERSITY

In order to actualize the positive potential of diversity, you must recognize that diversity exists and then learn to value and respect fundamental differences among people. This is especially true in countries in which widely diverse groups of people live. The United States, for example, has always been a nation of many cultures, races, languages, and religions. In the last eight years alone, over 7.8 million people journeying from over 150 different countries and speaking dozens of different languages made the United States their new home. America's pluralism and diversity has many positive values, such as being a source of energy and creativity that increases the vitality of American society. Diversity among collaborators has been found to contribute to achievement and productivity, creative problem solving, growth in cognitive and moral reasoning, perspective-taking ability, and general sophistication in interacting and working with peers from a variety of cultural and ethnic backgrounds (Johnson & Johnson 1989).

Within a relationship, a community, an organization, a society, or a world, the goal is not to assimilate all groups so that everyone is alike. The goal is to work together to achieve mutual goals while recognizing cultural diversity and learning to value and respect fundamental differences while working together to achieve mutual goals. Creating a *unum* from *pluribus* is done in bascially four steps. *First, you develop an appreciation for your own religious, ethnic, or cultural background.* Your identification with the culture and homeland of your ancestors must be recognized and valued. The assumption is that respect for your cultural heritage will translate into self-respect.

Second, you develop an appreciation and respect for the religious, ethnic, and cultural backgrounds of others. A critical aspect of developing an ethnic and cultural identity is whether ethnocentricity is inherent in your definition of yourself. An ingroup identity must be developed in a way that does not lead to rejection of outgroups. There are many examples where being a member of one group requires the rejection of other groups.

1

There are also many examples where being a member of one group requires the valuing and respect for other groups. Outgroups need to be seen as collaborators and resources rather than competitors and threats. Express respect for diverse backgrounds and value them as a resource that increases the quality of your life and adds to the viability of your society. The degree to which your ingroup identity leads to respect for and valuing of outgroups depends on developing a superordinate identity that includes both your own and all other groups.

Third, you develop a strong superordinate identity that transcends the differences between your own and all other groups. Being an American, for example, is creedal rather than racial or ancestral. The United States is a nation that unites as one people the descendants of many cultures, races, religions, and ethnic groups through an identification with America and democracy. Ever since exploring Europeans landed, the inhabitants of North America have represented a variety of races, religions, languages, and ethnic and cultural groups. And America has grown increasingly diverse in social and cultural composition. Each cultural group is part of the whole and members of each new immigrant group, while modifying and enriching our national identity, learn they are first and foremost Americans. America is one of the few successful examples of a pluralistic society where different groups clashed but ultimately learned to live together through achieving a sense of common nationhood. In our diversity, there has always been a broad recognition that we are one people. Whatever our origins, we are all Americans.

Fourth, you adopt a pluralistic set of values concerning democracy, freedom, liberty, equality, justice, the rights of individuals, and the responsiblities of citizenship. It is these values that form the American creed. We respect basic human rights, listen to dissenters instead of jailing them, and have a multiparty political system, a free press, free speech, freedom of religion, and freedom of assembly. These values were shaped by millions of people from many different backgrounds. Americans are a multicultural people knitted together by a common set of political and moral values.

Diverse individuals from different cultural, ethnic, social class, and language backgrounds come together primarily in school, career, and community settings. Sometimes the results are positive and individuals get to know each other, appreciate and value the vitality of diversity, learn how to use diversity for creative problem solving and enhanced productivity, and internalize a common superordinate identity that binds them together. If diversity is to be a source of creativity and energy, inviduals must value and seek out diversity rather than fear and reject it. Doing so will eventually result in cross-cultural friendships.

GAINING SOPHISTICATION
THROUGH RELATIONSHIPS

Some people are *sophisticated* about how to act appropriately within many different cultures and perspectives. They are courteous, well-mannered, and refined within many different settings and cultures. Other people are quite *provincial*, knowing how to act appropriately only from their narrow perspective. To become sophisticated a person must be able to see the situation from the cultural perspective of the other people involved. Much of the information about different cultural and ethnic heritages and perspectives cannot be attained through reading books and listening to lectures. Only through knowing, working with, and personally interacting with members of diverse groups can individuals really learn to value diversity, utilize diversity for creative problem solving, and work effectively with diverse peers. While information alone helps, it is only through direct and personal interaction among diverse individuals and developing personal as well as professional relationships with them that such outcomes are realized. Understanding the perspective of others from different ethnic and cultural backgrounds requires more than information. It requires the personal sharing of viewpoints and mutual discussion of situations.

To gain the sophistication and skills required to build relationships with diverse peers you need to develop friends from a wide variety of cultural, ethnic, social class, and historical backgrounds. There are many aspects of relating to individuals different from you that are learned only by a friend being candid about misunderstandings you are inadvertently creating. To gain the sophistication and skills you need to relate to, work with, and become friends with diverse peers, you need the following.

1. *Actual Interaction:* Seek opportunities to interact with a wide variety of peers. You do so because you value diversity, recognize the importance of relating effectively to diverse peers, and recognize the importance of increasing your knowledge of multicultural issues.

2. *Trust:* Build trust by being open about yourself and your commitment to cross-cultural relationships and being trustworthy when others share their opinions and reactions with you. Being trustworthy includes expressing respect for diverse backgrounds and valuing them as a resource that increases the quality of your life and adds to the viability of your society.

3. *Candor:* Persuade your peers to be candid by openly discussing their personal opinions, feelings, and reactions with you. There are many events that seem neutral to you that are offensive and hurtful

to individuals from backgrounds different from yours. In order to understand what is and is not disrespectful and hurtful, your peers must be candid about their reactions and explain them to you.

If you are not sophisticated and skilled in building relationships with diverse peers, you are in danger of unconsciously colluding with current patterns of discrimination. *Collusion* is conscious and unconscious reinforcement of stereotypic attitudes, behaviors, and prevailing norms. People collude with discriminatory practices and prejudiced actions through ignorance, silence, denial, and active support. Perhaps the only way not to collude with existing discriminatory practices is to build the friendships with diverse peers that allow you to understand when discrimination and prejudice ocurs.

COOPERATIVE CONTEXT

Bringing diverse individuals into the same room does not ensure that constructive relationships will result. The discords of diversity are not automatically transformed into a symphony when people are brought face-to-face. Prejudice, stereotyping, and discrimination often increase with proximity. What largely determines whether interaction results in positive or negative relationships is the context within which the interaction takes place. Basically, the context can be cooperative, competitive, or individualistic. In a *cooperative* context individuals work together to achieve mutual goals; in a *competitive* context individuals strive to outperform each other; in an *individualistic* context individuals seek their own benefit independently of what others are doing.

Perhaps the surest way of building relationships with diverse people is to involve yourself and the other people in a situation where you have to cooperate with each other to achieve mutually desired goals. *Cooperation* means that you and the other person engage in joint action to accomplish a goal you both want. Two people who both wish to build a sand castle and who help each other do so are in cooperative interaction. The members of a football team take cooperative action to win a game. A teacher and a student planning an assignment to maximize the student's learning are in cooperative interaction. Two people who wish to deepen their relationship and thus spend time on a joint project are in cooperative interaction. Any time that you and another person have the same goal and help each other accomplish it, you are in cooperative interaction.

Cooperative interaction has very powerful and positive effects on relationships. Friendships are based largely upon cooperation. The development of a fulfilling friendship rests upon the ability of two people to define mutual goals (even if the goal is to fall in love) and then to cooperate in obtaining them. When people cooperate, they tend to like each other more, trust each other more, are more candid with each other, and are more willing to listen to and be influenced by each other. When people compete or work individualistically, then liking, trust, influence, and candor tend to decrease. There is considerable evidence that cooperative experiences, compared with competitive and individualistic ones, promote more positive, committed, and caring relationships regardless of differences in ethnic, cultural, language, social class, gender, ability, or other differences (Johnson & Johnson 1989). In addition, joint efforts to achieve mutual goals (that is, cooperation) increase individuals' self-esteem and psychological health, ability to act independently and exert their autonomy, and interpersonal and small-group skills.

Strength through diversity does not automatically occur. It is only within a cooperative context that positive relationships among diverse individuals develop (Johnson & Johnson 1989). Individuals must believe that they "sink or swim together" in striving to achieve important mutual goals if positive relationships among diverse individuals are to develop. In order to create a cooperative context you must identify and highlight:

1. Important goals that everyone wants to achieve
2. A set of common procedures and norms that help coordinate efforts to achieve the goals

Once a cooperative context has been established, the next step is to clarify misunderstandings that arise as diverse individuals work together.

CLARIFYING MISCOMMUNICATIONS

Imagine that you and several friends went to hear a speaker. Although the content was good, and the delivery entertaining, two of your friends walked out in protest. When you asked them why, they called your attention to the facts that the speaker continually said "you guys" even though half the audience were women, used only sports and military examples, only quoted males, and joked about senility and old age. Your friends were insulted.

Communication is actually one of the most complex aspects of managing relationships with diverse peers. To communicate effectively with people from a different cultural, ethnic, social class, historical background than yours you must increase your:

1. *Language Sensitivity:* knowledge of words and expressions that are appropriate and inappropriate in communicating with diverse groups. The use of language can play a powerful role in reinforcing stereotypes and garbling communication. To avoid this, individuals need to heighten their sensitivity and avoid using terms and expressions that ignore or devalue others.

2. *Awareness of stylistic elements of communication:* knowledge of the key elements of communication style and how diverse cultures use these elements to communicate. Without awareness of nuances in language and differences in style, the potential for garbled communication is enormous when interacting with diverse peers.

Your ability to communicate with credibility to diverse peers is closely linked to your use of language. You must be sophisticated enough to anticipate how your messages will be interpreted by the listener. If you are unaware of nuances and innuendoes contained in your message, then you will be more likely to miscommunicate. The words you choose often tell other people more about your values, attitudes, and socialization than you intend to reveal. Receivers will react to the subtleties conveyed and interpret the implied messages behind our words. The first step in establishing relationships with diverse peers, therefore, is to understand how language reinforces stereotypes and to adjust our usage accordingly.

You can never predict with certainty how every person will react to what you say. You can, however, minimize the possibility of miscommunicating by following some basic guidelines:

1. Use all the communication skills discussed in this book.
2. Negotiate for meaning whenever you think the other persons you are talking with misinterpreted what you said.
3. Use words that are inclusive rather than exclusive such as women, men, participants.
4. Avoid adjectives that spotlight specific groups and imply the individual is an exception, such as black doctor, woman pilot, older teacher, blind lawyer.
5. Use quotes, references, metaphors, and analogies that reflect diversity and are from diverse sources, for example, from Asian and African sources as well as from European and American.

6. Avoid terms that define, demean, or devalue others, such as crip-
    ple, girl, boy, agitator.
7. Be aware of the genealogy of words viewed as inappropriate by oth-
    ers. It is the connotations the receiver places on the words that is
    important, not your connotations. These connotations change over
    time so continual clarification is needed. There are "loaded" words
    that seem neutral to you but highly judgmental to people of diverse
    backgrounds. The word "lady," for example, was a complement
    even a few years ago, but today it fails to take into account wom-
    en's independence and equal status in society and, therefore, is
    offensive to many women. Words such as girls, ladies, or gals are
    just as offensive.

SUMMARY

In a global village highly diverse individuals interact daily, study and
work together, and live in the same community. Diversity among your
acquaintances, classmates, coworkers, neighbors, and friends is increasingly inevitable. You will be expected to interact effectively with people
with a wide variety of characteristics and from a wide variety of backgrounds. In order to gain the sophistication and skills needed to do so
you must accept yourself, lower the barriers to building relationships
with diverse peers, recognize that diversity exists and is a valuable resource, build friendships with diverse peers, highlight important mutual
goals that require cooperative action and develop a common ground on
which everyone is co-oriented, and clarify misunderstandings.

All people need to believe that they are unique and separate individuals who are valued and respected in their own right. In order to do
so, you must accept yourself as you are and build a coherent, stable, and
integrated identity. Your identity helps you cope with stress, it provides
stability and consistency to your life, and it directs what information is
attended to, how it is organized, and how it is remembered. Your identity is built through your current relationships and identifications with
real, historical, and fictional people. Actually, you have many interre-
lated identities. You have a family identity, a gender identity, and a
country identity. An important aspect of your identity is your identification with your cultural, ethnic, historical, and religious background.

The more accepting you are of yourself, the more able you are to
be accepting of others. But there are barriers to building positive relationships with diverse peers. The most notable barriers are prejudice, blaming the victim, and culture clash. Minimizing these barriers makes it easier to recognize that diversity exists and fundamental differences among

people are to be both respected and valued. To do so you must respect your own heritage, respect the heritages of others, develop a superordinate identity that transcends the differences, and a pluralistic set of values.

Accepting yourself, minimizing the barriers, and respecting and valuing diversity set the stage for actually gaining cross-cultural sophistication. Being able to relate effectively to people from a variety of cultures depends on seeking opportunities to interact cross-culturally, building trust, so that enough candor exists that you can learn what is and what is not disrespectful and hurtful to them. It is only through building friendships with diverse peers that the insights required to understand how to interact appropriately with people from a wide variety of backgrounds can be obtained. Two requirements for developing such friendships are highlighting cooperative efforts to achieve mutual goals and clarifying miscommunications that arise while working together.

Exercise 10.1: Stereotyping

Once you realize that everyone is socialized to be prejudiced and to stereotype others, you need to clarify just what stereotypes you now hold. The following exercise is aimed at clarifying (a) what stereotypes you have been taught about other groups, (b) what stereotypes they have been taught about you, and (c) how the process of stereotyping works.

1. Post the following list of words on sheets of paper around the room:

Over age 60	Man
Asian-American	Woman
African-American	Middle income
Native American	Lower income
Puerto Rican	Southerner
Gay	Midwestern
Lesbian	Californian
Blind	Roman Catholic
Deaf	Muslim

2. Each participant is to circulate around the room, read the various categories, and write one stereotype he or she has heard under each heading. Participants are told not to repeat anything that is already written down. They are not to make anything up. They are to write down *all* the stereotypes they have heard about each of the groups listed.

3. After everyone is done writing, participants are to read all the stereotypes under each category.

4. Participants discuss:
   a. Their personal reactions.
   b. How accurate the stereotypes of their identities are.
   c. What they have learned about stereotyping others.

Exercise 10.2: Interacting on Basis of Stereotypes

Stereotypes are rigid judgments made about other groups that ignore individual differences. The purpose of this exercise is to demonstrate how stereotypes are associated with primary and secondary dimensions of diversity.

1. Divide participants into groups of five. The group is to role play a discussion among employees of a large corporation of the ways in which the percentage of people of color and women in higher level executive positions may be increased from 10 percent to 50 percent.

2. Give each member of the group a headband to wear with a particular identity written on it for other group members to see. *Group members are not to look at their own headbands.* The five identities are:

Single Mother Of TwoYoung Children

Physically Handicapped Employee

Women, Age 62

White Male, Group Leader

Black Union Official

3. Stop the discussion after 10 minutes or so. Then have the groups discuss:
   a. Guess what the label on their headband was.
   b. Their personal reactions.
   c. The participation pattern of each member—Who dominated, who withdrew, who was interrupted, who was influential.
   d. What they have learned about stereotyping others.

Exercise 10.3: How Self-Accepting Are You?

How do you tell if you are self-accepting? One way is to list all the assets you have. If you can list 200 to 300 assets, then you are very self-accepting. Another way is to see if you can plan how to use your assets when you get into a stressful or problem situation. Finally, you can measure yourself against the following checklist, which summarizes much of the research conducted on self-accepting people (Hamachek 1971). Write yes if the item fits you, write no if it does not.

_____ I strongly believe in certain values and principles. I am willing to defend them, even in the face of strong group opposition. I feel personally secure enough to change them if new experiences and new evidence suggest I am in error.

_____ I am capable of acting on my own best judgment. I do this without feeling overly guilty or regretting my actions, even if other people disapprove of what I have done.

_____ I do not spend a lot of time worrying about what is coming tomorrow, what has happened to me in the past, or what is taking place in the present.

_____ I am confident in my ability to deal with problems, even in the face of failure and setbacks.

_____ I feel equal to other people as a person. I do not feel superior or inferior. I feel equal even when there are differences in specific abilities, family backgrounds, job prestige, or amount of money earned.

_____ I take for granted that I am a person of interest and value to others, at least to the people I associate with.

_____ I can accept praise without the pretense of false modesty; I can accept compliments without feeling guilty.

_____ I am inclined to resist the efforts of others to dominate me.

_____ I am able to accept the idea and admit to others that I am capable of feeling a wide range of impulses and desires. These range from being angry to being loving, from being sad to being happy, from feeling deep resentment to feeling deep acceptance.

_____ I am able to genuinely enjoy myself in a wide variety of activities. These include work, play, loafing, companionship, and creative self-expression.

_____ I am sensitive to the needs of others, to accepted social customs, and particularly to the idea that I cannot enjoy myself at the expense of others.

Exercise 10.4: Strength-Building

Accepting and appreciating yourself is related to being aware of your strengths and assets. We all have many strengths. We all have strengths we are not using fully. We all can develop new strengths. A *strength* is any skill, ability, talent, or personal quality that helps you be effective and productive. You increase your self-acceptance as you become more aware of your strengths and develop new ones. The more you see yourself as having real skills, abilities, talents, and other personal strengths, the more you will value and accept yourself.

In this exercise you will concentrate on identifying your strengths and determining how they can be used most productively to build personal relationships. The objectives of this exercise are to increase your self-acceptance through the increased awareness of your strengths and to increase your awareness of how your strengths can be used to develop fulfilling relationships with other individuals. In this exercise you will be asked to discuss your strengths openly with the other group members. This is no place for modesty; an inferiority complex or unwillingness to be open about your positive attributes is not a strength. You are not being asked to brag, only to be realistic and open about the strengths that you possess. The procedure for the exercise is:

1. Think of all the things that you do well, all the things which you are proud of having done, all the things for which you feel a sense of accomplishment. List all your positive accomplishments, your successes, of the past. Be specific.

2. Divide into pairs and share your past accomplishments with each other. Then, with the help of your partner, examine your past successes to identify the strengths you utilized to achieve them.

3. In the group as a whole, each person should share the full list of his strengths. Then ask the group, "What additional strengths do you see in my life?" The group then adds to your list other qualities, skills, and characteristics that you have overlooked or undervalued. The feedback should be specific; that is, if one member tells another he has a strength, he must back his feedback up with some evidence of behavior that demonstrates the strength.

4. After every group member has shared her strengths and received feedback on what further strengths others see in her life, each member should then ask the group, "What might be keeping me from utilizing all my strengths?" The group then explores the ways you can free yourself from factors that limit utilizing your strengths.

5. Think about your past successes and your strengths. Think about how your strengths may be utilized to improve the number or quality of your close relationships. Then set a goal for the next week concerning how you may improve

either the number or the quality of your close relationships. Plan how utilizing your strengths will help you accomplish this goal.

Exercise 10.5: Standing Ovation

The purpose of this exercise is to provide you with the opportunity to receive considerable recognition and acceptance by your peers. The procedure is:

1.   Stand in a circle of at least six people. The larger the group, the better.
2.   One at a time, each member goes to the center of the group, states his or her name, and then the group cheers and claps for that person. Make each member feel special, valued, and recognized.

Exercise 10.6: Off Balance

The purpose of this exercise is to experience mutual physical support with another person. The exercise is taken from the excellent book *Playfair*, written by Weinstein and Goodman (1980). The procedure is:

1.   Find a partner who was born in a different month from you. Make sure no walls, furniture, or objects are near you. This is an exercise that calls for starting slow, staying in complete control, and taking responsibility for your partner's well-being.
2.   Stand facing your partner, firmly grasping each other's hands or wrists. The object of this exercise is for both of you to be off balance, yet totally supporting each other the whole time. Lean your weight backward so that if it were not for your partner supporting you, you would fall over. Be careful not to put too much strain on your partner. Work out an effective counterbalance between the two of you. Move around together, exploring different levels, different points of balance for your body. Use the support from your partner to do things you could not do by yourself.
3.   Stand back-to-back with your partner, leaning into each other, so you are off balance and supporting each other's weight. Move around and explore this new position so that you are both continually off balance yet continually supporting each other.
4.   Combine into a group of four with another pair. Repeat steps 2 and 3. Again, start out carefully. Make sure you do not have an unpleasant crash landing.

Exercise 10.7: Gaining Acceptance Nonverbally

Sometimes other people do not just give you acceptance; you have to earn it. We often spend a great deal of time and energy trying to gain the acceptance of individuals we like and admire. This exercise gives you an opportunity to experience gaining acceptance from the group nonverbally. The procedure for the exercise is:

1. One member volunteers to be an outsider. The other members of the group form a tight circle by locking arms and pressing close to each other's sides.

2. The outsider has to break into the group by forcing his or her way to the center of the circle. This is quite an active exercise. You should, therefore, be careful not to hurt anyone by becoming too rough. Anyone with a physical handicap or injury should not take part in this exercise.

3. After everyone who wishes to has been an outsider, discuss the experience. The discussion may center upon:

    a. How did you react to being an outsider? What did you learn about yourself from the experience?

    b. How did you react to trying to keep the outsider from gaining entry into the group? What did you learn about yourself from the experience?

Exercise 10.8: Expressing Acceptance Nonverbally

The purpose of this exercise is for you to have an opportunity to experience fully the acceptance felt toward you by others. At the same time, the members of the group are given an opportunity to express acceptance nonverbally. The procedure for the exercise is:

1. One member volunteers to stand in the center of a circle made up of the other members of the group. She is to shut her eyes and be silent.

2. The other members of the group are all to approach her and express their positive feelings nonverbally in whatever way they wish. This may take the form of hugging, stroking, massaging, lifting, or whatever each person feels.

3. After everyone who wishes to has been the center of the circle, the group may wish to discuss the experience. The discussion may center on the following two areas:

    a. How did it feel to receive so much acceptance and affection? What were the reactions of each person in the center? Was it a tense situation for you or was it an enjoyable one? Why do you react as you do? What did you learn about yourself?

   b. How did it feel to give so much acceptance and affection to other members of the group? What are your reactions to such giving? Why do you react this way? What did you learn about yourself from this experience?

Barriers to Interpersonal Effectiveness

We pay a heavy price for our fear of failure. It is a powerful obstacle to growth. It assures the progressive narrowing of the personality and prevents exploration and experimentation. There is no learning without some difficulty and fumbling. If you want to keep on learning, you must keep on risking failure—all your life. It's as simple as that.

John Gardner, Self-Renewal

INTRODUCTION

There are a number of barriers to engaging in effective interpersonal interaction that have their origins in interpersonal relationships. When you are troubled by these barriers your interpersonal effectiveness is seriously impaired. The barriers are

1. Fear and anxiety
2. Shyness
3. Self-blame.

Fear and anxiety, more than any other emotions, incapacitate interpersonal interaction. They cause avoidance of the anxiety-provoking situation and an immobilization of interpersonal interaction within the situation. Fears can persist year after year, chronically interfering with constructive relationships and effective interaction. Learning to overcome fear and anxiety is an essential ingredient of being effective interpersonally. One specific type of problem arising from fear and anxiety is shyness. The excessive caution and overly self-consciousness in interpersonal relationships produced by shyness can stand as a major barrier to developing and maintaining friendships and effective working relationships. When interpersonal interaction is inhibited, interpersonal skills either never appear or are underutilized. Finally, self-blame, the directing of anger toward yourself for not living up to your expectations and hopes, results in depression that interferes with effectively relating to other people. This chapter focuses on overcoming the inhibition and avoidance created by these three barriers.

MANAGING ANXIETY AND FEAR

Of all the emotions humans experience, fear is perhaps the most chronic and troublesome. All of us, many times during our lives, are afflicted with fear, anxiety, nervousness, phobia, or worry. Anger can quickly flare up and quickly die down. Depression may hang on, but sooner or later it will be replaced with a neutral feeling or even a positive one. A fear of failure, however, can influence practically everything you do every day of your life. It may not hurt as much as depression, or flare up like anger, but it will be there all the time, ready to disturb, year in and year out. It is fear that has the unique power of preventing you from fulfilling your potential. It is fear that can suppress talents and prevent genius from being actualized. Stage fright can prevent a great singer from being recognized; fear of failure can prevent an Einstein from entering a doctoral program or beginning a research project; fear of humiliation can prevent a young inventor from submitting his or her ideas to a potential manufacturer. Fear can be devastating in a special way that anger and depression cannot.

Fear exists when a person is afraid and knows what he or she is afraid of. *Anxiety* exists when a person is afraid but does not know what he or she is afraid of. The fears and anxieties that rule our lives the most are not spectacular ones. Most of us do not chronically fear having to fight a great white shark with a letter opener. What we do fear is being rejected and failing. We all experience anxiety at times—a troubled uneasiness of mind mixed with uncertainty and doubt. But when the feeling is persistent, with an intensity out of proportion to the object or situation that caused it, the anxiety is called a *phobia*. Phobias can develop in at least three ways. They can result from anxiety attacks, because people associate their feelings of panic with the places and situations in which they occur. A panic attack that occurs while you are driving your car, for example, may result in a phobia about driving. Phobias can also grow out of specific experiences. If you were bitten by a dog when you were a young child, for example, you may develop a phobia about dogs. Finally, phobias can be learned from others, such as by observing parents who fear lightning or bugs. In some cases the fear involved in a phobia is displaced from its original source to a different place or situation. A fear of falling in social status, for example, may be repressed and displaced into a fear of falling in an elevator.

Fear and anxiety usually involve two kinds of pain. One type of pain comes from doing what you are afraid of. The other type of pain comes from avoiding what you are afraid of. Either way you experience pain. The pain connected with doing an activity is generally less in the long run than the pain connected with avoiding an activity. Replacing the unpleasantness of rejection with the pain of loneliness usually is not a good bargain. Simply avoiding anxiety-provoking situations does not remove discomfort. There is discomfort in combatting the fear and there is discomfort in giving into the fear. The discomfort connected with overcoming your fears has an ending, whereas the annoyance connected with not changing your fears can persist for as long as you live.

The procedures for managing and overcoming your fears and anxieties include the following:

1. Do not fear anxiety. Once you become afraid that your anxiety may come back, it will. Fearing that you may become anxious creates anxiety. The more you worry about the possibility of experiencing an anxiety attack, the more likely it is that you will have one. Generally, the more you worry about something, the worse it gets.

2. Accept your fear and anxiety as natural feelings that are to be experienced but not fought or resisted. The key to managing fear and anxiety is simply to accept them. The harder you fight them the worse they become. The more you try to fight to get rid of your fears, the more unacceptable and shameful you see them to be, the worse they will become. The more you ignore them, pay no attention to them, and accept them for what they are, the less hold they will have over you.

3. Own your fear and anxiety. Accept them as your feelings. Do not view anxiety as "it," something separate and apart from you that descends on you and takes control, but rather as one of your feelings that you sometimes experience and is within you and, therefore, subject to your control.

4. Accept yourself as you are. Rejection from others cannot hurt unless you reject yourself as a result. Failing cannot hurt unless you reject yourself for it. Being an anxious person or a person who has anxiety attacks does not make you a horrible outcast. You do not have to be loved and accepted by others to like yourself, you do not have to be perfect in order to respect yourself, and you do not have to be in perfect control of your feelings in order to feel worthwhile.

5. Recognize that fear is learned and, therefore, it may be unlearned.

6. Challenge the idea that you must worry over something unpleasant just because it "might" happen to you. Do not engage in "what if?" Avoid the neurotic idea that it is important to think about a possible danger. Fight the idea that you should constantly think of, dwell upon, and worry over a frightening situation. Do not fix upon "a grain of truth" and magnify it out of proportion. Vigorously attack the mental nonsense (neurotic misconceptions) that:

   a. You ought to be terribly upset about something.

   b. Worrying helps.

   c. The more you focus on the dreaded event, the better it is; that is, it is important to think about potential danger just because it "might" happen.

   d. Outside events can upset you. Remember that it is your thinking about things that disturbs you, not the things themselves.

7. Avoid "catastrophizing." The moment you tell yourself that something is awful or terrible, or that you are facing a catastrophe, you are going to become disturbed. The two things you can do are:

    a. Convince yourself that the situation is not a catastrophe after all. Accept your fear as being a minor, not a major, inconvenience.

    b. Convince yourself that even if the situation is a catastrophe there is really no need to become terribly upset over it because it only makes your situation worse.

8. Remember that being afraid does not mean that you are crazy. Many people fear that experiencing an anxiety attack will drive them crazy. They are afraid that experiencing anxiety means that they are losing their minds. They see themselves as going out of control and running berserk down the street. Being afraid and being psychotic are two separate things entirely. An anxiety attack may feel strange and puzzling, but it does not mean you are going crazy.

9. View the fear and anxiety as a problem to be managed and solved, not as a catastrophe to hide from. When you overreact and become overconcerned, the anxiety takes control. When you are working on solving a problem, you are merely concerned.

10. Systematically desensitize yourself to the fearful situation by doing the following:

    a. Learn how to relax systematically. A relaxed person cannot be an anxious person.

    b. After you are relaxed, imagine yourself overcoming your fears by engaging in the behavior you are afraid of.

11. Flood yourself with actual experiences of doing what you are most afraid of. Such "flooding" involves at least three elements:

    a. Taking risks by repeatedly exposing yourself to the very thing you are most afraid of. You overcome your fear when you do the thing you are afraid to do and are willing to face the dangers involved. People who do not take risks in facing their fears live in a constant state of anxiety and apprehension. If you are afraid of riding an elevator, you must do so anyway. People who have ridden in elevators thousands of times do not have the same nervousness as a person who rarely takes an elevator.

    b. Not blaming yourself if you perform less than perfectly in the situation. Separate your actions and performance from yourself.

    c. Practicing facing the fearful situation and then practicing some more. Practice makes you the master. If you have not mastered the situation you are afraid of, you have not practiced it enough. To master an activity you have to:

        (1) Practice it.

(2) Examine the performance to find out where you can improve.

(3) Change.

(4) Practice it again.

In other words, stick your neck out and do the thing you are afraid of. Then, after you have done less than perfectly, sit back objectively and look over your mistakes so that you can improve next time. Progress is built on mistakes. The person who does not make mistakes does not learn.

12. Distract yourself when the anxiety becomes too high. It is impossible to be upset about something unless you are thinking about it. Anything that diverts you from your troubles will give you relief.

13. Work on developing a broad view of life and a wide variety of experiences. The more you know about the world, and the more you have experienced, the more comfortable you tend to be in any situation. The person with the most experiences is the person who can compare the next experience to those that he or she has already had.

14. Do not be afraid of being independent. Do not ask for sympathy from other people. There is a tendency to use one's fear and anxiety to control others by expecting them to feel sorry for you or to make excuses and exceptions for you, because you are terrified. People who are afraid and who lean upon others to help them with their fears are not always quick to give them up, because to do so means they have become independent, which they are sometimes reluctant to do.

15. Accept reality. Life is full of danger, heartache, and injustice. Every living creature has to go through some suffering, and you are no different. If you are not facing some suffering today, you will be tomorrow. There is no need to be terrified or nervous or worried about these possibilities. Remind yourself that:

a. Most frustrations are really not as bad as you think they are.

b. Even if some are that bad, you do not have to lose your mind over them and thus make matters worse. If you focus on danger, heartache, and injustice unduly, you will create unnecessary additional suffering for yourself and for the people around you.

16. Do not expect great improvement. Measure improvement in terms of:

a. Duration of anxiety

    b. Intensity of anxiety

    c. Frequency of anxiety

17. Others will be too busy to pay much attention to how you are doing on your self-improvement program. Reward yourself for your progress.

18. As you confront your fears, they will get worse for a while. Learning usually takes place in an erratic way, and you will never know from one time to the next just how you are going to do.

19. Watch out for spontaneous recovery. There is a strong tendency for neurotic symptoms to return after you think you have gotten rid of them. This usually means you have gotten careless about fighting your fear.

BREATHING

Breathing is essential to life. Proper breathing is an antidote to stress. It is through proper breathing that your blood is purified of waste products, infused with oxygen, and purged of carbon dioxide. Poorly oxygenated blood contributes to anxiety states, depression, and fatigue, making it many times more difficult to cope with stressful situations. Proper breathing habits are not only essential for good mental and physical health but are a key to relaxing effectively. When you are faced with an anxiety-provoking situation, deep and proper breathing is one of your first lines of defense. Breathing exercises have been found to be effective in reducing anxiety, depression, irritability, muscular tension, and fatigue.

Exercise 11.1: Learning How to Breathe Deeply

The objective of this exercise is to help you relax systematically when you are anxious by controlling your breathing. You may wish to complete this exercise with a partner. Take turns reading the exercise while the other does it. The procedure for the exercise is:

1. Sit up straight in good posture in a hard-backed chair.

2. Slowly breathe inward through your nose counting from one to four as you do so.

a. First, fill the lower section of your lungs. Your diaphragm will push your abdomen outward to make room for the air.

b. Second, fill the middle part of your lungs. As you do so you will feel your lower ribs and chest move slightly forward to accommodate the air.

c. Third, fill the upper part of your lungs. Raise your shoulders and collarbone slightly so that the very top of your lungs are replenished with fresh air.

Practice until these three steps are performed in one smooth, continuous inhalation.

3. Hold your breath for 4 seconds.

4. Exhale slowly counting to eight while you do so. Pull in your abdomen slightly and lift it slowly as the lungs empty. When you have completely exhaled, relax your abdomen and chest.

5. Continue deep breathing for about 5 to 10 minutes at a time.

6. Scan your body for tension. Compare the tension you feel at this time with the tension you felt at the beginning.

7. Use this deep-breathing procedure whenever you feel yourself getting tense.

PROGRESSIVE MUSCLE RELAXATION

You cannot have a warm feeling of well-being and relaxation in your body and at the same time experience anxiety and psychological stress. As your muscles relax your pulse rate becomes slower, your blood pressure drops, and you breath deeper and slower. When it is successfully learned, deep-muscle relaxation is an excellent antidote to anxiety and fear.

There are two steps in using deep-muscle relaxation:

1. Learning to distinguish between sensations of tension and deep relaxation

2. Learning to relax any major muscle group on demand, even within highly anxiety-provoking situations

Exercise 11.2: Systematic Muscle Relaxation

The objective of this exercise is to train you in a procedure for systematic muscle relaxation. You may wish to complete this exercise with a partner. Take turns reading the exercise while the other does it. Go through the following procedure daily until you have it memorized and are able to relax any set of muscles at will. Then use it whenever you are in an anxiety-provoking situation. The procedure is:

1. Lie down on a blanket or rug or sit in a comfortable chair with a back high enough to support your head. When you tense a muscle group do so enough to clearly feel the tension, but do not strain any muscles.

2. Tense your hands, forearms, and biceps by clenching both fists and curling both arms as if you were in a Charles Atlas pose. Hold for 5 to 7 seconds. Concentrate on how the tension feels. Notice each detail of the tension in your hands, forearms, and biceps. Feel the tension.

3. Relax your hands and arms, letting them rest on the floor or on the arms of the chair. Concentrate on relaxing your hands, forearms, and biceps as much as possible. Continue the relaxation for 20 to 30 seconds. Notice the difference between the tension and relaxation. Enjoy the pleasant and soothing feeling of relaxation.

4. Repeat this procedure.

5. Tense all your facial, neck, throat, and shoulder muscles by wrinkling up your forehead and, at the same time, press your head as far back as possible, rotate it clockwise in a complete circle, and then rotate it counterclockwise in a complete circle. Now wrinkle up the muscles of your face by frowning, squinting your eyes, pursing your lips, pressing your tongue on the roof of the mouth, and trying to touch your ears with your shoulders. Hold for 5 to 7 seconds. Notice the tension. Study how it feels. Enjoy it.

6. Relax all the muscles in your face, neck, throat, and shoulders. Concentrate on how the relaxation feels. Continue the relaxation for 20 to 30 seconds. Enjoy the relaxation and study each detail of how each relaxed muscle feels.

7. Repeat the procedure.

8. Tense your chest, stomach, and lower back muscles by arching back as you take a deep breath into your chest. Hold your breath for 5 to 7 seconds. Study how the tense muscles feel. Then relax for 20 to 30 seconds. Notice the difference between the tension and the relaxation. Take a deep breath, pressing out your stomach, and tensing your muscles. Hold your breath and the tension for 5 to 7 seconds. Then relax for 20 to 30 seconds. Notice the difference between the tension and the relaxation. Study the difference. Enjoy the soothing and enjoyable feeling of relaxation.

9. Repeat this procedure.

10. Tense your thighs, buttocks, calves, and feet by pointing your feet and toes back toward your face and tightening your shins. Hold for 5 to 7 seconds. Study the tension. Then relax the muscles. Let them go completely relaxed. Notice the difference between the tension and relaxation. Enjoy the warm and soothing feeling of relaxation. Now curl your toes downward while at the same time tightening your calves, thighs, and buttocks. Hold for 5 to 7 seconds. Study the details of how each tensed muscle feels. Then relax. Let the muscles go completely relaxed. Notice and enjoy the difference between the tension and relaxation.

11. Repeat this procedure.

12. Let your whole body go completely relaxed. Feel the relaxation in your hands

and arms, your face and neck, your chest and stomach, and your legs and feet. Notice how comfortable and enjoyable it feels.

SHYNESS

Every person, experiencing as he does his own solitariness and aloneness, longs for union with another.

Rollo May, Love and Will

There is no joy except in human relationships.

Antoine de Saint-Exupéry
Wind, Sand, and Stars

Answer the following questions yes or no:

____ 1. I often become anxious when I am the center of attention.
____ 2. I am often concerned about being rejected by others.
____ 3. I tend to be very self-conscious in interacting with other people.
____ 4. When I am with people I do not know, I hesitate before expressing my thoughts and feelings.
____ 5. I am very conscious of whether people like me or not.
____ 6. I need to be more aggressive in forming relationships with other people.

If you answered yes to several of the above questions, you may be suffering from a very common problem—shyness. *Shyness* is an excessive caution in interpersonal relations. Specifically, shy people tend to (1) be timid about expressing themselves, (2) be overly self-conscious about how others are reacting to them, (3) embarrass easily, and (4) experience physiological symptoms of their anxiety, such as a racing pulse, blushing, or an upset stomach (Zimbardo 1977). Shyness involves excessive caution in social interaction and may include timidity, self-consciousness, anxiety, and sensitivity to embarrassment.

If you are shy, you are not alone. Most people have been shy during some stage of their lives, and up to 40 percent of Americans report being currently troubled by shyness. Most people, furthermore, experience shyness only in certain situations, such as when asking someone for help, when interacting with a member of the opposite sex, or when attending large parties. Shyness has a number of undesirable consequences, such as contributing to difficulty in making friends, being lonely and depressed, and being sexually inhibited. It is no surprise, therefore, that the vast majority of shy people do not like being shy.

Shyness can be successfully overcome. Although shyness tends to be a deeply entrenched part of a person's personality, and it takes a great deal of hard work to overcome, most shy people believe that they have succeeded in conquering their shyness. The three steps in doing so are (1) understanding your shyness, (2) building your self-esteem, and (3) improving your social skills.

UNDERSTANDING YOUR SHYNESS

To understand why you are shy, you should analyze your shyness. Try to pinpoint exactly what kinds of peope tend to elicit your shy behavior. In his study on shyness, Zimbardo (1977) found the people who generated shyness (in order of decreasing importance) were:

1. Strangers
2. Members of the opposite sex
3. Authorities by virtue of their knowledge
4. Authorities by virtue of their role
5. Relatives
6. Elderly people
7. Friends
8. Children
9. Parents

Next, try to ascertain what situations tend to elicit your shyness. Situations in which people tended to feel shy (in order of decreasing importance) were when they were:

1. The focus of attention of a large group (such as when giving a speech)
2. A member of a large group
3. Of lower status than the other people present
4. In social situations in general
5. In new situations in general
6. In situations requiring assertiveness
7. In situations in which one was being evaluated
8. The focus of attention of a small group

9. In small social groups
10. In one-to-one interactions with a member of the opposite sex
11. Vulnerable (needing help)
12. In small task-oriented groups
13. In one-to-one interactions with a member of the same sex

Once you understand which people and situations cause your shyness, you are ready to work on overcoming it.

BUILDING YOUR SELF-ESTEEM

Your shyness lies primarily within your evaluation of your self-worth. Increased self-confidence is an important aspect of combatting shyness. Some of the guidelines for building higher self-esteem are as follows:

1. *Control your self-esteem through how you see yourself.* Changing the way in which you think about yourself (see chapter 8) will change your self-esteem.

2. *Set your own standards for evaluating yourself.* Do not fall into the common trap of letting others set the standards by which you evaluate yourself. People with low self-esteem tend to be particularly susceptible to persuasion and too readily accept others' standards for their own.

3. *Set realistic goals.* Do not demand too much of yourself. Do not expect yourself to perform always at your best. Compare your performance against that of average individuals, not superstars.

4. *Modify negative self-talk and attributions.* Individuals with low self-esteem tend to think in counterproductive ways and make negative statements to themselves. When they succeed at something, for example, they may attribute it to good luck rather than to their ability and effort. Make sure you take credit for your successes and consider seriously the possibility that failures may not be your fault. Make self-enhancing conclusions about the way in which you applied your abilities and effort and tell yourself what a competent and good person you are.

5. *Emphasize your strengths.* People with low self-esteem often derive little satisfaction from their accomplishments and virtues. They pay little heed to their good qualities while emphasizing their defeats and faults. Accept your personal shortcomings that you are powerless to change and work to change those that are change-

able. At the same time, you should increase your awareness of your strengths and learn to appreciate them.

6. *Work to improve yourself.* Efforts at self-improvement can be used to boost your self-esteem. Many personal shortcomings can be conquered. Although it is important to reassess your goals and discard those that are unrealistic or are imposed by others, this book is an example of how you can improve your interpersonal skills and your confidence in relating to others.

7. *Approach others with a positive outlook.* Negativism toward yourself can result in negativism toward others. Faultfinding and criticism destroy relationships with others. They lead to tension, bitter exchanges, and rejection, which, in turn, lower your self-esteem. When you approach people with a positive, supportive outlook, you will promote rewarding interactions and gain acceptance. There is nothing that enhances self-esteem more than acceptance and genuine affection from others.

Exercise 11.3: Understanding Your Shyness

The objective of this exercise is to help you analyze not only the social situations in which you feel shy but also the causes of your shyness. Without understanding your shyness you cannot build an effective strategy to overcome it. The procedure for the exercise is:

1. Divide into pairs. Complete the following steps for both of you.

2. *Specify your target behaviors.*

   a. Examine the list of Zimbardo's findings on which people and situations tend to generate reticence in others (see page 341). List the ones that seem most characteristic of you. Add any others which apply to you.

   b. Decide which of the following may be reasons for your shyness:

   Concern about negative evaluation

   Fear of rejection

   Lack of self-confidence

   Lack of specific interpersonal skills

   Fear of intimacy

   Preference for being alone

   Emphasis on and enjoyment of nonsocial activities

   Personal inadequacy or handicap

   Other _____

c. Which of the following negative thoughts are typical of you and help prevent you from pursuing relationships in an active and positive way? Each of these thoughts undermines or precludes productive interpersonal behavior.

I am undesirable.

I am dull and boring.

If I ever admitted this thought to anyone, that person would reject or ridicule me.

Other people are not interested in my thoughts and feelings.

I cannot relax, be spontaneous, and enjoy myself.

I cannot seem to get what I want from this relationship.

If I said how I feel, that person might leave me and I will be all alone.

I will not risk being hurt again.

There must be something wrong with me if he/she left me.

I do not know how to act around other people.

I will make a fool of myself.

Other _____

d. Generate a number of specific behaviors you wish to increase in frequency within the problem situations and with the problem people. Initiating a conversation, asking someone to dance, and paraphrasing a person's remarks are examples.

3. *Gather baseline data.* The *baseline period* is a span of time, before the actual beginning of your efforts to change, during which you systematically observe your target behaviors. Gathering baseline data includes (1) measuring the specific frequency of the behaviors targeted to be increased, (2) noting the situations or events that happen before the targeted behavior, and (3) noting the typical consequences of the targeted behavior.

a. Place yourself in the situation in which you feel shy. Count how often you engage in the behavior targeted to be increased (such as initiating a conversation). You need to know the initial frequency of the target behavior in order to evaluate later how effectively you are increasing it. Because it is crucial that you have accurate data about the initial frequency of your behavior, it is important that you be honest with yourself and count all instances of the targeted behavior. It may be necessary to carry a portable device for recording your behavior, which may be simply an index card. The information should then be transferred to a permanent written record sheet or a graph. Do this for a week or for a minimum of five times.

b. For each instance of the targeted behavior, note the situations, events, feelings, or thoughts that precede the occurrence of your targeted behavior. These questions may help:

What did I think or say to myself?

What behavior of other people occurred?

What were the physical circumstances of the past few minutes?

4. Based on your tentative conclusion as to the causes of your shyness and the data you have gathered about the frequency with which you naturally initiate and build a relationship, design a plan to increase the frequency of your targeted behavior. The plan should include:

    a. How you will reinforce or reward yourself for engaging in the desired behavior.

    b. The conditions you have to meet in order to earn the reward. Set a behavioral target and frequency that are both challenging and realistic.

5. Complete a contract for each member of the pair.

Self-Change Contract

I, _____, do hereby agree to initiate my action plan as of (date) _____ and to continue it for a minimum period of (weeks) _____ or until (date)_____.

My specific action plan is to _____

_____.

I will do my best to complete this action plan to my utmost ability and to evaluate its effectiveness only after it has been honestly tried for the specified period of time.

For every _____ times I successfully comply with my action plan, I will reward myself with _____.

I hereby request that the witness who has signed below support me in my action plan and encourage me to comply with the specifics of the contract.

Signed _____

Witness _____

IMPROVING YOUR INTERPERSONAL SKILLS

Improved interpersonal skills are vital to overcoming shyness. All the skills listed in this book are relevant. Finding extroverted models to imitate, developing an area of expertise so that you have something to contribute in conversations, and being an active and attentive listener are three of the strategies commonly used to overcome shyness.

HELPING OTHERS LEARN INTERPERSONAL SKILLS

Reach out and touch someone.®

AT&T advertisement

Relationships are built because they are reinforcing to the people involved. However, the interpersonal skills necessary for building and maintaining fulfilling relationships do not appear magically when a person reaches a certain age. They are learned throughout a person's life and are based on the person's history of interpersonal interactions. Interpersonal skills are learned according to the specific principles of learning, which include reinforcement theory. Many people with whom you become involved may be lonely or isolated from their peers because they have not learned the skills necessary for positive interactions with others.

Because current behavior is the product of past experience (that is, learning history), individuals can recondition themselves to replace bad habits with constructive behaviors. The bad habits that have been acquired through conditioning yesterday can be dislodged today through reconditioning. Using the principles of learning theory, you may encourage individuals to increase their positive interactions with others. Reinforcement principles may be used to increase, maintain, reduce, or teach new behaviors. The principle of reinforcement is the process of increasing or strengthening a response by following that response with a consequence. There are two kinds of reinforcement, both of which increase the likelihood that a response will reoccur. *Positive reinforcement* is presenting an object or event that increases, strengthens, or maintains a response. *Negative reinforcement* is withdrawing or removing an object or event that, by its removal, encourages or strengthens a response. When using reinforcement principles it is important to determine reinforcers or reinforcing events that are appropriate for that individual.

Reinforcement theory is based on the simple rule that behavior is controlled by its consequences. If you say hello to a person you are just getting to know and receive a warm smile and a hello back, you are

likely to repeat the behavior in the future. If you receive a blank look and silence, however, you will be less likely to repeat the behavior in the future (you will be extinguished). When we engage in a particular behavior, it is to create the consequences we want. If those desired consequences do not result, we tend not to repeat the behavior but rather to switch to a new behavior that may be more effective in the future. This means that through the control of consequences you may increase, decrease, or keep constant the frequency of your own or another person's behavior. The procedure for the use of learning theory in influencing the behavior of yourself or another individual consists of the following:

1. Specify the target behavior.
2. Gather baseline data.
3. Design your program.
4. Execute and evaluate your program.
5. End your program.

Specifying the Target Behavior

The first step in any systematic effort to modify behavior is to specify the behavior targeted to be increased, stabilized, or decreased. It is important that the behavior is observable and measurable. You may decide that your objective is to increase the number of times John paraphrases or to decrease the number of times Jane frowns. To change the frequency of the target behavior you must control its consequences. Most problems can be characterized as either behavioral deficits or behavioral excesses (Martin and Poland, 1980). A *behavioral deficit* involves a response that is a problem because it does not occur often enough. The failure to use any of the interpersonal skills discussed in this book is an example. A *behavioral excess* involves a response that is a problem because it occurs too often. For example, people who frequently criticize others, smoke constantly, or talk all the time are troubled by behavioral excesses. In many cases, the target behavior may be characterized as either a deficit or an excess, depending on the perspective you choose to take. A problem with shyness, for example, may be described as socially withdrawing too often or initiating a conversation too rarely. When you have the choice, it is better to describe the target character as a deficit. Designing a program to increase a deficit has advantages over designing a program to decrease an excess (which often depends on the use of punishment).

Gathering Baseline Data

The *baseline period* is a span of time before the actual start of your program during which you systematically observe the target behavior. Gathering your baseline data involves monitoring

1. The initial response level of the target behavior
2. The typical antecedents of the target behavior
3. The typical consequences of the target behavior

You need to know the preprogram response level of the target behavior in order to evaluate the effectiveness of your program later. In most cases you simply keep track of how often the target behavior occurs in a predetermined time interval. In some cases the duration of responding is a more meaningful measure than simple frequency. It may be necessary to carry some kind of portable device for recording the target behavior, such as an index card, but your data should be transferred to a permanent written record and then placed on a graph. One week is usually the minimum for gathering baseline data.

Antecedents are situations or events that typically come before the target behavior. Recognizing the links between triggering events and the behavior to be modified can be very helpful in designing your program. In analyzing antecedents it may be helpful to ask the following questions:

1. What were the physical circumstances?
2. What was the social setting?
3. What behavior of other people occurred?

Finally, it is important to recognize what is currently reinforcing the behavior targeted for modification.

Designing the Program

To increase the frequency of the target behavior, give a positive reinforcer (such as warmth, acceptance, or praise) immediately after the person has engaged in the behavior. Be sure to choose a reinforcer that is appealing to the other person, that is relatively potent, and that is available to you to give. Then set up the *reinforcement contingencies*, which are the conditions that have to be met in order for the person to earn the reinforcer. A reinforcement contingency specifies the exact nature of the target behavior that must be emitted and the reinforcement that will then be awarded. Set up a behavioral goal that is both challenging and realistic. In helping other people learn more effective interpersonal skills, you may wish to model or demonstrate the skill and then reinforce the other person for engaging in it. Nothing teaches like a good example. Learning new behaviors by imitating others is a major means of acquiring new skills. By engaging in the needed skills you can encourage others to do likewise, and then you can reinforce them for doing so.

To decrease the frequency of a target behavior, reinforce the person for not emitting the target behavior, eliminate the triggering situations, or reinforce an incompatible response.

Executing and Evaluating Your Program

Put your plan into action and observe whether the target behavior changes in the desired direction. If the program does not work, revise it until it does.

Ending Your Program

Once your program is clearly successful, it will often become self-maintaining. The person may internalize the target behavior and his or her increased positive interactions with others may become intrinsically reinforcing. Sometimes it is a good idea to phase out your program gradually. However, some programs will need to go on indefinitely. A periodic check to make sure that the target behavior is being maintained is always constructive.

Exercise 11.4: Reinforcing Another Person's Strengths

The objective of this exercise is to give you practice in reinforcing another person for behaving in ways that demonstrate one of his or her basic strengths or attempts to overcome a barrier to expressing his or her strengths. The procedure is:

1. Think of a person you know (1) whose relationship skills you could help improve, (2) who lacks the self-confidence to use these relationship skills, or (3) to whom you would like to express more support. On a sheet of paper, describe this person's basic strengths.

2. What are the barriers that keep this person from expressing his or her strengths in interpersonal situations? List them on a sheet of paper. Examples of possible barriers are a lack of self-confidence, fear of rejection, fear that friends will think he or she is foolish, wanting to be overly nice, or lack of self-acceptance.

3. What possible strengthening consequences could you give this person? Examples of possible strengthening consequences are expressing warmth, acceptance, encouragement, understanding, self-disclosure about your positive reactions to his or her behavior, and many of the other behaviors that have been discussed in this book. List the behaviors you could engage in that are possible strengthening consequences.

4. Reviewing what you have listed in steps 1, 2, and 3, write out a series of behavioral objectives for your interactions with the person for the next week. Such a list should include a statement that describes the countable behavior on the part of the other person, indicates the desired change in the countable behavior, and specifies countable behavior by you to provide a strengthening consequence. An example of such a behavioral objective is: Increase the number of times John initiates a conversation by expressing warmth toward him immediately after he does so in my presence.

5. Review your objectives. It is important that they are not attempts to manipulate the other person but rather expressions of support for behaviors you feel will help the person express his or her strengths or eliminate barriers to showing these strengths. Your objectives should reflect a sincere attempt to be supportive, not an attempt to remake the other person. On the basis of your review, rewrite any objectives that may seem more manipulative than supportive.

6. In the group as a whole, discuss the objectives you have listed. Review what you wrote on steps 1, 2, and 3 in order to provide background for the objectives written in step 4. Help each other increase the specificity and concreteness of your objectives. Suggest new ideas for strengthening consequences for each other; help each other write new objectives that may be more effective in helping the other person.

7. During the next week, keep the record sheet that follows. Bring the sheet back to the group meeting and discuss the results. Is there any relationship between the number of strengthening consequences you engaged in and the number of times the other person engaged in behaviors that demonstrated his or her strengths or attempts to overcome barriers to the expression of these strengths?

Record Sheet: Reinforcing Another Person's Strengths

	Number of times other person engaged in behavior to be increased	Number of times I engaged in a strengthening consequence
Day One	_____	_____
Day Two	_____	_____
Day Three	_____	_____
Day Four	_____	_____
Day Five	_____	_____
Day Six	_____	_____
Day Seven	_____	_____

Exercise 11.5: Reinforcing Your Own Strengths

In addition to reinforcing another person's strengths, you can set up situations in which your own behavior gets reinforced. Through such reinforcement systems you may maximize your strengths and facilitate the development of your interpersonal skills. The process is the same for reinforcing another person's behavior; when your behavior is followed by a strengthening consequence, you will tend to repeat the behavior. The more immediately the strengthening consequence follows your behavior, the more likely you will be to repeat the behavior in the future. If you consistently receive a strengthening consequence immediately after engaging in the behavior, you will increase the number of times you engage in the behavior at a rapid rate. To maintain the frequency of your behavior, it is better to receive strengthening consequences immediately, but inconsistently. When you have important goals you are trying to accomplish, it is often helpful to find ways of receiving reinforcers for engaging in the behavior that will help you accomplish your goal.

In this book we discuss a variety of interpersonal skills that will increase the quality of your relationship if put to use. But in order to apply what is learned you need to have some personal goals about building better relationships and to apply the skills in a systematic way and build systems to receive reinforcement for engaging in the skills. Such a process involves being aware of, and building upon, your present strengths and skills. This does not mean you cannot develop new strengths; indeed, the purpose of this book is to help you develop new strengths in interpersonal skills. But developing new strengths is helped by being aware and using your present strengths.

The objective of this exercise is to give you an opportunity to use reinforcement theory to increase the number or quality of your strengths in relating to other people. The procedure for the exercise is:

1. Using the skills presented in the previous chapters of this book, set a goal for increasing the quality of your relationship with one or more people.

2. What specific behaviors will you have to engage in to accomplish your goal? What specific behaviors will indicate that the goal is accomplished?

3. What personal strengths will you utilize to accomplish your goal?

4. What are the barriers to your using your strengths to accomplish your goal?

5. Review what you have written for steps 1, 2, 3, and 4. Set a series of behavioral objectives for yourself. Make sure that they are countable and have direction.

6. In the group as a whole, review each person's objectives. Set aside some time during the next several group meetings to review each member's progress toward accomplishing his or her objectives. All possible support should be given to the members of the group who make progress toward achieving their objectives. It is the support and praise of the group that will serve as the major strengthening consequences for engaging in the behavior that helps to accomplish your objectives.

Summary Questionnaire: Reinforcing Your Own Strengths

1. My long-term objectives for building better relationships are:

    _____

    _____

    _____

    _____

2. My short-term objectives for building better relationships are:

    _____

    _____

    _____

    _____

3. The strengths and skills I will use to accomplish my objectives are:

    _____

    _____

    _____

    _____

4. The way in which I will know when my objectives are accomplished is:

    _____

    _____

    _____

    _____

5. The system of reinforcement for the behavior I engage in to accomplish my objectives is:

    _____

    _____

AVOIDING SELF-BLAME

A major threat to self-acceptance and good interpersonal relationships is a blame orientation. *Self-blame* exists when you say "bad me" to yourself or when you judge your basic self-worth on the basis of your inadequate or rotten behavior. Self-blame is, in effect, being angry at yourself. Blame involves a double attack: one against your actions and the other against yourself as a person. If you spill coffee on your desk, you can see your behavior as being uncoordinated, or you can see your behavior as clumsy and yourself as rotten and no good. Self-blame is similar to giving yourself a grade on the basis of a behavior you do not like. When you blame yourself you believe it is catastrophic that you are not getting what you want, that it is your fault, and therefore you are a bad person who should be severely punished. When you blame yourself (or others) you have to carry the anger around inside you, subjecting yourself to a great deal of stress and even making yourself sick. Perhaps most important, blaming yourself distracts you from finding a solution to your problems. All the punishment in the world does not promote creative insight into how a situation may be more constructively managed.

You should never blame yourself (or others) for:

1. *Not having the intelligence to do as well as you would like.* If the intellectual ability is not there, you cannot blame yourself. Either it is in your genes or it is not.

2. *Being ignorant.* Ignorance means that you have not yet learned a skill. You cannot blame yourself if you did not know better.

3. *Having behaved badly.* You should separate your behavior and your self-worth. You are not your actions. Engaging in bad behavior does not make you a bad person.

4. *Not being perfect.* In perfectionism, you attempt to be all things rather than who you are. A perfectionist never has developed an internal sense of how much is good enough. Only when you can stop trying to be perfect do you ever become free to be who you are.

5. *Being psychologically disturbed at the time.* Everyone at times enters psychological states such as anger, depression, grief, fear, and even extreme tiredness that result in behavior that is destructive to the best interests of ourselves or others. Psychological problems do

not result from being possessed by demons. Being psychologically disturbed does not make you an evil person.

To combat self-blame you must first (1) change your basic assumptions about it being a catastrophe when you do not get what you want and that whoever is to blame must be severely punished, and (2) engage in an internal debate to replace your old assumptions with the new, more constructive, ones (the specific procedures for doing so are covered in the previous chapter). Secondly, you must forgive yourself (and others) for everything. The sooner you forgive yourself the better. Sooner or later you forgive yourself and those you disagree with. Since you will eventually forgive, the sooner you do so the better for you. Finally, be problem oriented, not blame or fault oriented. Never blame anyone (including yourself). Always separate the person from his actions. Focus on the problem to be solved, not on the failure of you or others to live up to your expectations. Remember that when you blame others they become much more hostile and angry with you, escalating conflicts into destructive directions.

TAKING RISKS, TOLERATING FAILURE, PERSISTING, AND CELEBRATING SUCCESS

> Even if the breath of hope which blows on us from that new continent were fainter than it is and harder to perceive, yet the trial (if we would not bear a spirit altogether abject) must by all means be made. For there is no comparison between that which we may lose by not trying and that by not succeeding.
>
> Sir Francis Bacon, on
> Settling the New World

To be successful in interacting with other people, you must take risks. You must leave the beaten track and wander through the jungle of creative interaction, flirting with the not-yet-mastered and the unknown. For effective and successful people, risk taking is a way of life. To live a creative, interesting, challenging, and successful life, you have to gamble, take some risks, and experiment.

Special attributes of successful people are

1. A willingness to take risks
2. A substantial tolerance for failure
3. Persistence
4. The personal celebration of success

Growth demands commitment. To change your life even in small ways requires energy, participation, and enthusiasm. You cannot grow while you are inert. Overcoming the barriers to interpersonal effectiveness requires that you take risks. It is your first step to increased interpersonal competence. The essential advice for risk taking is:

1. Take risks often.
2. Start small. Small risks, with small penalties for failure, may be attempted first. If successful, you will increase in both self-confidence and knowledge and, therefore, can take on bigger risks.
3. The most appropriate risk is one in which there is a fifty-fifty chance of success or failure. This means that on the average, you will fail half of the time and succeed half of the time.
4. Prepare for your risks. Do not try to swim the English Channel without studying how it is done, practicing, getting into shape physically, and obtaining the proper equipment and support systems. The more experienced and better equipped you are, the more likely that your risk will succeed. You can control the outcome of your risks by being prepared and well-informed.

After taking a planned risk, you then accept failure gracefully, reflect on and learn from it, and persist in your efforts until you succeed. Once you have succeeded, celebrate! You have earned it.

> With the good people, you can see the learning juices churning around every mistake. You learn from mistakes. When I look back, my life seems to be an endless chain of mistakes.
>
> Edward Johnson, millionaire businessman

A basic tenet of all individuals who wish to become more effective interpersonally is, ''I have to be willing to fail.'' You cannot learn, you cannot improve your interpersonal effectiveness, you cannot build better relationships, and you cannot try new procedures and approaches unless you are willing to accept your mistakes. You need the ability to fail. Tolerance for failure and the ability to learn from it are very specific characteristics of any highly successful person. The important things to remember about failure are:

1. See failure as a positive indication that you are in the process of becoming more competent and effective.
2. Analyze your failure, reflect on it, and learn from it. Use it to plan your next attempt to do the same thing.
3. Give failure its due, but no more. Do not see it as catastrophic. Do not see it as the perfect indicator of your personal worth.
4. Do not make the penalty for failure worse than the reward for suc-

cess. The worse penalty should be reserved for doing nothing at all.

Failure and success are intimate relatives. If you want to dine on success you must occasionally sit down to failure.

> *A bright and energetic self-starter can make all the mistakes in this business in five years. With fools and sluggards, it may take a lifetime.*
>
> > *Unknown stockbroker*

The third step to successful growth is persistence. Try and try again. Keep practicing. Never (or almost never) give up.

> *Do what you can, with what you have, where you are.*
>
> > *Theodore Roosevelt*

Finally, when you are successful, celebrate! Reward yourself. Tell all your friends. Make sure the rewards you give yourself for success are far greater than the punishment you give yourself for any failure along the way.

MISTAKES AND SELF-TALK

Many people, when they make a mistake, make discouraging, critical, and blaming statements to themselves almost automatically. You may be one of them. In many cases it is difficult for you to identify your negative self-talk. But in order to feel better, it is important to train yourself to engage in positive self-talk after making mistakes. This behavior change can be initiated by:

1. Looking at negative self-talk in general
2. Identifying as best you can your negative self-talk
3. Formulating productive self-talk
4. Practicing it until it becomes automatic

The purpose of these four steps is to develop an on-going, energetic, encouraging inner speech.

There are times when many people are really hard on themselves when they make a mistake. They forget that while it feels good to succeed, it is not "awful" to make a mistake. Mistakes tell them that certain things may need to be done in a different way or with more time and concentration. Mistakes are the means for learning to do things better.

Mistakes are an important part of long-term success, especially when people challenge themselves to accomplish something difficult.

You have a choice. You may see mistakes as negative (something awful that proves you are stupid, a loser, or a failure) or as positive (a source of information about how to modify current behavior to be more effective in the future). What choice you make determines how you react to your mistakes. Genuine happiness is only possible to the degree that you feel good about yourself despite your mistakes and failures. The sooner you realize that failure is not bad in itself but is rather a natural part of achieving and living, the better able you will be to challenge yourself, grow, develop, and achieve.

Critical Thoughts	Encouraging Thoughts
(Circle the self put-down that you might use when you make a mistake.)	(Circle the comments you like best for handling a mistake.)
You stupid idiot. Why can't you do something right!	That didn't work. What shall I try next?
I'll never get it.	Everyone makes mistakes. Just try it again.
I really blew it this time.	I'll see if I can do better next time.
I hate myself.	I only did one thing poorly. Look at everything I did right!
Why am I such a loser?	I'm learning from my mistakes and that makes me a winner!

Exercise 11.6: Being Positive About Yourself While Trying Again

1. Form a group of three.

2. Ask members to identify a failure or two they have experienced recently. These failures need to be written out on a slip of paper. Place all the failures in a hat.

3. Each member draws a failure out of the hat. The member then

   a. Makes a series of negative self-statements about the failure

   b. Makes a series of positive self-statements about the failure.

4. This procedure is repeated until every member has gone through the sequence at least twice.

5. Discuss how hard or easy it is to change negative self-statements to positive ones and how important it is to learn to do so.

Epilogue

To live is to reach out to others. We all need other people. Striving to maximize the quality of our life requires that we also strive to maximize the quality of the lives of our friends and loved ones. We engage in relationships because we have goals we wish to pursue that require the participation of other people as well as ourselves. Many young adults have seemed to become obsessed with themselves. Their rampant individualism exists without any commitment to the common good. Concern for oneself without concern for others produces depression and meaninglessness. Life without friends is not much of a life.

Relationships are not optional luxuries, to be enjoyed when time allows. They are a necessity for our growth and development as a person, for the clarity of our self-identity, for our career success, for seeing life as meaningful, for our physical and psychological health, for our ability to cope with adversity and stress, for the actualization of our potential, and for our humaneness. In our life, furthermore, we will need to build relationships with a wide variety of individuals from many different backgrounds and cultures. The increasing interdependence of the world means we will need the interpersonal skills to build effective relationships with diverse individuals and then to resolve constructively any conflicts that occur while working to achieve mutual goals.

Relationships do not magically appear when needed. They are initiated, built, developed, and maintained through the application of interpersonal skills. Forming and maintaining relationships is not easy. With every interaction the relationship changes. When we do not have the required interpersonal skills, close, personal, intimate relationships are unlikely. Negative or destructive relationships may result.

It takes work to maintain a relationship. Many relationships fade away and are lost along the way. First, to maintain a relationship you have to be concerned about the well-being of the other person. If the relationship is not meeting his or her needs, then he or she will deemphasize it and fade away. Second, you have to invest time, energy, and resources in the relationship. Relationships have to be nurtured. Individuals you are always too busy to see will look for a relationship elsewhere. Schedule time together for matters of mutual interest. Quality time must be regularly scheduled if the relationship is to remain vital and a priority. Third, you have to accept, support, care for, and encourage the other person. We criticize most harshly those people we love. Many relationships fade away because one person never hears anything positive from the other. Small attentions and tokens of affection count for a lot. Fourth, maintain direct and open communication patterns. Whenever a problem arises, deal with it immediately while it is small. Do not let small grievances build into major resentments. Fifth, forgive the past and focus on the present and the future. Apologize and ask for forgiveness if it is necessary. Finally, regularly discuss how well the relationship is going and constructively resolve any conflicts that surface. Relationships are often damaged by silence, withdrawal, and unspoken hurt and anger. Regular processing of relationships is always helpful.

You have now completed a variety of experiences aimed at improving our interpersonal skills. You should now be more self-aware, self-accepting, and self-disclosing. You have had a variety of experiences in building trust, in giving and receiving constructive feedback, and in communicating ideas and feelings accurately and without ambiguity. You have had practice in expressing support and acceptance, confronting other people, and modeling appropriate behavior. You have been exposed to ways of reinforcing your own and another person's behavior. You have had practice in resolving conflicts constructively. You may find that you wish to repeat many of the exercises and reread much of the material in this book in order to learn how to utilize it fully in our relationships. There is, however, a concluding exercise that may be helpful in applying the material covered in this book to our relationships.

Relationship Survey

The objectives of this exercise are to help you become more aware of the qualities of the relationships in your life and to commit you to applying the skills and insights you have gained from this book to increase the richness of them. You will need a large sheet of paper and a felt-tipped pen for the exercise. The procedure for the exercise is as follows:

1. Write your name at the top of the paper and divide it into two columns. On one side, list four of your relationships that you value highly, and on the other side, write what it is that you value about the relationship. These could be relationships you are presently involved in or ones you have had in the past.

2. Share this information with the group as a whole. This gives you an opportunity to practice self-disclosure and listening skills. After each person has shared his information, the group should suggest what they perceive as the essential qualities of a good relationship for that person. The person should then write down the suggestions of the group in the appropriate column on the sheet of paper.

3. Divide into groups of three. Within the triad have each person review the strengths, skills, and insights learned from this book. Each person then picks several of the relationships she is now involved in and sets a series of goals about how she will behave in order to improve them. Discuss the goals within the group.

4. Address an envelope to yourself. Plan how you will behave in the next 6 months to accomplish the goals you have just set. Write a letter to yourself specifying your goals and your behavior in the relationships selected during the next 6 months. Seal the letter. Open it 6 months from today.

SUMMARY OF INTERPERSONAL SKILLS

1. Self-Disclosure
   a. Be aware of and accept your thoughts, feelings, needs, and actions.
   b. Express your thoughts, feelings, reactions, and needs to other people when it is appropriate; let other people know you as you really are.
   c. Seek out feedback from other people.
   d. Give feedback to other people when they request it.

2. Trust
   a. Take risks in self-disclosure when it is appropriate.
   b. Respond with acceptance and support when other people self-disclose.
   c. Reciprocate other people's self-disclosures.

3. Communication
   a. Speak for yourself by using personal pronouns when expressing thoughts, feelings, reactions, and needs.
   b. Describe other people's actions without making value judgments.
   c. Use relationship statements when they are appropriate.
   d. Take the receiver's perspective into account when sending your message.
   e. Ask for feedback about the receiver's understanding of your message.

f. Make your nonverbal messages congruent with your words.

g. Describe your feelings.

h. Describe what you think the other person is feeling and then ask if you are correct.

i. Paraphrase accurately without making value judgments about the sender's thoughts, feelings, and needs.

j. Negotiate the meaning of the sender's message.

k. Understand what the message means from the sender's perspective.

l. Make your nonverbal messages communicate clearly what you are feeling.

4. Responses
   a. When appropriate, engage in an evaluative response.
   b. When appropriate, engage in an interpretative response.
   c. When appropriate, engage in a supportive response.
   d. When appropriate, engage in a probing response.
   e. When appropriate, engage in an understanding response.

5. Acceptance and support
   a. Describe your strengths when it is appropriate to do so.
   b. Express acceptance of other people when it is appropriate to do so.

6. Influence
   a. Reinforce others' actions in order to increase, decrease, or maintain the frequency of their behavior, depending on what is in their best interests.
   b. Arrange for your behavior to be reinforced in order to increase, decrease, or maintain the frequency of desired behavior.
   c. Model interpersonal skills for others who wish to acquire them.

7. Conflicts   .
   a. Be aware of your habitual conflict style. Modify your conflict style according to the situation and the person you are dealing with. Whenever possible, manage conflicts like an Owl. View conflicts as a problem to be solved. Be aware of their potential value. And seek a solution that achieves both your own goals and the goals of the other person. Try to improve your relationship with the other person by resolving the conflict.
   b. Define conflicts constructively:
      (1) Describe the other person's actions without labeling or insulting her.
      (2) Describe the conflict as a mutual problem to be solved, not as a win/lose struggle.
      (3) Describe the conflict as specifically as possible.
      (4) Describe *your* feelings and reactions to the other person's actions.
      (5) Describe *your* actions that help create and continue the conflict.
   c. Know when and how to confront—to begin open discussions of the conflict aimed at resolving it constructively.

d. Define the conflict jointly with the other person.

e. Be sure the conflict is defined according to issues, not person-alities. Make it clear that you disagree with the other person's ideas or actions, not with him as a person. Do not take criticism of your ideas and actions as criticism of you as a person.

f. Find out how you and the other person differ before seeking to resolve the conflict.

g. See the conflict from the other person's viewpoint.

h. Increase both your motivation and the other person's motiva-tion to resolve the conflict.

i. Manage your feelings so that they do not make the conflict worse.

j. Reach an agreement about how the conflict is to end and not recur.

k. Avoid common misperceptions that intensify the conflict.

8. Stress and anger

a. Follow the rules for the constructive management of anger.

(1) Recognize and acknowledge that you are angry.

(2) Decide whether or not you wish to express your anger.

(3) Have ways of responding to provocations other than anger and depression.

(4) Express your anger directly and effectively when it is ap-propriate to do so.

(a) Make the expression cathartic.

(b) Ask for clarification before responding to a provoca-tion.

(c) Make it to the point and express it to the appropriate person.

(d) Take responsibility for the anger, owning it as yours, and becoming more involved with the other person in expressing it.

(e) Remember that heightened anger makes you agitated and impulsive.

(f) Beware of the righteousness of your anger.

(g) Stay task oriented rather than letting yourself get sidetracked by taking others' actions personally.

(h) Take into account the impact your anger will have on the other person.

       (i) Use the skills of accurate communication and constructive feedback.

       (j) Express positive feelings as well as your anger while discussing the situation.

    (5) Express your anger indirectly when direct expression is not appropriate.

    (6) Analyze, understand, and reflect on your anger.

    (7) Congratulate yourself when you have succeeded in managing your anger constructively.

b. Assert your anger through behavior descriptions, descriptions of your own feelings, congruent nonverbal messages, and good listening skills.

c. Manage your feelings constructively:

    (1) Recognize your irrational assumptions that lead to negative feelings.

    (2) Build more rational assumptions.

    (3) Argue with yourself, replacing your irrational assumptions with your rational ones.

Appendix

Instructions: The sender is to study the figure to the left below. With his back to the group, he is to instruct the members of the group on how to draw them. He should begin with the top square and describe each in succession, taking particular note of the placement relationship of each to the preceding one. No questions are allowed.

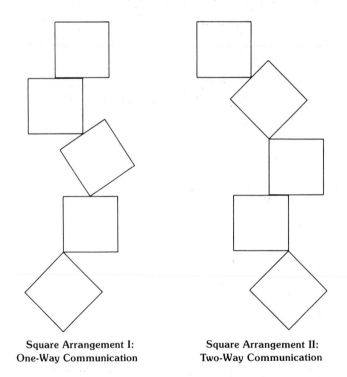

Square Arrangement I:
One-Way Communication

Square Arrangement II:
Two-Way Communication

Instructions: The sender is to study the figure to the right above. Facing the group, she is to instruct the members on how to draw them. She should begin with the top square and describe each in succession, taking particular note of the placement relationship of each to the preceding one. She should answer all questions from participants and repeat her descriptions if necessary.

Picture A

Picture B

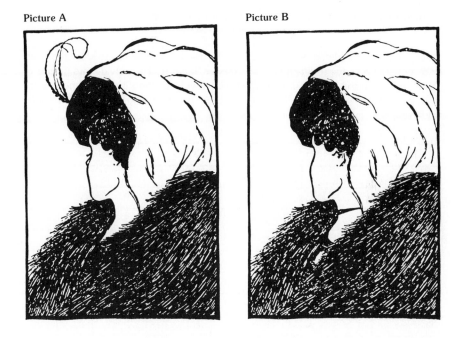

Picture C

Scoring Key: Identifying the Intent of a Response

After you have completed Answer Sheet 7.1B, use this scoring key to score the types of responses you gave for each item on Answer Sheet A. Then divide into groups of three and score the accuracy with which you identified the different responses for each item on Answer Sheet B. In groups of three, discuss each answer until everyone understands it.

Item	1	2	3	4	5
1.	I	S	E	U	P
2.	E	U	I	P	S
3.	U	I	P	S	E
4.	P	U	E	S	I
5.	S	P	U	I	E
6.	P	U	I	E	S
7.	E	I	P	S	U
8.	S	E	U	P	I
9.	U	P	E	S	I
10.	P	U	E	S	I
11.	I	E	S	U	P
12.	U	P	S	E	I

Scoring Key: Phrasing an Accurate Understanding Response

After you have completed Answer Sheet 7.3B, use this scoring key to score the type of phrasing you personally gave for each item on Answer Sheet A. Then divide into groups of three, score the accuracy with which you identified the different types of phrasing for each item on Answer Sheet B, and discuss each answer in your group until everyone understands it.

Item	1	2	3	4
1.	*I*	*A*	*P*	*S*
2.	*S*	*I*	*P*	*A*
3.	*A*	*S*	*I*	*P*
4.	*P*	*A*	*S*	*I*
5.	*I*	*P*	*A*	*S*
6.	*P*	*S*	*A*	*I*
7.	*A*	*P*	*I*	*S*
8.	*P*	*I*	*S*	*A*
9.	*I*	*S*	*A*	*P*

MANAGING PROVOCATIONS BY TALKING TO YOURSELF

Given below are a number of statements that you could say to yourself to help yourself manage a conflict situation constructively. Working as a triad, classify each statement given below as belonging in one of Novaco's four stages of managing a provocation constructively.*

Stage → Self-Statement

1. __1__ I can work out a plan for handling this.
2. __2__ As long as I keep cool, I'm in control here.
3. __3__ Getting upset won't help.
4. __4__ It worked!
5. __1__ If I find myself getting upset, I will know what to do.
6. __2__ You don't need to prove yourself.
7. __3__ It's not worth it to get so angry.
8. __4__ I could have gotten more upset than it was worth.
9. __4__ I actually got through that without getting angry. Way to go!
10. __3__ My anger is a signal that it's time to start talking to myself.
11. __2__ If I start to get mad, I will just be banging my head against the wall. So I might as well just relax.
12. __1__ This could be a bad situation, but I believe in myself.
13. __4__ I'm doing better at handling myself in these situations all the time.

*This test appears in Chapter 9, pp. 288–89.

14. __3__ My muscles are starting to feel tight. Time to relax and slow things down.

15. __2__ Don't assume the worst or jump to conclusions. Look for positives.

16. __1__ Before I go in, I need to take a few deep breaths, relax myself, make sure I feel comfortable and at ease.

17. __4__ I didn't take anything personally. I sure feel better that way!

18. __2__ I'm not going to let them get to me.

19. __3__ He would probably like me to get really angry. Well, I'm going to disappoint him.

20. __1__ I'll be able to manage this situation. I know how to regulate my anger.

21. __3__ Calm down. I can't expect people to act the way I want them to.

22. __4__ I've been getting upset for too long when it wasn't necessary. I have really improved in not getting angry!

23. __1__ There won't be any need to get angry or upset.

24. __2__ Don't get upset; just keep thinking about what I want to do to make sure I get what I want out of this situation.

25. __3__ Keep focused on the task. Don't let them distract you into a quarrel.

26. __1__ What is it I have to do to stay calm and be effective?

27. __2__ There is no need to doubt myself. What he says doesn't matter.

28. __4__ I am excellent at not reacting with anger when people provoke me.

REFERENCES

California Department of Mental Health (1981). *Friends can be good medicine*. Sacramento: State of California, Technical Report.

DEUTSCH, M. (1962). Cooperation and trust: Some theoretical notes. In M. Jones, ed., *Nebraska symposium on motivation*, pp. 275–319. Lincoln, Nebr.: University of Nebraska Press.

DEUTSCH, M. (1973). *The resolution of conflict*. New Haven, CT: Yale University Press.

ELLIS, A. (1962). *Reason and emotion in psychotherapy*. Secaucus, N.J.: Lyle Stuart.

FISHER, R., and URY, W. (1981). *Getting to yes*. Boston: Houghton Mifflin.

GLASSER, W. (1984). *Control theory*. New York: Harper & Row.

HAMACHEK, D. (1971). *Encounters with the self*. New York: Holt, Rinehart, and Winston.

JACKSON, D. (1959). Family interaction, family homeostasis, and some implications for conjoint family therapy. In J. Masserman, ed., *Individual and familial dynamics*, pp. 112–141. New York: Grune & Stratton.

JOHNSON, D. W. (1971). Role-reversal: A summary and review of the research. *International Journal of Group Tensions*, 1: 318–34.

JOHNSON, D. W. (1973). *Contemporary social psychology*. Philadelphia: J. B. Lippincott.

JOHNSON, D. W. (1974). Communication and the inducement of cooperative behavior in conflicts. *Speech Monographs*, 41, 64–78.

JOHNSON, D. W. (1979). *Educational psychology*. Englewood Cliffs, NJ: Prentice Hall.

JOHNSON, D. W. (1991). *Human relations and your career*, 3d ed. Englewood Cliffs, N.J.: Prentice Hall.

JOHNSON, D. W., and JOHNSON, F. (1991). *Joining together: Group theory and group skills*, 4th ed. Englewood Cliffs, N.J.: Prentice Hall.

JOHNSON, D. W., and JOHNSON, R. (1989). *Cooperation and competition: Theory and research*. Edina, MN: Interaction Book Company.

JOHNSON, D. W., and JOHNSON, R. T. (1991). *Teaching students to be peacemakers*. Edina, MN: Interaction Book Company.

JOHNSON, D. W., and JOHNSON, R. T. (1992). *Creative controversy: Intellectual challenge in the classroom*. Edina, MN: Interaction Book Company.

JOHNSON, D. W., and MATROSS, R. (1977). Interpersonal influence in psychotherapy: A social psychological view. In A. Gurman and A. Razin, eds., *Effective psychotherapy*, pp. 395–432. Elmsford, N.Y.: Pergamon Press.

JOHNSON, D. W., McCARTY, K., and ALLEN, T. (1976). Congruent and contradictory verbal and nonverbal communications of cooperativeness and competitiveness in negotiations. *Communication Research*, 3, 275–92.

JOHNSON, D. W., and NOONAN, M. (1972). The effects of acceptance and reciprocation of self-disclosures on the development of trust. *Journal of Counseling Psychology*, 19: 411–16.

KERR, N. (1983). The dispensability of member effort and group motivation losses: Free-rider effects. *Journal of Personality and Social Psychology*, 44, 78–94.

LEAVITT, H. (1958). *Managerial psychology.* Chicago: University of Chicago Press.

LUCE, R., and RAIFFA, H. (1957). *Games and decisions.* New York: John Wiley & Sons.

LUFT, J. (1969). *Of human interaction.* Palo Alto, Calif.: National Press.

MARTIN, R., and POLAND, E. (1980). *Learning to change.* New York: McGraw-Hill.

MCCROSKEY, J., LARSON, C., and KNAPP, M. (1971). *Introduction to interpersonal communication.* Englewood Cliffs, N.J.: Prentice Hall.

MILLER, S., NUNNALLY, E., and WACHMAN, D. (1975). *Alive and aware: Improving communication in relationships.* Minneapolis: Interpersonal Communication Programs.

NOVACO, R. (1975). *Anger control.* Lexington, Mass.: D. C. Heath & Co.

POWELL, J. (1969). *Why am I afraid to tell you who I am?* Niles, Ill.: Argus.

ROGERS, C. (1965). Dealing with psychological tensions. *Journal of Applied Behavioral Science,* 1:6–25.

ROGERS, C., and ROETHLISBERGER, F. (1952). Barriers and gateways to communication. *Harvard Business Review,* July–August: 28–35.

ROTTER, J. (1971). Generalized expectancies for interpersonal trust. *American Psychologist, 26,* 443–52.

WEINSTEIN, M., and GOODMAN, J. (1980). *Playfair.* San Luis Obispo, Calif.: Impact.

ZIMBARDO, P. (1977). *Shyness.* Reading, Mass.: Addison-Wesley.

GLOSSARY

Action theory. A theory as to what actions are needed to achieve a desired consequence in a given situation.

Aggression. An attempt to hurt someone or destroy something.

Anger. A defensive emotional reaction that occurs when we are frustrated, thwarted, or attacked. Anger is a righteous but defensive reaction to frustration and aggression based on a unidimensional perceptual focus, a physical demand to take action, and a belief that we must get our way.

Antecedents. Situations or events that typically come before the target behavior.

Anxiety. A feeling that exists when you are afraid but you do not know what you are afraid of.

Assertiveness. Describing your feelings, thoughts, opinions, and preferences directly to another person in an honest and appropriate way that respects both yourself and the other person.

Arbitration. The submission of a dispute to a disinterested third party who makes a final and binding judgment as to how the conflict will be resolved.

Attribution. An inference about the cause of a person's action.

Attribution theory. A social psychological explanation of how individuals make inferences about the causes of behaviors and events.

Autonomy. Ability to decide how to apply personal values and principles flexibly in order to act appropriately in the current situation.

Baseline period. A span of time before the actual start of an intervention program during which the target behavior is systematically observed.

Basic self-acceptance. A belief that you are intrinsically and unconditionally acceptable.

Behavioral description. A statement that includes a personal statement (referring to "I," "me," or "my") and a description of the specific behaviors you have observed.

Behavioral deficit. A response that is a problem because it does not occur often enough.

Behavioral excess. A response that is a problem because it occurs too often.

Belief in a just world. A belief that there is an appropriate fit between what people do and what happens to them.

Beneffectance. The tendency to take credit for success and deny responsibility for failure; from *beneficent* plus *effectance*.

Blame. Believing that the cause of your frustration is wicked people (including yourself) who deserve to be punished for their evil acts.

Blaming the victim. Attributing the cause of discrimination or misfortune to the personal characteristics and actions of the victim.

Categorizing. A basic human cognitive process of conceptualizing objects and people as members of groups.

Catastrophizing. Believing that you must have your way and that it is awful not to get everything you want.

Causal attribution. The process of explaining or inferring the causes of events.

Channel. A means of conveying the message to the receiver; the sound waves of the voice or the light waves of seeing words on a printed page are examples of channels.

Cognitive conservatism. Effect where, once your view of yourself has developed, there is a conservative tendency to maintain and reinforce it and to resist changing it.

Collusion. Conscious and unconscious support of prejudice, stereotypes, and discrimination, and prevailing norms. People collude with discriminatory practices and prejudiced actions through ignorance, silence, denial, and active support.

Communication. A message sent by a person to a receiver(s) with the conscious intent of affecting the receiver's behavior.

Communication networks. Representations of the acceptable paths of communication between persons in a group or organization.

Competitive goal structure. A negative correlation among group members' goal attainments; when group members perceive that they can obtain their goals if and only if the other members with whom they are competitively linked fail to obtain their goal.

Compliance. Behavior in accordance with a direct request. Behavioral change without internal acceptance.

Compromising. Giving up part of your goal while the other person does the same in order to reach an agreement. You seek a solution in which both sides gain something and settle on an agreement that is the middle ground between your two opening positions.

Conditional self-acceptance. Making conclusions about yourself on the basis of how well you meet external standards and expectations.

Conflict of interest. When the actions of one person attempting to maximize his or her needs and benefits prevent, block, interfere with, injure, or in some way make less effective the actions of another person attempting to maximize his or her needs and benefits.

Confrontation. The direct expression of one's view of the conflict and one's feelings about it and at the same time an invitation to the opposition to do the same.

Consensus. A collective opinion arrived at by a group of individuals working together under conditions that permit communications to be sufficiently open and the group climate to be sufficiently supportive for everyone in the group to feel that he or she has had a fair chance to influence the decision.

Conformity. Changes in behavior that result from group influences. Yielding to group pressures when no direct request to comply is made.

Cooperation. The means by which you and other people engage in joint action to accomplish a goal you all want.

Cooperative goal structure. A positive correlation among group members' goal attainments; when group members perceive that they can achieve their goal if and only if the other members with whom they are cooperatively linked obtain their goal.

Co-orientation. Operating under the same norms and adhering to the same procedures.

Culture clash. Conflict over basic values that occurs among individuals from different cultures. The most common form is when members of minority groups question the values of the majority.

Cycle of social interaction. Perceiving the other person's actions, deciding how to respond, taking action, and perceiving the other person's response.

Discrimination. An action taken to harm a group or any of its members.

Double Standard. Believing what you do is legitimate while identical actions by the opponent in a conflict are illegitimate.

Effective communication. When the receiver interprets the sender's message in the same way the sender intended it.

Egocentrism. Embeddedness in one's own viewpoint to the extent that one is unaware of other points of view and of the limitations of one's perspectives.

Emotional isolation. Not having deep relationships.

Ethnocentrism. The tendency to regard our own ethnic group, culture, or nation as better or more "correct" than others.

Experiential learning. Generating an action theory from your own experiences and then continually modifying it to improve your effectiveness.

False consensus bias. A belief (often false) that most other people think and feel very much as we do, such as sharing our stereotypes (such as believing that poor people are lazy).

Fear. A feeling that exists when you are afraid and you know what you are afraid of.

Feedback. Disclosing how you are perceiving and reacting to another person's behavior to provide him or her with constructive information to help the person become aware of the effectiveness of his or her actions.

Feelings. Internal physiological reactions to your experiences.

Forcing. Overpowering opponents by requiring them to accept your solution to the conflict. You seek to achieve your goals at all costs and without concern with the needs of others.

Fundamental attribution error. The attribution of the causes of other's behaviors to personal (disposition) factors and the causes of one's own behavior to situational (environmental) factors. In explaining the causes of the other's behavior the attributer overestimates the causal importance of personality, beliefs, attitudes, and values, and underestimates the causal importance of situational pressures. The opposite is done in explaining the causes of one's own behavior.

Hit-and-run. You start a conversation about the conflict, give your definition and feelings, and then disappear before the other person has a chance to respond.

Identity. A consistent set of attitudes that defines "who you are."

Illusory correlation. An overestimation of the strength of a relationship between two variables. Variables may not be related at all, or the relationship may be much weaker than believed.

Impression management. The process by which you behave in particular ways to create a desired social image.

Individualistic goal structure. No correlation exists among group members' goal attainments; when group members perceive that obtaining their goal is unrelated to the goal achievement of other members.

Inner directed. Controlled by a small number of values and principles set early in life that are rigidly adhered to, no matter what the situation.

Interdependence. Sharing mutual goals and needing to coordinate actions to achieve a goal.

Integration. Combining several positions into one new, creative position.

Intentions. Guides to action, immediate goals as to what you want to have happen.

Interest. Need, goal, benefit, profit, advantage, concern, right, or claim.

Interpersonal effectiveness. The degree to which the consequences of your behavior match your intentions.

Interpersonal skills. The sum total of your ability to interact effectively with other people.

Interpretation. Deciding what the information gathered by your senses means.

Irrational assumption. A belief that makes you depressed, anxious, or upset most of the time.

Message. Any verbal or nonverbal symbol that one person transmits to another.

Mirror image. Both parties in a conflict believing they are an innocent victim who represents truth and justice and who is being attacked maliciously by an evil enemy.

Mote-beam mechanism. Each person in a conflict seeing all the vicious acts of the opponent while being blind to identical actions they are taking.

Negative reinforcement. Withdrawing or removing an object or event that, by its removal, encourages or strengthens a response.

Negotiation. A process by which persons who have shared and opposed interests and want to come to an agreement try to work out a settlement.

Nonnegotiable norms. Norms individuals are expected to follow without exception, such as those outlawing physical violence against oneself or another person, public humiliation and shaming, and lying and deceit.

Nonassertiveness. You say nothing in response to a provocation, keeping your feelings to yourself, hiding feelings from others, and perhaps even hiding your feelings from yourself.

Norm of mutual responsiveness. Rule that you should be committed to fulfilling each other's goals and concerned about each other's interests.

Norm of reciprocity. A norm that a negotiator should return the same benefit or harm given him or her by the other negotiator; "an eye for an eye and a kiss for a kiss" is an example of a norm of reciprocity.

Norms. Shared expectations about the behavior that is appropriate within the situation.

One-step negotiations. Each person (a) assesses the strength of his or her interests, (b) assesses the strength of the other person's interests, and (c) agrees that whomever has the greatest need is given his or her way.

Objective self-awareness. Becoming aware of some aspect of yourself and evaluating it by considering how it measures up to some internal rule or standard.

Outer-directed. Controlled by other's expectations and pressure to conform.

Paraphrasing. Restating, in your own words, what the person says, feels, and means.

Perception-checking. Asking for clarification or correction to make sure your understanding is accurate. It involves describing what you think the other person's feelings are, asking whether or not your perception is accurate, and refraining from expressing approval or disapproval of the feelings.

Perceiving. The process of gathering sensory information and assigning meaning to it.

Personal statements. Statements that refer to "I," "me," "my," or "mine."

Perspective. A person's way of viewing the world and his or her relation to it.

Perspective reversal. Presenting the perspective and position of another person as if it were yours.

Polarized thinking. An oversimplified view of a conflict in which everything you do is good and everything the other person does is bad.

Positive reinforcement. Presenting an object or event that increases, strengthens, or maintains a response.

Prejudice. An unjustified negative attitude toward a person based solely on that individual's membership in a group other than one's own.

Problem-solving negotiations. When each negotiator has as his or her goal the reaching of an agreement that benefits everyone involved. You negotiate to solve the problem when you have an ongoing cooperative relationship with the other person, must negotiate an agreement to resolve the current conflict, and then will continue the cooperative efforts and the relationship.

Provincial. Knowing how to act appropriately only with one's own narrow perspective and culture.

Psychological health. The ability to build and maintain cooperative, interdependent relationships with other people.

Racism. Any attitude, action, or institutional structure that subordinates a person because of his or her ethnic membership.

Real-ideal comparison. A judgment about how your real self compared with your ideal self.

Reflected self-awareness. Making conclusions about yourself on the basis of how you think other people see you.

Reinforcement. Rewards given for approved behavior that tend to increase the likelihood that the behavior will be repeated.

Reinforcement contingencies. The conditions that have to be met in order for the person to earn the reinforcer.

Relationship statements. Personal statements that describe some aspect of the way the two of you are interacting with each other.

Role. A set of expectations defining appropriate behaviors associated with a position within a group. The "part" played by a member of a group. Rules or understandings about the tasks persons occupying certain positions within a group are expected to perform.

Role reversal. Having two participants in a conflict reverse roles and play each other during a role play.

Self-acceptance. A high regard for yourself or, conversely, a lack of cynicism about yourself.

Self-actualization. The drive to develop our potential to its fullest extent to find joy and a sense of fulfillment.

Self-awareness. The paying attention to and being aware of oneself. Focused self attention.

Self-blame. When you judge your basic self-worth on the basis of your inadequate or rotten behavior.

Self-disclosure. Revealing how you are reacting to the present situation and of giving any information about the present that is relevant to an understanding of your reactions to the present.

Self-evaluation. Your estimate of how positively your attributes compare with those of your peers.

Self-fulfilling Prophecy. A set of actions that provokes the other into engaging in behavior that confirms one's original assumptions. An example is assuming that the other is belligerent and then proceeding to engage in hostile behavior thereby provoking the other into belligerent actions, which confirms the original assumption.

Self-schema. A set of cognitive generalizations about the self, derived from past experience, that organizes and guides the processing of self-related information.

Self-serving attribution bias. The tendency to accept greater personal responsibility for positive outcomes than for negative outcomes.

Self-verification. Presenting yourself to others as you believe yourself to be.

Sensing. Gathering information through your five senses—seeing, hearing, touching, tasting, and smelling.

Sexism. Any attitude, action, or institutional structure that subordinates a person because of his or her gender.

Shyness. Excessive caution in interpersonal relations.

Smoothing. Giving up your goals and letting the other person have his or her way in order to maintain the relationship at the highest level possible. When the goal is of no importance to you but the relationship is of high importance, you smooth.

Social comparison. Using the other person for comparison so that we can evaluate our own attitudes and abilities.

Social isolation. Not having a network of friends who share your interests and concerns and help provide a sense of community.

Social interaction. Patterns of mutual influence linking two or more persons.

Social loafing. A reduction of individual effort when working with others on an additive group task.

Social perspective taking. The ability to understand how a situation appears to another person and how that person is reacting cognitively and emotionally to the situation.

Social sensitivity. The ability to perceive and respond to the needs, emotions, and preferences of others.

Social skills training. A structured intervention designed to help participants to improve their interpersonal skills. It is generally conducted in group settings.

Sophistication. Knowing how to act appropriately (in courteous, well-mannered, refined ways) within many different cultures, perspectives, and settings.

Stereotype. A set of beliefs about the characteristics of the people in a group that is applied to almost all members of that group.

Time competent. Tying the past and the future to living fully in the present.

Triggering event. An event (such as two group members being in competition or the expression of criticism on a sensitive point) that triggers the occurrence of a conflict.

Trust. Perception that a choice can lead to gains or losses, that whether you will gain or lose depends on the behavior of the other person, that the loss will be greater than the gain, and that the person will likely behave so that you will gain rather than lose.

Trusting behavior. Openness and sharing.

Trustworthy behavior. Expressing acceptance, support, and cooperative intentions.

Win-lose dynamic. Seeing every action of the other as a move to dominate.

Index